FRATERNAL ENEMIES

CLIVE JONES
YOEL GUZANSKY

Fraternal Enemies

Israel and the Gulf Monarchies

HURST & COMPANY, LONDON

First published in the United Kingdom in 2019 by
C. Hurst & Co. (Publishers) Ltd.,
41 Great Russell Street, London, WC1B 3PL
© Clive Jones and Yoel Guzansky, 2019
All rights reserved.
Printed in India

The right of Clive Jones and Yoel Guzansky to be identified as
the author of this publication is asserted by them in accordance
with the Copyright, Designs and Patents Act, 1988.

A Cataloguing-in-Publication data record for this book
is available from the British Library.

ISBN: 9781787382121

This book is printed using paper from registered sustainable
and managed sources.

www.hurstpublishers.com

CONTENTS

CONTENTS

ACKNOWLEDGEMENTS

This volume is the result of a number of discussions and debates (and friendly arguments) the authors had with close colleagues and friends over several years. In particular, the sage advice and guidance of Nahum Admoni, Alan Craig, Anoush Ehteshami, Efraim Halevy, Rory Miller, Beverley Milton-Edwards, Tore Petersen, Itamar Rabinovich, Yehudit Ronen and Amos Yadlin proved invaluable. They all provided keen insights that otherwise would have eluded the authors and helped sharpen the argument and analyses. We remain very much in their collective debt. In a similar spirit, we thank the anonymous referees who carefully read the manuscript and made several invaluable suggestions that have undoubtedly helped to sharpen the argument. The authors also gratefully acknowledge the patience and advice of Michael Dwyer at Hurst Publishers whose guidance in seeing this project through to its conclusion has been very much appreciated.

BIOGRAPHICAL NOTES

Dr Yoel Guzansky is Senior Research Fellow at the Institute for National Security Studies at Tel Aviv University and formerly Visiting Fellow at the Hoover Institution, Stanford University 2016/17. Dr Guzansky was previously in charge of strategic issues at the National Security Council in the Office of the Prime Minister of Israel.

Professor Clive Jones holds a Chair in Regional Security (Middle East) in the School of Government and International Affairs, Durham University, and is Visiting Research Professor in the Department of Historical Studies, NTNU, Trondheim, Norway.

FOREWORD

On 1 March 1945, President Roosevelt famously told a joint session of Congress that "I learned more about the whole problem, the Moslem problem, the Jewish problem by talking to Ibn Saud for five minutes than I could have learned in an exchange of two or three dozens of letters." FDR referred to the meeting he had with the Saudi king on board a US navy ship, *Quincy*, in the Great Bitter Lake section of the Suez Canal in February 1945 in the aftermath of the Yalta Summit. The meeting was preceded by an exchange of letters. In his letters Ibn Saud tried to persuade FDR to abandon the notion of supporting Jewish statehood in Palestine at the war's end, and minced no words in expressing his negative attitude to Jews. Needless to say, FDR's effort to reconcile Washington's support for the notion of Jewish statehood in part of Palestine—in the aftermath of the Holocaust with its growing role in Middle Eastern politics—was to no avail. In the coming decades direct pressure from Saudi Arabia—exerted by US oil companies, State Department and other Arabists to distance the US from Israel—were a permanent and important dimension of the American–Israeli relationship. From this perspective the tacit Saudi–Israeli dialogue and Saudi complaint in Israeli ears about former President Obama's Middle Eastern policies sound ironic, to put it mildly.

We should all be grateful to Dr Guzansky and Professor Jones for taking us through the long and difficult route that the Israeli–Saudi relationship, and indeed Israel's wider relations with the Gulf monarchies, have taken since the 1940s. They also managed within a limited space to strike the right balance between the story of Israel's relationship with Saudi Arabia and that of the different relationships it has built with the smaller Arab Gulf monarchies. These relationships are discreet and fragile. Gulf Arabs today attach less significance to the Palestinian issue than they did thirty, even twenty years ago, but the issue still matters to them and it matters more to the public than to the ruling elites. The latter are more worried by the challenge of Iran and Jihadi Islam and by America's apparent withdrawal from the region than they are by the challenge of Israel. Still, as long as the Israeli–Palestinian conflict continues (let alone deteriorates), a normal open relationship is not on the cards. But the Israeli–Palestinian conflict can conceivably be turned into a key component in a new political diplomatic context in which the Gulf Arabs play a role in restarting a genuine Israeli–Palestinian peace process. This could be achieved if the Gulf Arabs offered

Israel some of the peace rewards that the Palestinians are barely able to offer, by taking part in the reconstruction and development of Gaza and by helping the Palestinian leadership make some of the political and symbolic concessions it could commit. Such developments could be fitted into a broader common vision for the region by Israel and the moderate Arab states. A new vigorous US policy in the Middle East is a requisite for such a scenario to materialise. The present book lays the ground for a thorough discussion of these issues. Much remains unchanged since the transition from the Obama Administration to the Trump Administration. President Trump has clearly assigned great importance to his relationship with the House of Saud, but as the Khashoggi affair painfully demonstrated, it is difficult to manage that relationship smoothly. But, as Prime Minister Netanyahu's visit to Oman in October 2018 showed, there is a prospect for further development of Israel's relationship with the Gulf.

Professor Emeritus, Ambassador Itamar Rabinovich,
Tel Aviv University, December 2018

INTRODUCTION
FRAMEWORK FOR ANALYSIS

It was to become an almost constant theme in his speeches before gatherings of the great and the good and articles penned for global magazines. Addressing the seventy-third session of the UN General Assembly in New York in September 2018, the Israeli Prime Minister, Binyamin Netanyahu, used this platform to warn the international community of Iran's nuclear ambitions and its continued regional malfeasance. He reminded the delegates assembled that Israel had opposed the Iran nuclear deal, signed with such fanfare back in 2015, precisely because it emboldened what he theatrically referred to as the "tyrants in Tehran." However, he did note that the Iran deal, more properly known as the Joint Comprehensive Plan of Action (JCPOA), had one notable consequence for Israel:

Ladies and gentleman, I have an important confession to make: this may surprise you but I have to admit that the Iran deal has had one positive consequence, an unintended one but a positive consequence. By empowering Iran, it brought Israel and many Arab states closer together than ever before in an intimacy and friendship that I have not seen in my lifetime and would have been unimaginable a few years ago. And you know, when you form friendships around a threat, around a challenge, you quickly see opportunities... Israel deeply values these new friendships and I hope the day will soon arrive when Israel will be able to expand peace, a formal peace, beyond Egypt and Jordan to other Arab neighbours, including the Palestinians.[1]

Few had any doubts that the intimacy, the closeness, the friendship that Netanyahu referenced was with several Arab Gulf monarchies. For over a decade, reports of varying provenance had pointed towards a confluence of interests emerging between Israel and Bahrain, the United Arab Emirates (UAE) and Saudi Arabia in particular over the security challenge of Iran. But shared perception of threat tells us little about the wider dynamic that underpins a set of relationships that have, in no small measure, reshaped security thinking across much of the Middle East. Indeed, these relations, at least in Israel's eyes, have moved beyond just *Realpolitik* to embrace other forms of engagement in their wake. Writing in *The Economist* in January 2018 where he extolled Israel as the epitome of a knowledge-based economy, Netanyahu opined that "Many Arab countries now see Israel not as an enemy but as an indispensable ally in our common battle against militant Islam. They also seek Israeli technology to help their economies. The potential normalisation with Arab states could help pave the way for peace with the Palestinians."[2]

Netanyahu's speech to the United Nations and his opinion piece in *The Economist* captured the blend of both hard-power interest and soft-power influence that by 2018 shaped Israel's ties with the Arab Gulf monarchies. It represented a profound recasting of much of the regional order. Since 2010 this order had undergone change so seismic and often so brutal that the relatively static state-based, autocratic political order that had dominated the Middle East prior to the Arab uprisings was shaken to its very core.[3] These upheavals were of course a response to a range of economic, social, political, religious and sectarian shifts that are reshaping the geopolitical landscape of much of the Middle East. Gone were the certainties of a regional order shaped by the legacy of the 'Sykes-Picot agreement' that configured the Middle East state system around former colonial interests; gone was the state system that was entrenched by the certainties of the Cold War when the United States and the Soviet Union competed for regional influence. A state—for example Egypt in the mid-1970s—might switch sides in such an order but it was relatively clear as to where national loyalties lay.

Within this milieu, the wholesale rejection of Israel by the Arab world as a legitimate sovereign entity was clear cut. No Arab state was willing to deal openly with

Jerusalem, a position best enshrined in the so-called Khartoum Declaration proclaimed by the Arab League in November 1967 and its infamous "Three No's:" no recognition of Israel, no negotiation with Israel, no peace with Israel. We now know that, behind this display of collective regional animus, several Arab states, notably Jordan and Morocco, did enjoy clandestine relationships with Israel over several decades. Even so, the severity of this wider rejection of Israel across a predominantly Arab Muslim Middle East was enough to gainsay policy-making in Washington when deciding on Middle East security issues.[4]

After 2011 the picture became more complex. To be sure, the pan-Arab rejection of Israel enshrined in the Khartoum Declaration had already begun to fragment well before the Arab uprisings. The signing of the peace treaty with Egypt in 1979, followed in 1993 and 1994 by agreements with the Palestine Liberation Organisation (PLO) and Jordan, respectively, all bear testament to the fragility of Arab unity where Israel was concerned. Cracks soon appeared elsewhere. Where once any semblance of Arab–Israeli co-operation was unthinkable, by 2002 some Arab Gulf monarchies led by the Kingdom of Saudi Arabia had begun to pursue a form of dual-track diplomacy: openly condemning the construction of Israeli settlements and the perceived infringements of Palestinian national rights on the one hand, while on the other, exploring the benefits to be had through discreet dialogue with Israel on a range of security issues. Where once a resolution to the question of Palestine was considered a prerequisite for any dialogue between Israel and its Arab neighbours, the realities of the contemporary Middle East created an environment in which pragmatism born of strategic need pushed the issue of Palestine to the margins. Nowhere has this become more pronounced than in the concerns shared by Israel and many of the Arab Gulf monarchies over Iran, its nuclear programme and its growing influence across the Middle East.

How best to understand these burgeoning relationships between Israel and the Gulf monarchies is therefore the focus of this study. There is much empirical evidence to demonstrate the rich diversity of Israel's bilateral ties with the Arab world in general and the Gulf monarchies in particular, much of it now scarcely hidden.[5] As Glenn E. Perry noted in 1984, "The Israelis were always able to penetrate the Arab system as tacit allies of one side against another, and at times Israeli help was discreetly sought by some regimes or movements long before the more visible involvement after the mid-1970s."[6] Even so, the extent to which contemporary relations with the Gulf monarchies can and should be seen as forming the contours of a new regional order is a key theme of this volume and needs to be fully contextualized. Certainly, no formal diplomatic relations—let alone anything approaching an open alliance—exists between the Gulf monarchies and Israel, but this is not to say that a collaborative framework is not apparent. The Gulf monarchies had already proved more open in their apparent willingness to embrace Jerusalem. In April 2008 the former Israeli foreign minister, Tzipi Livni, addressed the eighth Doha Forum on Democracy, where she expressed the hope that ties between Israel and Qatar might eventually be conducted on a more open basis. In 2010 a report in the Israeli national daily newspaper, *Ha'aretz*, based on cables released by *Wikileaks*, disclosed that Livni had also established a particularly close relationship with her counterpart from the UAE, Sheikh Abdullah bin Zayed al-Nahyan, despite the absence of formal diplomatic ties between the two states. A shared suspicion of the regional designs of Tehran undoubtedly underpinned these ties, but it now allegedly extended to a secret dialogue between Israel and Saudi Arabia, conducted under the auspices of the former director of Mossad, the late Meir Dagan.[7]

Inevitably, any study dealing with Israel's relations with the Gulf monarchies faces an epistemological challenge. There is no shortage of news reports, policy papers, think tank briefings and well-sourced anecdotes that have helped remove much of the veil of mystery, if not subterfuge, over these ties. The provenance of much of this reporting is often good and we draw on these sources in this study. Even so, much is speculative at best and ill-informed at worst. In part, this is understandable:

few government interlocutors on either side, and certainly none from the Arab Gulf monarchies, readily give public interviews confirming the level or type of interaction with Israel. Nevertheless, many officials in the Arab Gulf monarchies have been willing to offer informal comments off the record, whispered conversations in some cases that enjoyed anonymity amid the heightened chatter of academic symposia, or conversely, discreet conversations held in a quiet corner of a café or hotel lobby in particular Gulf monarchies. Though useful as vignettes and often confirming much of our argument, they have largely been omitted from this study.

Secondly, analysis of the available information is often dealt with in a piecemeal way, the underlying nuances of the variegated ties often lacking conceptual and methodological rigour that allows for the trajectory of these ties to be mapped and placed within a wider context. This is particularly important if we wish to understand how the very contours of regional security have been revised and redrawn across so much of the Middle East, the Gulf included. Even before the Arab uprisings, this was evident in the increasingly fractious relationship between several Gulf monarchies and Iran. For example, while some academics noted the approbation heaped on the leader of Hezbollah, Sheikh Hassan Nasrallah, by the Arab world both during and after the 2006 Israel–Lebanon war, little attention was paid to the growing unease among the Gulf monarchies over the growing power and influence of the Shi'a movement, long regarded as a surrogate of Tehran's wider regional ambitions.[8]

This unease is now manifested across the Arab Gulf monarchies and divides them precisely over the issue of Iran. The regional ostracism of Qatar in June 2017 by the triumvirate of Saudi Arabia, the UAE and Bahrain underscored the increasingly moribund nature of the Gulf Cooperation Council (GCC) as a collective security alliance. Doha supported and promoted a range of regional actors, the Muslim Brotherhood in Egypt and their Palestinian offshoot Hamas included, whose ideology remains the antithesis of monarchical rule based largely on familial ascendency. For such groups to receive financial support from a regime whose fabulous wealth remains configured around the absolute fiat of the Al-Thani is not without irony. Yet, more broadly, the legacy of the Arab uprisings has seen the breakdown of the GCC as both a security complex and a security community. If we take the former to mean the close correlation of security concerns among and between states that remain interdependent and where regional security challenges demand a collective rather than individual response, then the GCC is little more than an anachronism. And if a security community is defined as the embodiment of a collective consensus over the nature of the security issues faced, as well as agreement among all members over how these should be addressed, then the GCC has moved beyond an anachronism; it barely exists.[9]

This, of course, privileges a largely realist few of security. We should be aware that, as a concept, the very idea of security remains contested and embraces multiple meanings and normative positions—security for whom and for what—as well as challenges that are not immediately recognised as either strategic in nature or amenable to a military solution. Moreover, scholars have come to see conflict across much of the Middle East as a contest between the pre-modern and post-modern. Forces have emerged that, while happy to embrace the digital age to spread their message, look to return the region to an imagined past that brooks no compromise with modernity or dissent from its brutal interpretation of Islamic law. The violence and cruelty unleashed by Islamic State across Syria and Iraq became the epitome of such antediluvian thinking. Equally, post-modern forces, also harnessing the power of information technologies, have increasingly challenged the sacrosanct nature of the Arab state as global capital flows and powerful non-state actors—from global business to mass movements associated with the Arab uprising—look to usurp the established order.[10] Both of course have challenged the centrality of the state as the reference point of regional and international relations.

Of course, balance is required to understand the plethora of security challenges facing the Middle East. Unproductive autocratic states are ill-suited to meet the demands of increasingly knowledge-based economies, and inflexible in accommodating a growing and changing demographic across the Arab Muslim Middle East. But while not denying the appeal of the 'pre-' and the 'post-' modern, states still remain the most important actors in the Middle East, and define an order that continues to privilege sovereignty and power in a regional system increasingly at odds with itself. If, however, the labels 'security complex' and 'security community' have limited utility in describing the fractious reality of inter-Gulf relations, how can we configure our understanding of a security landscape that has come to embrace ever closer ties between the Gulf monarchies and Israel?

Tacit Security Regimes

Our approach lies in understanding Israel's ties with many of the Gulf monarchies, notably Saudi Arabia, the UAE and Bahrain, not as some formal alliance but rather as a manifestation of a Tacit Security Regime. This regime allows for the evolution of ties between Israel and the Gulf monarchies to be explored and analysed while allowing us to be mindful that these relations have rarely been linear, let alone underpinned by any shared normative values. Indeed, *Realpolitik*, however unfashionable this term might appear in the rarefied surroundings of universities across Europe and the United States, best captures the essence of such ties. It does not, however, deny the importance of ideational constraints in both

Israel and the Gulf monarchies that prevent such ties being placed on a more formal diplomatic footing. Whatever the true fidelity of the Gulf regimes to Palestinian statehood, for example, the symbolism of Palestine on the Arab street and the refusal of the right wing in Israel to countenance meaningful retrenchment from the West Bank and East Jerusalem place limits upon more open, tangible expressions of collective security between the erstwhile protagonists.

Understanding Israel–Gulf relations through the prism of a TSR therefore has an obvious utility: it allows security co-operation to be pursued between the actors involved (most notably over Iran) but without compromising sensitive political positions that might give rise to internal opposition. Yet if the idea of the TSR is to have validity as a conceptual tool, its intellectual origins need to be understood. Security regimes more generally are the progeny of that much criticised but enduring staple of international relations: realism. For some realist scholars, the difference between a security regime and a more formal military alliance might well just be one of emphasis, although the latter usually incorporates some codified form of co-operation in the shape of a treaty or the emergence of a defined institution, as in the case of NATO. While often grounded in the logic of the security dilemma, such regimes by contrast suggest that while the national interests of states may diverge on given issue areas, these 'are often mixed with other more compatible interests and goals, which can sustain some forms of international co-operation.'[11]

It should be noted that throughout the 1970s and 1980s, the study of security regimes moved beyond purely strategic concerns to embrace a more normative approach, placing emphasis increasingly not just upon convergence and agreement on hard-power issues, but upon the emergence of institutions that could help promote and cultivate more liberal, collaborative values among its adherents. Its apogee has perhaps been most visibly realised with the emergence of the European Union, which has clearly championed a rights-based approach both among its member states and more broadly in its conduct of international affairs. The typology of regime posited in this study, however, very much rests on a realist interpretation of the term, rather than this liberal institutional variant. Security regimes, we argue, exist as a reflection of power—economic and military—that allows the interested parties to promote long-term interests which happen to conflate. Unlike liberal institutional approaches that see regimes as collaborative mechanisms designed to offset the worst excesses of the security dilemma, and configured to produce a normative public good, the idea of a security regime involving Israel and the Gulf monarchies is underpinned by shared perceptions of state interests to be realised and threats to be countered. As Stephen Krasner would perhaps recognise, it is a regime driven by a classic security dilemma rather than one that has emerged to mitigate its worst excesses.[12]

Yet the literature surrounding the establishment of security regimes has emphasised the informal rules with which to comply, often within an agreed institutional setting that eventually gives rise to formal alliances. In his examination of the Concert of Europe that broadly secured European peace for almost a century following the Napoleonic wars, Robert Jervis highlighted the shared understandings and the desire to maintain the status quo among the great European powers. His typology embraced, firstly, a mutual recognition of vital interests; secondly, a propensity for longer-term strategic gain over immediate advantage produced by restraint; and thirdly, that the actual concert did not conform to the distribution of power capabilities but instead conformed to agreed principles governing state behaviour. From this, Jervis concluded that security regimes were configured around principles, rules and norms that engendered mutual reciprocity and restraint.[13]

At first glance, identifying any security regime in the Middle East that adheres to the above characteristics is not so easy. Even before the rupture with Qatar in 2017, the GCC hardly conformed to agreed principles governing security co-operation. Attempts in 1991 to establish a pan-Arab force designed to deter any future Iraqi aggression—the so-called Damascus Declaration—proved stillborn. Suspicion of Saudi dominance, coupled with fears that the presence of Syrian and Egyptian forces on the Arabian Peninsula as part of the force could prove destabilising, were enough to scupper the initiative.[14]

However, scholars of the Middle East, as well as international relations theorists, have long been interested in the distribution of power across the region, as well as the way in which this has shaped a particular security architecture between Arabs and Israelis. After all, full-scale interstate war between Israel and its Arab neighbours has not broken out since 1973. In the 1980s, building on the work of Jervis, Janice Gross Stein looked to apply the concept of a security regime to understand the broad contours of the Arab–Israeli conflict. Notwithstanding the animosities that in the mid-1980s still determined patterns of diplomatic discourse between the protagonists, Stein claimed that zero-sum competition no longer defined the conflict. Rather, the interests of Israel and its Arab neighbours were neither 'wholly competitive or compatible,' leading, she concluded, to a process of conflict management where all sides recognised the rules of a game and the underlying principle of reciprocity involved.[15]

But for Efraim Inbar and Shmuel Sandler, reciprocity alone was insufficient in explaining the relative stability of Israeli ties with the Arab states. They argued that Stein underestimated the role that deterrence played in the relationship, and in particular—through its exercise of overwhelming military power—the extent to which

Israel saw its regional-strategic position and interests as configured around maintaining the status quo. Such deterrent power had, they argued, been essential in bringing Egypt to the negotiating table and the conclusive bilateral peace treaty. This led both scholars to argue that Israel's relations with the wider Arab world were best defined as a *laissez-faire* security regime: order was maintained through the distribution of military power and the emergence of a decentralised deterrence relationship. This worked because the strongest actor—in this case, Israel—was able to maintain an effective deterrent posture as a status quo power. It ensured the acceptance by other actors, however reluctantly, of the clear limitations of using force to change the regional configuration of power. Finally, Inbar and Sandler concluded that such *laissez-faire* regimes lack the institutionalisation and formal concordance that defined the construct of security regimes—as defined by Jervis. Even so, they are no less real for that.[16]

While clearly useful, the characterisation of security regimes as *laissez faire* is problematic. To begin with, the primacy placed on deterrence as the dominant condition of the regime tells us very little about the level and type of interaction between the actors involved. If the *laissez-faire* regime is defined by a search for security *from* one another rather than *with* one another, it remains limited concerning other forms of interaction that underpin constructs of a security regime, notably co-operative behaviour. While accepting that rules can be informal and norms implied, they remain integral to a regime even if deterrence remains the bedrock of state interaction. Moreover, by emphasising the idea of the status quo, how regional security regimes change and adapt remains unclear, not least when *laissez-faire* regimes built on the basis of deterrence are faced by broader existential threats.

The need therefore to understand the actual interaction between erstwhile protagonists is crucial to embedding our understanding of a security regime as more than just a progeny of deterrence. Here, the work of Aharon Klieman in relation to Israel's ties with Jordan prior to signing the 1994 peace treaty offers a more fruitful point of departure for understanding the value of a security regime. Acknowledging that the study of international regimes often eschews "the traditionally normative, legalistic-formulistic and institutional focus on treaty alliances," Klieman placed the emphasis upon those areas of co-operation where "actor expectations converge."[17]

Taking this as his starting point, Klieman went on to develop the idea of a "tacit" international security regime, a paradigm he described as "non-superpower, non-hegemonic, non-Western, non-contractual and non-institutionalised cooperation."[18] With particular reference to Israel's relations with Jordan, Klieman went on to argue that, prior to 1994, this TSR managed relations between adversaries rather than enemies and where potential points of friction were arbitrated through a series of formal and informal agreements and understandings. More specifically, Klieman used the term "tacit" to convey the following:

> [T]he Israel-Jordan regime, although not entirely "unspoken or wordless," does arise and operate without any "express contract." The regime does possess the requisite collection of rights and rules, however these are unwritten and uncodified. ... Signals and subtleties are exchanged more often than not behind the scenes, between the lines, and under the table, via back channels involving indirect but also direct communication.[19]

Underpinning this construct of a TSR, argued Klieman, are three key elements: (1) recognition and substantive acceptance that the regime guides the actors towards particular types of action; (2) recognised mechanisms for resolving situations that require trusted modes of engagement; and (3) that implementation of any action or policy accords with mutually accepted methods of compliance. While the maintenance of national security (understood in its hierarchical sense) remains the prime goal of such a regime, it is not the only 'good' to be realised; neither, importantly, does it preclude continued competition (or co-operation) in a different realm, be it political or economic.[20]

The contours of such a regime are certainly apparent in at least some facets of the relations between Israel and the Gulf monarchies, with one important innovation: while the idea of the "unwritten" and the "uncodified" defined the clandestine nature of Klieman's TSR, the construct of the TSR between Israel and the Gulf monarchies allows for multiple modes of engagement—some of it open—between the actors involved. As such, our construct of the TSR as it applies to Israel and the Gulf monarchies is defined by the following:

1. Geographical distance need not determine the scope and varying intensity of the modes and means of exchange—be they strategic, political or economic—between the actors involved. Indeed, as we shall see, security and economic interests combined have come to shape the scope and level of interaction between Israel and several of the Gulf monarchies.

2. That the regime itself is a function of shared perception of threat, in this case Iran, rather than primarily geared towards managing relations between the states themselves. This highlights ongoing competition in other areas, co-operation in others (see point 5) but, importantly, the regime itself mitigates excess competition to ensure its own core aim is realised: the containment of Iran.

3. Through the TSR, the actors involved recognise ideational, even emotive, factors derived from domestic legitimacy that constrain moves towards more progressive ties. This is an important correction perhaps to the dominance hitherto exercised by classical

Realist accounts regarding security regimes that deny sufficient agency to domestic constraints.

4. That the intimacy of the regime reflects subjective perceptions surrounding Great Power commitment, notably by the United States, to the security of the actors involved.

5. That other modes and means of exchange do mark relations between the erstwhile protagonists, not least in areas of mutual business and commercial interest. The nature and diversity of the ties can be conceived as Israel's use of soft 'technical' power for hard diplomatic gain. Israel's undoubted technological superiority in cyber security is much valued by several Gulf regimes, notably the UAE, and has been incorporated into surveillance systems designed to bolster internal security.[21]

6. That the regime allows for open yet subtle signals to be exchanged that might engender public acceptance over time of more substantive dialogue and the exchange of strategic and political goods. This allows the regime to change and adopt as ideational context dictates: it is not static.[22]

Ultimately, however, it is shared concerns over three hard security issues that define the trajectory and scope of ties between these 'fraternal enemies': Iran's growing regional influence; the rise of non-state armed groups; and shared unease over Washington's engagement across the Middle East. Equally, an enduring theme of the ties that have emerged is the extent to which several Gulf monarchies have seen closer association with pro-Israel Jewish groups in the United States, as well as contacts with Israel itself, as means to court favour in Washington. Faced with such challenges, this volume also comes to some conclusions over the likelihood that ties between Israel and the Gulf monarchies can move beyond the 'tacit' to embrace something more durable and open. Despite the historic (and indeed religious) enmities, the likelihood of such arrangements emerging is not so far-fetched. While informed comment highlights the contingent relationship between progress on Palestinian statehood and the establishment of overt ties between Jerusalem and the Gulf monarchies, the trajectory and importance of the ties and contact established so far are equal to the sum of its many and varied parts.[23] As regimes across the Middle East face a crisis of legitimacy, state identities and therefore threat perceptions have become defined increasingly by religious, sectarian and ideational affiliations. At a time when Washington's commitment to the security of the region remains in flux, the emerging contours of a security regime between Israel and some Gulf members of the GCC are, we argue, challenging much of what we thought we knew about the security of the Middle East.

To be sure, Israel's current association with the Gulf is somewhat removed from the clandestine nature of previous ties with a host of sectarian and religious minorities across the region, and where illicit arms supplies were often the currency of diplomatic exchange and influence. But, even so, it is the principle of clandestine diplomacy that underpinned the 'periphery doctrine' of the 1950s and 1960s, rather than clandestine diplomacy per se that determined Israel's burgeoning contacts with the Gulf monarchies; where the shared perception of the Iranian threat generated such contacts out of need rather than any shared affinity to wider normative practice.[24]

This study fully accepts that the level of Iran's involvement in Syria, Iraq and Yemen, as well as with a range of non-state actors, is open to debate and covers a range of opinions from the benign to the malign. Even Israeli scholars, security officials and commentators offer a plethora of views as to Iran's regional goals and whether the past behaviour of the Islamic Republic is necessarily an accurate guide to current and future actions and intent.[25] While important, this should not detract from the fact that it is the very perception of an Iranian threat, exaggerated or not, that has shaped the context for increased engagement between Jerusalem on one side, and Abu Dhabi, Riyadh and particularly Manama on the other.

Indeed, as this book highlights, the ties between Israel and the Gulf monarchies are hardly ones that bind the parties together. As already noted, the continued legacy of the Palestine issue, the status of Palestinian refugees and the emotive dissonance surrounding the future of East Jerusalem impose obvious limits on the overt nature of diplomatic ties. Nevertheless, if Lord Palmerston's infamous quip that "states do not have friends, only interests" is still relevant, then the ties between the Gulf monarchies and Israel are certainly its contemporary expression. As such, this volume presents the first in-depth academic study of Israel's relations with the Gulf monarchies. By drawing upon a wide range of contemporary sources, it explores both the scope and limits of these ties and their influence on the contemporary Middle East. It also argues that while such ties pre-date his premiership, it has been Netanyahu who has increasingly driven Israel's outreach to the Gulf monarchies. This volume places this as part of a wider Israeli grand strategy that views these dynastic regimes as 'front line' state actors whose stability is now a core Israeli security concern in its confrontation with Iran.

In fact, the Israeli prime minister deliberately sought to promote an approach "from outside in." This looked to first foster closer ties with a range of Arab and Islamic states with which Israel had no formal diplomatic ties before progress could be made in any future negotiations with Palestine. As such, Israel would be entering such negotiations from a position of strength. This was not just wishful thinking. In the spring of 2018 and before his international reputation was tarnished by allegations of his complicity in the murder of Jamal Khashoggi, Crown Prince Mohammed bin Salman, the heir apparent to the Saudi throne, expressed quite openly positive views on Israel and the right of the Jewish people to their own homeland during an extensive interview with *The Atlantic*.[26] This followed on from apparently disparaging remarks he made before an audience of Jewish community leaders in the United States regarding the Palestinian leadership, in which he reportedly scolded them for "rejecting peace with Israel" before suggesting that either they accept peace proposals "or shut up."[27] The veracity of this account was never confirmed, but even so it reinforced an Israeli view: that, at the very least, reaching an agreement with Gulf monarchies was no longer contingent on moves towards peace with the Palestinians. These alleged comments came at a time when many in the Gulf had come to question Washington's commitment to regional security. By contrast, Israel represented a status quo power that was both capable of and—as it increasingly demonstrated—willing to use military force to push back against Iran in Lebanon and Syria.[28]

These themes, individually or collectively, are explored in this volume. Chapter One offers a brief overview of the vexed history of Israeli interaction with the Gulf monarchies, noting how the issues of Palestine, Iran and wider ties that all actors have enjoyed with Washington have come to influence the patterns of relations over several decades. Chapter Two provides more detailed analysis about how, after signing the Oslo Accords in 1993, Israel developed open (if low-level) ties with what might be termed the monarchies of the lower Gulf: Qatar, Oman, Bahrain and the UAE. Equally, we examine how the trajectory of these ties has been conditioned by growing concern over Tehran's increased regional influence, as well as the need to demonstrate continued fidelity to the cause of Palestinian statehood. Continuing with this theme, Chapter Three examines Israel's ties with the most important of the Arab Gulf monarchies: Saudi Arabia. It explores how, over time, such ties have come to be 'legitimised' through what might be termed 'academic' or 'former practitioner engagement,' but equally how the progression of this relationship remains subject to ideational constraints facing both actors.

Even so, until the brutal slaying of Khashoggi at Istanbul's Saudi consulate in October 2018, these ideational constraints appeared to be fraying. Crown Prince Mohammed bin Salman, seen by most as the likely successor to his octogenarian father King Salman, adopted an overtly interventionist policy from Lebanon to Yemen, driven by a desire to 'roll back' Iranian influence. Whether such influence in Yemen, for example, was ever on the grandiose scale claimed by Riyadh remains a moot point. But the actions of the crown prince were accompanied by warm words for Israel and an appreciation of its security needs. By contrast, his views of both Iran and the Palestinians went beyond the derogatory.[29] Netanyahu's reaction to the Khashoggi murder was therefore telling: while a horrifying event, he cautioned against what he regarded as the ill-judged international opprobrium directed against Riyadh. Refraining from directly attacking the Saudi Crown Prince, Netanyahu instead noted the value Israel realised in ensuring the stability of the Kingdom as part of the regional struggle against Iran. To emphasise his point, he noted Israel's role in preventing two terrorist attacks orchestrated by Iranian intelligence against dissident Iranian-Arabs in Denmark. Tehran, he opined, presented a global threat and was certainly a more pressing challenge facing the international community, let alone Israel and the Gulf monarchies.[30]

Chapter Four examines the reality of the diplomatic co-operation between all the actors involved, both in relation to the JCPOA signed between Iran, the five permanent members of the United Nations Security Council, and Germany (P5+1) in July 2015, as well as Israel's continued concern over the nuclear ambitions of the UAE and Saudi Arabia. It demonstrates the paradox captured by the construct of a TSR: the willingness of Israel and the Gulf monarchies to work together to oppose the JCPOA but, equally, the divergence over individual regional nuclear ambitions once the agreement crafted by the Obama administration had been repudiated by his successor, President Donald Trump. Chapter Five examines the impact of the Syrian civil war on Israel's relations with the Gulf monarchies. Again, it highlights core areas where interests converge, but also explores how individual state-based interests have determined the extent to which Israel has been willing to exercise its undoubted military superiority beyond the containment of Hezbollah and their Iranian patron.

At a time when the world was fixated with the rise of Islamic State amid the shattered infrastructure of Syria and Iraq, Israel's reluctance to be drawn into any wider conflagration with a range of Sunni jihadi groups was pronounced. Rather, Iran and its proxies remained the focus of Jerusalem's strategic deliberations, a regional perspective readily understood in Gulf capitals, notably Riyadh and Abu Dhabi. Yes, they may have been fearful of the challenge presented by Islamic State, but the tangible gains made by Iran in fostering regional alliances from Baghdad to Beirut remained the primary concern. Whether this in turn has nurtured a shared understanding of how the new regional security architecture between Israel and the Gulf monarchies might evolve remains to be seen. But as Salman al-Ansari, the head of the newly-formed Saudi–American Public Affairs Committee in Washington noted, Israel and Saudi Arabia could serve as "the new twin pillars of regional stability." In turn, he argued, they could foster peace and stability across the Middle East.[31]

1

ISRAEL'S RELATIONS WITH THE GULF MONARCHIES

HISTORY AND CONTEXT

That Israel has ties spanning several decades with a variety of actors, both state and non-state across the Middle East, is no secret. Nor has geographical distance ever proved an obstacle to these ties. Faced with the animus of a largely hostile Arab and Muslim Middle East upon its establishment, Israel looked to a series of clandestine ties with minority groups such as the Kurds in Iraq and Christian tribes in southern Sudan, but also with state actors—most notably Ethiopia, Turkey and Iran—as a means of weakening the idea of a united Arab front against the nascent Jewish state. What became known as the *Torat Ha'peripheria* or Periphery Doctrine was the brainchild of Israel's first prime minister, David Ben Gurion, and met with considerable success (yet tragedy in the case of Lebanon) as Israel looked to secure its position as a permanent fixture among the wider constellation of Middle East States.[1] Scholars have also subjected the vicissitudes of Israel's relations with several Arab Gulf monarchies to academic scrutiny.[2] Examining the position of the smaller members of the GCC towards Israel, Elisheva Rosman-Stollman concluded that their views of Israel, let alone any more formal ties, were inextricably bound up with the wider Middle East peace process and of course, the need to ensure Washington's goodwill.[3]

Unlike its immediate Arab neighbours, the Gulf monarchies only rarely engaged directly in combat operations against Israel, although Saudi Arabia sent symbolic military forces to ostensibly bolster the armies of Egypt, Jordan, Syria and Lebanon during the Arab–Israeli wars of 1948, June 1967, and October 1973.[4] They did, however, impose energy embargoes with varying degrees of success against several Western states, notably the United Kingdom and the United States, for their perceived support of Israel in the June 1967 war.[5] The most successful embargo imposed in the immediate aftermath of the October 1973 war provided exclusions only for those nations supportive of the Arab position or who were actively pressuring Israel to make substantial diplomatic and territorial concessions. The resulting hike in energy prices had an adverse impact on the global economy throughout the rest of the 1970s.[6]

From the mid-1970s onwards, Riyadh attempted to position itself at the forefront of Arab diplomatic efforts to resolve the Arab–Israeli conflict. In 1976, the Saudis, after great effort, brought together President Anwar Sadat of Egypt and President Hafez al-Assad Syria in an attempt to reconcile the two leaders. They diverged following Cairo's criticism of the Syrian invasion of Lebanon that year and condemnation by Damascus of the Separation of Forces Agreement along the Suez that Israel had signed with Egypt known as 'Sinai II.'[7] These initial successes for Saudi-led diplomacy resulted in the development of a more ambitious diplomatic goal of forming a unified Saudi–Syrian–Egyptian position with which they could pressure Israel through Washington to return to the ceasefire lines of 5 June 1967.

History, however, ran away from the Saudis. In March 1979 the signing of the Camp David Accords marginalised Riyadh's attempts to present their regional peace plan to the Americans. Refusing to accept this as a *fait accompli*, Riyadh now attempted to regain influence over the diplomatic agenda by pushing for a new initiative that had wider traction across the Arab world. While seemingly a bid to fill the Arab vacuum following Cairo's rapprochement with Jerusalem, Riyadh's move had a more prosaic if no less pressing rationale: a fear that the Soviet Union would use its ties to the so-called rejectionist Arab regimes—notably Iraq, Syria and Libya—to again increase its influence and embolden those regimes whose ideological basis remained the antithesis of monarchical rule. The failure to resolve the Arab-Israeli conflict would therefore only empower the rejectionist states, and in so doing, threaten once again the oil interests of the Kingdom.[8]

The eponymous 'Fahd Plan,' named after Crown Prince Fahd bin Abdul Aziz Al Saud and launched in August 1981, has to be seen in this context. It consisted of eight articles, but only the final two indicated anything new in the Saudi position towards Israel. Point Seven articulated the right of all Middle Eastern countries to live in peace, while Point Eight guaranteed the implementation of the plan by the UN. This introduced a new, radical proposal into the often volatile arena of inter-Arab political dialogue: in exchange for a full Israeli withdrawal from the territories occupied in 1967, including East Jerusalem, and the right of Palestinian refugees to either return to their homes or receive appropriate financial compensation, the Arabs would give *de facto* recognition to Israel. This was implicit in the plan, which noted that "All states in the region should be able to live in peace."[9] For the first time, the Saudis were attempting to establish a new pathway for resolving the Arab–Israeli conflict: an Israeli withdrawal from all the occupied territories and the establishment of a Palestinian state living peacefully alongside its neighbours.[10]

While implicit, this *de facto* recognition of Israel was historic. Up to this point no Arab country—with the exception of Egypt—had recognised Israel, and most Arab states remained bitterly opposed to any form of diplomatic contact with Jerusalem. Underpinning the Saudi initiative, however, was an element of instrumentalism too: Israeli–Egyptian negotiations were now at an impasse over the reluctance of Israeli premier Menachem Begin to embrace Palestinian autonomy in the West Bank and Gaza (a key element of the Camp David Accords). Riyadh's desire to improve its regional standing was also directed at Washington as it looked to purchase F-15 fighter-bombers and Airborne Warning and Control Systems (AWACs) aircraft. Given both the qualitative and quantitative nature of the proposed arms deal, the Saudis remained wary that the United States Congress, under pressure from pro-Israel lobby groups, would look to block a deal that might adversely impact Israel's regional military dominance.[11] The initiative therefore was calculated to send a signal, both to Washington and the wider region, that Saudi Arabia was a reliable partner for peace, and an actor willing and able to contribute towards regional stability within the wider context of the Cold War. As Joseph Kostiner noted, "These elements showed that Saudi Arabia was attempting to bring the entire Middle East into a stable order, hoping to position itself as the conductor of this concert and thus link itself to US policies in the region."[12]

However, the first iteration of the Fahd plan failed to garner much regional enthusiasm. Arab leaders were more preoccupied with the Iran-Iraq war while equally the radical Arab front-line states—notably Syria, whose ideological hostility to Israel underpinned its wider domestic and regional legitimacy—refused to entertain any thoughts of compromise with the 'Zionist entity.' Moreover, the Reagan Administration in Washington was preoccupied with its worsening ties with Moscow. As such, the Fahd plan gained little diplomatic traction, let alone the regional momentum that might have demonstrated to the United States that it represented an earnest attempt to finally resolve the Arab–Israeli conflict.

At the Arab League's second Fez summit the following year, a modified version of the 'Fahd Plan' was, however, adopted as the Arab League's peace proposal.[13] The Saudis took more care to consult with the Syrians before reintroducing the plan, and altered certain details to make the initiative more palatable to Damascus. The primary difference between the initial draft and its later iteration in 1982 was the level of recognition that Israel would receive from its hostile neighbours. The end result was a change in the language of Article 7, whose allowance for all states to live in peace was to be guaranteed by the United Nations rather than by the Arab states themselves, thus removing from the table problems caused by even implicit recognition of Israel.[14] In essence the acceptance of the legitimacy of Israel as a state was reduced to a subjective inference that had little hope of gaining wider diplomatic appeal.

However, more pressing concerns dictated the Saudi position. The Iran-Iraq war, by then well into its second year, had failed to deliver the quick victory that had been expected of Baghdad following the invasion of its predominately Shi'a neighbour in September 1980. It was now a conflict which divided the Middle East along religious and sectarian lines, a harbinger of the future violence that would later tear at the very fabric of the Arab state system. Given the cost that the war now exacted in lives, treasure, and with them an increased fear that the Shi'a theocracy in Tehran might now just be gaining the upper hand, Riyadh invested little time and effort in pushing a plan in the capitals of the Arab world whose returns were likely to be meagre. Any continued importance the Saudis attached to the Fahd plan was in the value of a multilateral approach that engaged all or most of the Arab world. The Camp David Accords, after all, proved that any bilateral agreements could easily create schisms in the Arab world that would be more difficult to bridge. While Riyadh hoped to demonstrate to Washington and the West that they were now a regional power of significance, the assassination of President Sadat of Egypt in October 1981 acted as a salutary reminder that rapprochement with Israel, however tentative, could well exact a bloody price in terms of regime stability.[15]

Israel's invasion of Lebanon in June 1982 and the widespread opprobrium it faced from across the Arab world, followed by the outbreak of the Palestinian intifada five years later, certainly underscored an entrenched pan-Arab antipathy towards Jerusalem.[16] Yet the Gulf War of 1990–1 changed the political balance across the region, not least because of the outright hostility felt by some Gulf monarchies, notably Kuwait, towards the PLO following its open support for the actions of Saddam Hussein. The consequent expulsion of over 400,000 Palestinians from the Emirate and, with it, the loss of remittance payments to Palestinian families in Jordan, the Occupied Territories and the deleterious impact upon the coffers of the PLO collectively constituted a major factor in shifting the movement towards a historic accommodation with Israel.[17]

Basking in its military and diplomatic triumph and enjoying unprecedented political capital across the Middle East, Washington now sought to break the deadlock in the peace process by bringing Israel and most of the Arab states together at what became known as the Madrid Peace Conference in October 1991. The Gulf monarchies responded favourably to the proposals now tabled by Washington, although the right-wing Likud-led government of Yitzhak Shamir, suspicious of multilateral negotiations that Israel knew would focus international attention on the future of the West Bank and Gaza, remained wary. Only their dependence on Washington's financial largesse to help absorb the increasing numbers of Jews now leaving the Soviet Union for a new life in Israel saw the hawkish Shamir finally agree to an Israeli presence at the conference which he insisted on leading personally.[18]

As a result, a partial rapprochement was reached between Israel and the broad panoply of Arab leaders over five key issue areas: water, environmental protection, economic co-operation, refugees, and arms control. However, the meagre progress made during the Palestinian–Israeli talks in the months following the conference now led the Gulf monarchies to harden their positions, manifested in the outright anti-Zionist and anti-Semitic rhetoric that questioned Israel's right to exist as a sovereign Jewish state. However symbolic it may have appeared, the narratives surrounding Palestine remained important tools in the court of domestic Arab public opinion and regime legitimacy. Nonetheless, with the election of a Labour-led coalition government under Yitzhak Rabin in 1992, and the signing of the Oslo Accords in September 1993 between Israel and the PLO, several Gulf monarchies, led initially by Oman, quietly abandoned their policies of boycotting companies that had economic relations with Israel (the secondary boycott), emphasising that this new policy was to be distinguished from the direct or tertiary boycott which would continue until Israel made a comprehensive peace agreement with the Palestinians.[19]

The diplomatic entrée that the Oslo Accords gave Israel to the Gulf was, in retrospect, modest. Nonetheless, the symbolism was profound and prompted clear hope that more tangible relations could now be realised. By 1996, Israel had established two trade missions to Muscat and Doha while the late Yossi Sarid, as Minister for Environment in the government of Yitzhak Rabin, headed an official Israeli delegation to Bahrain in 1994 as part of a wider multilateral accord on environmental co-operation that had developed out of the Madrid peace talks. For a short period, the Oslo process opened a window on the possibility of new regional horizons for Israel, a window whose latch had been Israel's ties with the Palestinians. As Sarid reported back to the Knesset,

> The Bahraini foreign minister asked me to convey a message of peace to the people of Israel, his determination and desire to see the peace process succeed, and to establish economic co-operation with Israel. He viewed the meeting (of the environmental working group) as the first in a number of stages that would lead to closer relations between the two countries.[20]

The promise that these low-level ties might translate into more tangible diplomatic gains soon foundered due to the increasingly fractious nature of Israel's relationship with the Palestinians, which culminated in the outbreak of the al-Aqsa intifada in September 2000. Amid the carnage visited by Palestinian suicide bombers on Israel's streets, and the inevitable human cost in retribution exacted by Israel against the various Palestinian militias, any hope of progressing ties with Oman, for example, proved stillborn. Muscat quietly shut the Israeli trade mission in response to the violence, but the Qataris proved more reluctant, perhaps demonstrating their growing confidence in foreign affairs. It was only after sustained pressure from both Riyadh and Tehran—who threatened to boycott a meeting of the Organisation of the Islamic Conference (OIC), then under the chairmanship of the Qataris—that Doha somewhat reluctantly closed the Israeli office in November 2000. Still, as Uzi Rabi notes, the Qataris continued to hold a series of meetings with Israeli officials, including former foreign ministers Shlomo Ben-Ami and Silvan Shalom in Geneva and Paris respectively.[21]

The shared position of Tehran and Riyadh on this issue was as much to do with playing the card of anti-Israeli feeling in the wider court of Arab-Muslim opinion as it was from any sense of fidelity to advancing the Palestinian cause. However, wider regional eddies, related directly to the fallout from the attacks of 9/11 and later from the 2003 Iraq war, soon overshadowed the ongoing al-Aqsa intifada. The war and consequent insurgency that bedevilled attempts to resurrect anything resembling a coherent state in Iraq created a vacuum increasingly filled by sectarian interests backed by competing regional powers. King Abdullah II of Jordan may have sounded alarmist when, in 2004, he expressed fears of an emerging "Shi'i crescent," comprising both state and non-state actors that now stretched from Tehran to Beirut. Yet, for the Gulf monarchies, the warning from the Hashemite monarch carried a keenly felt veracity.[22]

This growing antipathy towards Iran and its sponsorship of its Shi'a surrogates across the Middle East surfaced most visibly during the 2006 Lebanon war. While mindful of the image of heroic resistance against the 'Zionist aggressor' that Hezbollah enjoyed across the Arab world, Riyadh made clear its displeasure with the group's rash actions that precipitated the crisis. Amid the violence across southern Lebanon and northern Israel, the Saudi government announcement condemning the "reckless adventurism" of the Lebanese Shi'a movement and that such adventurism was liable to "bring ruination down on all the Arab states" came as an unpleasant surprise to the Hezbollah leadership amid the wider approbation it had hitherto enjoyed on the Arab street.[23]

Partly because of fears surrounding the recrudescence of Iranian-inspired influence across the Middle East, and partly because of lingering sensitivity to accusations that Saudi Arabia remained an incubator of extremism given the identity of fifteen of the nineteen hijackers on 9/11, Riyadh had looked to actively promote a more moderate image of the Kingdom across the world.[24] Now, by championing a peace initiative that looked to broker an agreement between Israel and the Palestinians, the Saudis hoped both to ameliorate these concerns and shore up its influence among Sunni Arabs increasingly uneasy at the emerging sectarian shifts in power in Iraq as well as Lebanon. The announcement in February 2002 of the Abdullah Plan, named after the then Crown Prince

Abdullah bin Abdulaziz Al-Saud and now more commonly known as the Arab Peace Initiative (API), has therefore to be seen in this context.[25] While in accordance with the various United Nations resolutions demanding Israeli withdrawal to the lines held by the protagonists on 5 June 1967, the plan promised normalisation between Israel and the Arab world. One further concern prompted the Abdullah Plan: an acute fear that the violence of the al-Aqsa intifada might inspire unrest among Saudi Arabia's own restive Shi'a minority.[26]

The plan interested some in Israel, including the late president and Prime Minister Shimon Peres, but its appeal remained limited and perhaps even politically toxic amid the ever-increasing bloodshed of the al-Aqsa intifada. Moreover, its inclusion of UN Resolution 194, championing the right of return of Palestinian refugees, was seen by its critics for what it really was: denial of Israel's right to exist as a predominantly Jewish dispensation.[27] However, there remained for many Israelis the question of Saudi sincerity. In a country where security (*bitachon*) remains the totem of daily political discourse, Riyadh never publicly disavowed the use of suicide-bomb attacks by Palestinian militant groups that had wreaked such carnage on Israel's streets.

However, the plan was greeted with diplomatic plaudits in the capitals of Europe, and even informed the 'Road Map,' the moribund peace initiative launched by former US President George W. Bush. Even the so-called rejectionist Arab states led by Syria cautiously welcomed the Saudi initiative; the return of the Golan Heights symbolically allowed Damascus to engage with the initiative under the fig leaf of Arab solidarity. Despite the consequent vicissitudes of Israeli–Palestinian relations—including Israel's unilateral withdrawal from Gaza in 2005, the 2006 Lebanon war, the Hamas take-over of Gaza in 2007 and a series of Israeli military operations into the Gaza Strip itself from 2008 onwards—the API has remained on the table ever since.

Still, the aftermath of the 2006 Lebanon war now witnessed a more benign attitude towards Jerusalem emerge among some of the Gulf monarchies. In the wake of the conflict, the Deputy Director of the Israeli Ministry of Foreign Affairs Ya'acov Hadas-Handelsman opined to his American counterparts that Israel's views of Iran, Syria and Hamas were now shared by many of the Gulf monarchies, with Tehran's regional ambitions now the root cause of much of the turmoil across the region. With Washington experiencing its own difficulties with Iranian-backed Shi'a militias in Iraq, there is a sense that the Israeli was playing to the gallery. Even so, Hadas-Handelsman warned that an equally pervasive feeling among the capitals of the Gulf was that the United States appeared no longer able or willing to extend effective security guarantees to the Gulf monarchies. As such, friendly ties with Tehran were not a choice but a necessity. Quoting an unnamed Gulf official in close contact with Jerusalem, the Israeli diplomat went on to note that, "Our target [Iran] is mutual but we beg to differ on how to achieve it [countering its military power]."[28]

Having become preoccupied with fighting two bloody military campaigns in Afghanistan and Iraq, the perception that the United States, now under the Obama Administration, was becoming increasingly wary (and weary) of further military commitments across the Middle East, appeared pervasive among the Gulf monarchies. This sense of retrenchment was itself testament to a growing belief among the actors involved that Pax Americana was increasingly tenuous. These perceptions had begun to influence attitudes towards both Iran and Israel even before the onset of the Arab Spring. Jerusalem was never naïve enough to ascribe unity of purpose to the position of the Gulf monarchies; Oman and Qatar in particular remained outliers in their public endorsement of close ties with Tehran. But behind closed doors, the Qataris were convinced that only the threat of military action could curtail Tehran's regional ambition and nuclear programme, the scope and scale of which Iran had only revealed under considerable pressure from the international community.[29]

To add to the mix, the Arab uprisings and their aftermath also acted as an important contextual driver behind Israel's burgeoning ties with the Gulf monarchies. What started in December 2010 as a series of

Tunisian anti-government protests quickly spread to other countries in the region, notably Egypt, Yemen, Syria and Bahrain. By the second half of 2011, however, the initial optimism generated in the Middle East and elsewhere by this series of popular rebellions against authoritarian regimes in the Arab world was dashed by the realities of the Arab upheavals. Indeed, the removal of President Hosni Mubarak from office, and his replacement by an Islamist government in Egypt led by Mohammed Morsi, raised acute concerns not only in Israel but equally in Riyadh, Abu Dhabi and Manama in particular.[30]

Israel now needed to adapt to this fast-changing regional environment. One focus was what Itamar Rabinovich and Itai Brun called the "amorphous relationship with the Sunni bloc in the Middle East."[31] The Gulf States too were increasingly preoccupied with the Iranian threat, the challenge of jihadi terrorism, as well as their increasing unease with the policies of the Obama administration. Against this background, the confluence of interests with Israel was becoming readily apparent. All shared a similar strategic outlook concerning threatening scenarios presented not just by Iran and its proxies, but a threat to the very regional order. In particular, Israel, Saudi Arabia and the UAE were concerned about one overriding trajectory following the overthrow of the regimes in Tunisia and Egypt: the fear that much of the Arab world, including the Gulf monarchies, might be swept by a radical, mostly Islamist wave. All clearly preferred an 'old order' and the preservation of conservative, autocratic regimes; all saw Islamist groups as their regional rivals—be it the Muslim Brotherhood in Egypt, Hamas in Gaza, al-Islah in the UAE and of course Hezbollah in Lebanon.

The wider impact of the upheaval triggered by the Arab uprising, however, was to expose the major rupture in the Middle East order: sectarian politics. This now flourished in the increasingly febrile atmosphere as tensions escalated amid a renewed contest for regional hegemony: Iran against Saudi Arabia, the UAE and Bahrain. While this tension reached its bloody apogee in Iraq, Syria and later in Yemen, the violence did much to shape elite attitudes across the Gulf monarchies about the value of seeking closer ties with Israel if the perceived threat from Iran was to be contained. As the scholar Mamoun Fandy noted in the Saudi-owned Arab daily *Asharq Al-Awsat*: "The good news, were [sic], that if Israel wants to strike a grand deal with the Arabs, now is the time to do it. Arab states are in their weakest political positions for a long time, and given their internal political upheavals they are ready to sign a comprehensive deal."[32]

This fear of unchecked Iranian ambition emboldened by a nuclear programme designed to underpin those selfsame goals only heightened concern that Washington, particularly under the Obama Administration, now looked to lessen its commitment to the security of the Gulf. Israel's relations with individual member states of the GCC now emerged increasingly from the shadows and with it, the contours of a TSR whose realm was independent of geographical proximity or, crucially, the development of normative principles designed to regulate the behaviour of the actors involved. As the next chapter argues, Israel's burgeoning relations with the states of the lower Gulf increased both quantitatively and qualitatively from 2009 onwards. While, as noted, this was a response to the rise of Iranian influence across the Gulf and the wider Middle East, other factors associated with Israel's own 'soft power,' as well as a perception of Jerusalem's influence in Washington, increasingly came to the fore.

2

ISRAEL AND THE LOWER GULF

SMALL-STATE DIPLOMACY

In July 2009 *The Washington Post* published an opinion piece by the heir to the Bahraini throne, Crown Prince Sheikh Salman bin Hamad al-Khalifa. He pointedly declared the need for creative thinking on the part of all parties concerned if the API was to have traction and mitigate a conflict that "needlessly impoverishes Palestinians and endangers Israel's security."[1] The article was significant for two reasons: firstly, it was explicit recognition by an Arab state of Israel's genuine security concerns, expressed in an influential publication; secondly, such an article—despite being authored by a leading member of the al-Khalifa dynasty—was most likely approved by Bahrain's suzerainty, Saudi Arabia.

To be sure, not all the states of the lower Gulf shared a consensus over ties with Israel, or indeed the extent and reach of Tehran's influence throughout the region.

Of the small Arab Gulf monarchies, Bahrain was always most likely to be the foremost advocate of discreet if durable ties with Jerusalem. Even before the protests that rocked the small island Kingdom in 2011, informed sources noted that Israel had developed links with Bahrain through *Tevel*, the foreign liaison division of Mossad. Such was the intimacy of these ties that the Bahraini monarch Hamad ibn Isa al-Khalifa instructed officials in Manama to refrain from reference to the "Zionist entity" or the "enemy," derogatory nomenclature used to refer to Israel more widely across the Arab world.[2] Initially at least, even Kuwait, long seen as among the more conservative monarchies of the Gulf, curbed its long-established propensity to condemn Israel and Zionism at any given opportunity. While no official government edict was ever declared, influential journalists such as Ahmad al-Sarraf were now critical of those imams who engaged in ritual condemnation of Jews and Christians in their Friday Sermons. Of one such individual he opined:

> I am intrigued by his curse beseeching Allah to also enable our 'mujahedeen brothers' or more accurately, 'ISIS and al-Qaeda,' to behead the Jews and Christians. It is they [the Jews and Christians] who gave this preacher the prayer mat on which he stands, who invented the microphone through which hundreds and thousands of people hear his curse ... It was also they that invented and produced the most complex medical

instruments and discovered the best serums and drugs which have healed millions of Muslims, and without which they could have died due to lack of care ... This preacher is entitled to curse who he wants. But leave the Jews and Christians alone.[3]

This outspoken attack on members of the Sunni clergy, and with it the championing of values associated with tolerance and respect for the other, demonstrated a discernible shift in the popular status quo as related to Jews and Israel. While some, such as Abdullah al-Nafisi, continued to condemn Israel, the marked increase in public discourse around it demonstrated a growing *de facto* acceptance of the state itself, often discernible in the casual yet defined use of the very term 'Israel' in public speeches. Of course, open hostility towards Israel remained: in 2016 Kuwait Airways suspended flights between the Emirate and New York to prevent Israeli passengers boarding their flights to the United States while transiting through Europe.[4] More recent moves by Kuwait to expel the Israeli Knesset from the Inter-Parliamentary Union appeared to resonate with a continued animus towards Jerusalem. However, such cases merely disguised a wider truth: the extent to which rising fears among the Gulf monarchies towards Iran's perceived regional malfeasance diluted their antipathy—collective and individual—towards Israel.[5]

Further evidence emerged that this wider societal acceptance (though not outright embrace of Israel) now had a wider traction across the region. As highlighted by the eighth annual Asda'a Burson-Marsteller Arab Youth Survey conducted in 2016, the Israeli–Palestinian conflict ranked only seventh when young Arabs were asked to identify the biggest challenges now facing the Middle East; Israel only elicited a mention by name on two occasions.[6] Yet it is Oman, Qatar, Bahrain and the UAE that best highlight the variated nature of Israel's ties with the regimes of the lower Gulf. Oman and Qatar, for example, have followed foreign policy goals and objectives that have often placed them at odds with other Gulf neighbours, and nowhere has this been more apparent than in their relations with Israel. For many years, both tried to avoid entanglement in the Palestinian–Israeli conflict, and both avoided ever fully enforcing the Pan-Arab economic boycott of Israel. Equally, Muscat and Doha have pursued what might be termed strategic hedging designed to "reduce the danger of conflict with Iran in the short term, while preserving contingency plans that address the severity of the threat and the uncertainty of the relationship in the long term."[7]

This in turn allowed Oman and Qatar to maintain their economic ties with Iran whilst protecting their own sovereignty and regional interests. This balance is pivotal to understanding the foreign policy of these smaller nations and how all parties, in developing and managing those ties, remain wary of paying too great an ideational price in pursuit of wider regional security.

However, they remain mindful that ties with the United States need to be preserved. Like other Gulf monarchies, both Oman and Qatar have come to realise the utility of ties to both pro-Israel groups and individuals in the United States, as well as Israel itself, as a conduit for ensuring their own security interests.

Oman: A Mercurial Ally?

Open contacts between Israel and Oman did not begin until after the 1991 Madrid Conference, but even so, Israel was no stranger to the sultanate. In the 1970s, Jerusalem provided discreet military assistance and advice to Sultan Qabus as part of his wider efforts to suppress the Marxist-inspired rebellion in Dhofar, aid that the Omanis were grateful to receive.[8] In 1975, a small advisory mission was sent to Oman, its presence remaining entirely hidden from the sultan's main military benefactor, the British government.[9] The following year, Oman began to distinguish itself by its willingness to enter into agreements with Western powers for the benefit of its own security, even if such deals courted controversy in the wider Arab world, including the Gulf states that saw this as little more than continued neo-colonialism. One such example was the military basing agreements that Oman signed with Washington in June 1980, the first of its kind in the Middle East, despite opposition from some of Oman's neighbours who were at the time negotiating the GCC's establishment. Equally, Muscat has always sought to balance this pro-Western orientation with a desire to maintain cordial ties with both Riyadh and Tehran, two powerful neighbours with historical claims on Omani territory. Given its geopolitical locale, it could not have been otherwise.[10]

Even so, the legacy of the Iranian revolution and the Soviet invasion of Afghanistan saw Oman align itself with the broader regional interests of the United States and the United Kingdom, best seen in the close military co-operation that has marked these relations ever since.[11] What was part of an Israeli outreach to second-tier states in the region paid dividends years later when Oman decided to support the Camp David Accords. In contrast to most other Gulf countries, Oman was one of only three Arab states (along with Morocco and Sudan) that did not break off relations with Cairo over its peace treaty with Israel, a position that inevitably attracted the ire of some of its Gulf neighbours.[12] Nevertheless, Oman remained unbowed: it agitated openly for Egypt's return to the wider Arab fold following its expulsion from the Arab League; and called for the use of the Camp David Accords as a template for future Middle East peace agreements, they being "the only means that achieved a constructive step in the direction of reaching a peaceful solution to the Middle East Issue."[13]

Although Oman had no formal public relations with Israel up until the early 1990s, both states co-operated in certain areas where Israeli expertise was most valuable, including drip-irrigation technology and other agricultural techniques that Israel had pioneered in similar climatic conditions. There were also hints of continued clandestine co-operation between Israel and Oman in the realm of intelligence collaboration and training, although the scope and extent of such ties remains a matter of conjecture.[14] Even before formal relations were established, Muscat held a relatively benign view of Israel, devoid of the latent anti-Semitism often masquerading as anti-Zionism that had, hitherto, marked so much commentary of Israel in the Arab press. Oman appeared ready to embrace closer ties with Israel even while the Oslo negotiations were ongoing, a position at odds with the other Gulf monarchies who felt such moves were premature without formal comprehensive peace having first been reached between Israel and the Palestinians.

There were several informal meetings between Israeli and Oman officials that preceded the visit of Prime Minister Yitzhak Rabin to Muscat in December 1994, during which he was given an official state welcome in Muscat while returning from the Far East. This opening to Muscat had been made possible by the signing of the peace treaty between Israel and Jordan, a country with whom Sultan Qabus had enjoyed particularly close relations.[15] In April 1994, Oman hosted the Middle East multilateral group on water resources and for the first time hosted an Israeli delegation led by the deputy

Foreign Minister Yossi Beilin.[16] Beilin returned in November to lay the groundwork for Rabin's eventual visit in December of the same year. As Raphael Ahren noted, "Although the trip lasted less than twenty-four hours, its very occurrence showed Oman's intention to follow its own path with regard to Israel."[17]

Further discussions followed the meeting, leading to speculation in the Israeli media that Oman and Israel were on the verge of establishing full diplomatic relations. By the spring of 1995, however, such hopes had yet to be realised. Muscat now argued that further progress was required in peace negotiations with the Palestinians before such ties could be established. Still, by September 1995 reciprocal trade missions were established, followed by the announcement that Israel would have a financing role in the Middle East Desalination Research Center (MEDRC) that was to be headquartered in Muscat. In October 1995 Oman and Israel finally reached agreement on the mutual establishment of commercial missions, once again raising hopes that formal diplomatic ties between the two states might now be concluded.[18]

However, events in Israel dictated otherwise. The assassination of Rabin in November 1995 by a young Jewish militant, Yigal Amir, who was bent on preventing any peace deal with the Palestinians that required Israeli territorial retrenchment, brought strong public condemnations from officials in Oman. Foreign Minister

Yusuf Ibn Alawi was one of several senior Arab representatives at Rabin's state funeral, before being hosted
in Jerusalem by Acting Prime Minister Shimon Peres. In
a subsequent interview given by Ibn Alawi to Israeli
media, he opined that "Oman will soon have diplomatic
relations with Israel; Oman was never in a state of war
with Israel so there is no need for a peace agreement."[19]
The intent appeared genuine. In January 1996, Israel
and Oman reached an agreement to open trade offices
in Muscat and Tel Aviv. They have continued to maintain quiet, but uninterrupted, low-level diplomatic ties
ever since, most notably through the MEDRC, which
came to double as a multilateral forum for Arab–Israeli
track II diplomacy.[20]

An organisation which in the truest sense of the term
has aimed to realise an epistemic community dedicated
to addressing water scarcity across the Middle East, the
MEDRC was established as a direct result of the Madrid
Conference and the Oslo Accords. Even though Muscat
forced the closure of the Israeli trade mission in Muscat
following the outbreak of the Al-Aqsa intifada in
September 2000, the continued participation of Israeli
scientists in the MEDRC has remained crucial to its
work, also allowing Israeli diplomats to continue to meet
with their Omani and Qatari counterparts under the
auspices of the Centre's collaborative ventures.[21] This
despite 'official ties' being held in suspended animation
for nearly two decades amid Muscat's stated desire to

strike a more nuanced position on the Palestinian–Israeli conflict, as well as its role in facilitating the strategic (and, for the most part, clandestine) dialogue between Iran and the Obama Administration that led to the signing of the JCPOA.[22]

Given Netanyahu's vehement opposition to this international agreement—an opposition that informed the decision of President Trump to withdraw the United States from its provisions in May 2018—the visit of the Israeli premier along with the head of Mossad, Yossi Cohen, to Oman in October 2018 caught most observers by surprise. As Zvi Bar'el, the veteran Israeli commentator on Arab affairs, noted, it certainly "crack[ed] the wall" of no public meetings between Arab Gulf leaders and an Israeli prime minister.[23] Of course, the meeting at one level was a classic iteration of Omani foreign policy: co-operation with a range of regional actors, including Iran, to ensure its own security, much to the irritation of Riyadh. The personal role played by Qabus in facilitating the secret talks that led to the signing of JCPOA under President Obama consequently did little to endear Qabus to Trump's administration, which saw the nuclear agreement as emboldening Iran's regional power.[24]

Netanyahu's very public trip was therefore as much about Oman re-engaging with President Trump as it was about diplomatic leverage, beyond a public relations coup, that Jerusalem hoped it could accrue. Speculation inevitably focused on whether Qabus, with his close ties to the Iranian regime, would act as an intermediary between Israel, Iran and even Syria. While this could not be ruled out, Iran was quick to criticise the meeting; Israel, meanwhile, had always preferred to use other actors, notably Germany, to 'converse' with Iran. However, it is telling that Israel, with the agreement of the Omanis, made the visit so public. It was a signal to other Gulf Arab leaders (and the wider Arab world) that they could be more open in their relations with Israel and that, faced with the Iranian challenge, they should follow in the sultan's wake. As one commentator noted:

> Exposing the ties with Oman is another layer in [Netanyahu's] strategy, which includes creating covert alliances—and public ones wherever possible—with moderate Sunni nations and movements, in an effort to prevent Iran's spread throughout the region, as well as undermine Tehran's regional power, all the while proving that Israel can normalise its ties with Arab nations even without solving the Palestinian issue.[25]

For their part, the Omanis remained keen to ensure that Netanyahu's visit was not seen as a radical departure from their support for a Palestinian state. Qabus was quick to send a letter of reassurance to Palestinian President Mahmoud Abbas, assuring him of Oman's continuing support for a Palestinian state. Mindful, however, that the visit had attracted opprobrium from those who felt that Israel's growing influence in the capitals of the Gulf came at the expense of the Palestinians,

Omani Foreign Minister Yusuf Ibn Alawi highlighted that both pragmatism and principle guided Muscat's approach towards resolving the Israel-Palestine conflict. At the end of October 2018 and before the gathering of the Manama Dialogue—a regional conference organised and held in Bahrain by the London-based think tank, the International Institute for Strategic Studies—Alawi rebuked those who believed past grievances had to determine a pan-Arab approach on the issue of Palestine. Israel, he noted, was a permanent state fixture in the Middle East and had a positive role to play in regional security. Palestinian rights and statehood had to be facilitated through state-to-state relations and Muscat was well placed to fulfil this role. From Jerusalem's perspective, however, it was proof that ties with the sultanate need not be contingent on tangible progress being made towards Palestinian statehood.[26]

Qatar: Reluctant Dependence?

For much of the twentieth century, Qatar's freedom to determine its own foreign policy remained limited, its rulers largely reliant on British retainers who advised the al-Thani and determined the scope of its foreign relations. As a creation of British imperial interests in the Gulf, London heavily influenced foreign policy-making in Doha while simultaneously exercising a degree of diplomatic latitude; this at least created a veneer of quasi-Qatari control over its external relations.

While British tutelage had ensured the defence, security and longevity of the ruling dispensation, the al-Thani, Qatar found it difficult to compete with its immediate neighbours, notably Saudi Arabia. Once independence had been gained, the priority of Qatari foreign policy was to seek alliances with stronger states in order to ensure its security, a form of 'bandwaggoning' that came to distinguish Qatari foreign policy and its propensity to shift allegiances in order to maintain the greatest amount of autonomy.

A major change came in 1995 following a bloodless palace coup that saw Crown Prince Hamad Bin Khalifah Al Thani remove his father, Khalifa bin Hamad Al Thani, and accede to the throne. Hamad was made the Crown Prince in 1977 and he carefully accumulated increasing power through the late 1980s. He had profoundly different ideas concerning Qatar's regional role and global reach, which were nothing if not ambitious. Following the coup, he looked for ways in which these ideas could be realised. In spite of its actual geographical size and relatively small native-born demographic, Qatar began attempting to "punch above its weight" in regional affairs.[27] Having one of the highest per capita incomes in the world, and sitting atop vast natural-gas reserves, gave the Emirate the financial wherewithal to realise its regional ambitions. The emergence of *Al Jazeera* as a global news channel willing to report on unpalatable events across the Middle East, much to the discomfort of its Gulf neighbours, proved the most visible expression of such ambitions.

In parallel, from the early 1990s Qatar, like Oman, looked to develop warm if low-level ties with Israel, in pursuit of an independent foreign policy that often placed it at odds with its Arab neighbours, notably Saudi Arabia. Doha openly engaged Israel following the Madrid conference, a position that became more substantive in the immediate aftermath of the Oslo Accords in 1993. Two years later and following the palace coup, Qatar's attitude towards the Jewish state had changed noticeably into a *de facto* process of limited normalisation. In part, this process was propelled by inter-Arab rivalries and the shifting dynamics in Gulf politics that now pushed the gas-rich but tiny emirate to establish relations with partners who could help Doha court closer ties with Washington.[28] A more nuanced position towards Israel was part of this strategy. Like Oman, Qatari representatives attended Yitzhak Rabin's funeral as well as hosting his successor, Shimon Peres, in Doha the following year in his role as Deputy Prime Minister. This position lay at odds with most Arab Gulf monarchies, who still resisted such overtures towards Israel before a peace agreement had been reached with the Palestinians.[29] As Uzi Rabi noted, by the late 1990s Doha was in serious talks with Israel over the mutual exchange of trade legations, as well as the potential purchase of liquefied natural gas.[30]

Still, following the outbreak of the Palestinian al Aqsa intifada in September 2000, Israeli–Qatari relations soured even though Doha proved reluctant to cut all ties with Jerusalem. It was only after pressure to do so from other Arab and Muslim states who, led by Riyadh, threatened to boycott the November meeting of the Organization of Islamic Conference (OIC) in Doha that Qatar finally succumbed. The Israeli trade office in Doha, while never a substantial operation, was nevertheless forced to close. Discreet contacts were maintained, however, and although the Israeli mission had been officially 'expelled,' trade relations continued to operate below the radar. A secret meeting was held in Geneva between Israeli foreign minister Shlomo Ben-Ami and a senior Qatari official in December 2000. Three years later, his successor, Silvan Shalom, met his Qatari counterpart, Hamad bin Jassim, at a time when the al-Aqsa intifada was still raging across Israel, the West Bank and Gaza.

An element of instrumentalism undoubtedly informed dealings between Doha and Jerusalem. In particular, the continued presence of the Israeli trade delegation, however unpopular, allowed Doha to curry favour in Washington while carving out a distinct regional identity that challenged Saudi dominance among the Gulf monarchies. Yet, despite the willingness of Doha to follow its own interests and deal favourably with Israel over particular issues on a bilateral basis, this did not prevent

Doha from being one of Jerusalem's staunchest critics following the outbreak in 2006 of the Second Lebanon War. While pro-Western governments, including Saudi Arabia, Jordan and Egypt, retained an air of studied ambivalence during the conflict, Qatar offered several times to try and mediate between the protagonists. When these entreaties failed, it chose to openly support Hezbollah and Hamas, becoming in the process the most vocal critic across the Arab world of the 'disproportionate' use of force by Israel against Hezbollah in southern Lebanon. During the conflict, it held a seat as a non-permanent member of the United Nations Security Council. It used this as a platform from which to criticise not just Israel's actions, but equally what it regarded as the moribund stance of the permanent members of the Security Council, who appeared unwilling, let alone able, to intercede in a concerted attempt to halt the violence: "It is most saddening that the council stands idly by, crippled, unable to stop the blood bath ... what is happening will sow the seeds of hatred and extremism in the area."[31]

Such views, however, were not confined to the Security Council. Most Sunni Arab states were both surprised and alarmed that Hezbollah emerged from the war intact, its very survival portrayed across the Arab street as a victory against the might of the IDF. It merely underscored the view in Riyadh that Lebanon had become the vassal of Hezbollah, a view given short shrift in Doha. In the immediate aftermath of the war and amid the deliberate indifference of other Sunni Arab states towards Lebanon's predicament, Qatar now contributed a small number of troops to the United Nations peacekeeping force (UNIFIL) in southern Lebanon, as well as sending supplies and financial aid to the Lebanese communities displaced by the violence. By 2008, it had even become the focus of efforts to underpin Lebanon's unwieldy and increasingly unrepresentative confessional system that had threatened to unravel under its many sectarian contradictions. This was best exemplified in the popular approbation enjoyed by Sheikh Nasrallah and the Hezbollah following the 2006 war, and the continued public outcry in Lebanon over the 2005 assassination of Rafik Hariri, the billionaire Lebanese businessman and former president of Lebanon. Both these events continued to reverberate not just in Lebanon itself, but internationally too. With his close business ties to the Saudis, the alleged involvement of both Hezbollah and Syria in Hariri's violent demise heralded the more public cleavages that were to mark inter-Arab relations from 2011 onwards.[32]

The deterioration in Israeli–Qatari relations continued following the 2008–9 Operation Cast Lead, as Israel launched a widespread military operation against Hamas and its assets across the Gaza Strip. Initial offers made to both sides by Doha to broker a ceasefire failed. In response, Qatar announced it was freezing all ties with Israel, threatened to close down the remnants of the Israeli trade office in the Qatari capital and called on all Arab states to reconsider their diplomatic ties with Israel.[33] But such moralising often ran parallel with a more pragmatic streak in the conduct of Qatari foreign policy. With the possibility of a seat on the UN Security Council as the Asian representative, Qatar approached Israel to support its bid. Israel actually responded positively to the request. This acknowledged that despite the tensions over Qatari links to Hamas and Hezbollah, Israel's low-level diplomatic representation in Doha had traction, a position in marked contrast to other countries that had demanded the closure of Israeli diplomatic missions (however low-level) across the Middle East. In turn, Jerusalem expressed the hope that, as a non-permanent member of the UNSC, Qatar would remain loyal to the "principles of fairness" and avoid using its new-found influence to further any anti-Israel resolutions or agendas.[34]

It was a diplomatic investment that appeared to pay some dividend. In 2010, the former Israeli Minister for Industry, Trade and Labour, Benjamin Ben Eliezer, made a surprise trip to Doha. Shortly after his visit, Qatar reportedly offered to upgrade diplomatic ties with Israel on the condition that Doha be allowed to carry out extensive reconstruction work in Gaza. Prime Minister Netanyahu, as well as Foreign Minister Avigdor Lieberman, baulked at this proposal, arguing that "allowing such massive amounts of construction material into the Strip, of the sort that Hamas uses to build bunkers and reinforced positions for missile launches against Israel, runs counter to Israel's security interests."[35] It is also likely that Israel's rejection came about because of pressure exercised by the former Egyptian President Hosni Mubarak, whose relations with Doha over its support for the Muslim Brotherhood, a semi-proscribed organisation in Egypt, had now reached a new nadir. Indeed, Qatar's offer of building materials and financial aid was viewed in Cairo as only giving succour to Hamas and its main sponsor, Iran. Both Cairo and Jerusalem now opined that "the Qataris had opted for an alliance with Iran and Hamas, so there was no reason to give them [diplomatic] gifts."[36] As such, the renewal of relations with Qatar was never a priority for Israel and certainly not one to be pursued at any price.

By contrast, Qatar viewed its relations with Iran and Hamas as providing useful political leverage and security cover: it allowed Doha to exercise influence with Tehran and the Palestinian militant movement and, crucially, place clear water between Doha and Riyadh over the latter's increasingly malign view of Iranian regional intent. However, Qatar's close ties with Hamas, coupled with *Al Jazeera*'s increasingly hostile coverage of Israel, led Jerusalem to sever its remaining ties with Qatar in March 2011, banning all Qatari passport holders from visiting the West Bank, and freezing what limited co-operation existed between Qatar and Israel's hi-tech security industries.[37] One year later, Qatar's ruler Hamad bin Khalifa Al Thani became the first head of state to visit Gaza since Hamas took control in 2007. During his visit, he pledged $400 million towards reconstruction projects, including two housing complexes and road building, resources Jerusalem believed would be of direct benefit to Hamas both economically and militarily. But Doha still signalled a willingness to reach an accommodation with Israel on the condition that Jerusalem at least demonstrate the intent to invest sufficient diplomatic effort in peace talks with the Palestinians.[38] Given the conditions set by the Arab League under the API for open ties with Jerusalem, this proved a relatively low threshold for continued engagement with Israel.

Still, by 2012 tensions over Gaza and the Qatari push for a greater regional role saw tensions between Doha and Jerusalem increase, but even so the embers of a relationship still flickered. In early March 2014, Israel permitted the entrance of 450,000 litres of fuel into the Gaza Strip, paid for by Qatar. This allowed Gaza's only electricity generating plant—closed in November 2013 following Cairo's crackdown on the tunnels used to smuggle the majority of fuel into Gaza under the Egyptian border fence—to resume operations.[39] This was one piece of the underlying dynamic that now determined Doha's regional engagement. As Lina Khatib noted, "Qatar has been involved in so many conflicts in the region—mainly as a mediator and provider of humanitarian aid—that it has almost become expected that, whatever the conflict facing the region, the tiny emirate will find a role for itself within it."[40] This highlighted a wider truth: underpinning Qatari foreign policy had been the "motivation not to succumb to the perils of small-state anonymity and vulnerability—perils of the kind from which Kuwait suffered in 1990," as well as a desire to offset Saudi influence within the GCC that now defined Qatari regional strategies.[41]

However, Israel remained wary of closer engagement with Qatar. In 2016, Netanyahu openly expressed his government's opposition to the proposed purchase of the F-15SE Silent Eagle by Doha and informed the Obama administration that if pushed, it would seek to lobby the US Congress to veto the sale should a commensurate Unites States military aid package to Israel not be increased by at least $10 billion. This amount would allow the Israeli Air Force to purchase two further squadrons of advanced F15 aircraft, deemed necessary if Israel's qualitative military edge (QME) was to be maintained in the all-important domain of air power relative to its Arab neighbours. As one Israeli government source noted, "Our American friends understand that we have serious problems with Qatar."[42]

But rather than taking a firm stance alongside the triumvirate of Riyadh, Abu Dhabi and Manama in countering what they regarded as Iran's aggressive regional ambitions, Qatar's "[I]nvolvement in conflicts across the Middle East and beyond represented an effort to present itself as a viable alternative to Saudi Arabia and a potential new leader in the Middle East."[43] By their sponsorship of regional non-state actors—notably the Muslim Brotherhood, regarded as a terrorist organisation by the Emiratis and Saudis in particular—and an independent line taken towards Iran, Qatar set itself on a course that would only lead to a confrontation with Bahrain, the UAE and Saudi Arabia. The decision of all three, plus Egypt, to withdraw their ambassadors from Doha in 2014 for consultations, was followed in June 2017 with the decision to break off all diplomatic and economic ties with Qatar and impose a land, air and sea blockade of the emirate until it complied with thirteen key demands, including the closure of *Al Jazeera* and a cessation of funding to 'terrorist groups,' a euphemism for the Muslim Brotherhood. These decisions marked a new nadir in inter-Gulf relations.[44]

By the beginning of 2019, relations between Doha and what might be called the anti-Qatari quartet remained tense, but Qatar had yet to succumb to their collective diplomatic, economic and indeed military pressure.[45] Its ties to the United States, despite the mercurial and often contradictory statements of the Trump Administration, gave it political cover and military assurance as Qatar continued to host the largest United

States military base in the region at Al-Udeid.[46] By allowing Qatar access to its airspace, Iran helped Doha mitigate the impact of the blockade while, alongside Muscat, Tehran increased the export of foodstuffs that had previously flowed into Qatar from their larger Gulf neighbour. But more than anything else, the inter-Gulf crisis and the continuing standoff between Doha and Riyadh underscored the "divergent and even conflictual security perceptions of its members," with Qatar and even Oman unwilling to accept the "hegemonic diktats" of Riyadh.[47]

This split among and within the Gulf monarchies, plus moves towards closer ties with Tehran, only reinforced Jerusalem's suspicions of Qatar's regional agenda. Given its largesse towards Hamas and support for the Muslim Brotherhood, both Israel and Egypt had long accused Qatar of being "the world's largest [state] funder of terror."[48] Such accusations were shared across Israel's otherwise fractious political divide. The late Israeli President Shimon Peres, long associated with peace-making efforts, was outspoken in his criticism of Doha's support for Hamas. Hosting a visit by the former UN Secretary General Ban Ki-moon to Israel, Peres was strident in his denunciation of the Gulf Emirate: "Qatar does not have the right to send money for rockets and tunnels which are fired at innocent civilians."[49] Following attempts by Doha to provide funds for the development of a Hamas-controlled civil service in Gaza, something blocked by the influence Washington was able to leverage over the Doha-based Arab Bank, Peres noted that "Their [Qatari] funding of terror must stop: if they want to build then they should but they must not be allowed to destroy."[50]

Yet Qatar knew it had strong diplomatic and economic cards to play that effectively neutered Saudi Arabia and the UAE from using force to bring Doha into line. Aside from Washington's military presence which, while largely directed towards Iran, had the added bonus of deterring Riyadh from enforcing regime change, Qatar realised that the dependence of much of the global economy on liquefied natural gas meant the international community was unlikely to countenance further regional instability. Its apparent success in mitigating the impact of the Saudi-led blockade now saw Qatar looking to leverage its diplomatic and global economic assets in the United States to ensure a continued hearing in Washington. This included outreach activities by the Qatari government to prominent Jewish–American figures known to be sympathetic to Israel—including Mort Klein, president of the Zionist Organisation of America—who were brought over to Qatar in 2017 and 2018. Some saw these trips as mere exercises in Qatari propaganda designed to obscure Doha's alleged ties to groups ranging from Hamas through to Al-Qaeda and the Taliban. The trips were met with outright condemnation by the Israeli embassy in Washington, although in his own defence Klein stated that he had pushed the Qataris on their support for Hamas as well as alleged cases of anti-Semitic incitement broadcast on *Al Jazeera* Arabic.[51]

But at a time when ties between the Trump Administration and the Saudis appeared to be getting ever warmer—personified in the close friendship between Trump's son-in-law and roving Middle East ambassador Jared Kushner, and Crown Prince Mohammed bin Salman—the Qatari strategy made sense. Under successive Obama administrations, developing ties with pro-Israel organisations in the United States as well as Israel itself were seen as a practical move for a president who appeared to understand and care little for their security predicament. The same logic now determined the Qatari approach. As Zvi Bar'el noted: "Qatar understands that it must strengthen its ties with the Jewish community and Israel if it is to maintain the strength of its ties in Washington."[52]

Its protestations of Qatar's support for a range of militant groups notwithstanding, Israel knew that Qatar had an influential role to play in the Gaza Strip, not least in the payment of salaries to Palestinians and the funding of infrastructure projects, notably a new power station. It remained in Israel's interests to forestall any conflict, and to that end improving basic living conditions in Gaza remained crucial. While previously Qatar was accused of sending money and material to Hamas, it remained the only actor whose immediate largesse was of a magnitude sufficient to prevent the total collapse of the Gaza economy following the September 2018 announcement by the Trump Administration that it was ceasing all aid to the United Nations Works and Relief Agency (UNWRA). This placed Israel in a quandary: while publicly welcoming Washington's stance, humanitarian distress in Gaza inevitably spilled over into the security realm, not least in the intermittent rocket attacks from Gaza into Israel. The permutations caused by Qatari involvement in brokering a deal between Israel and Hamas were truly Byzantine. Doha's efforts attracted the opprobrium of the Palestinian Authority in Ramallah, who regarded any deal between Israel and Hamas to have likely been reached at their expense. Short of reoccupying Gaza itself, with the human and material costs this entailed, political and economic pragmatism determined a clear Israeli need to engage with the Qataris over Gaza, despite the tensions this generated with Egypt. Indeed, as a ready go-between with Hamas, Qatar's usefulness as an interlocutor seemingly trumped whatever concerns Israel had over how much of their financial and material aid emboldened Hamas. By 2019, wary engagement best summed up this rather vexed bilateral relationship.[53]

Bahrain: Testing the Water

In 2010 it was reported that an unidentified female member of the al-Khalifa, the ruling dynasty in Bahrain, had elected to have 'life-saving' surgery at the Rambam Medical Centre in Haifa, rather than travel to the United States. A report that subsequently appeared in *The Times of Israel* quoted Ayoub Kara, Israel's Minister for Regional Cooperation, that "Israel was the best place for her to get better," most likely from a form of cancer, having turned down the offer to have the necessary treatment in the United States.[54] Netanyahu agreed to what clearly had been a delicate request and senior ministers subsequently helped to facilitate the trip, a humanitarian gesture that underscored a burgeoning relationship of some regional significance.

Like the rest of the Arab Gulf, Bahrain's ties with Israel had always been shaped by the issue of Palestine but not determined by it. For the al-Khalifa, more pressing and enduring were the tensions with Iran, born from Bahrain's close geographic proximity and fears that the Kingdom's own Shi'a majority remained, in effect, a fifth column, able and willing to do Tehran's bidding in subverting this Sunni dispensation. There is, of course, an element of caricature in this assessment: denial of basic human rights and the wider participation of Bahrain's largely Arab Shi'a population in determining an order based on primogeniture explained much of the unrest that festered across this tiny island.[55] Even so, evidence does exist of Iran's involvement with a number of militant cells, which, alongside its territorial claims to the island that long predate the Iranian revolution, proved enough to convince the al-Khalifa of Tehran's malfeasance, however inflated this might appear.[56]

This context shaped Bahrain's view of Israel. Its size, and increasing economic and security reliance on Riyadh as its oil resources diminished, meant that it never developed an avowedly independent foreign policy, and certainly not one that would upset relations with its immediate neighbour and biggest patron, Saudi Arabia. Equally, the fact that Bahrain made overtures towards Israel and pro-Israel groups over a number of years suggests that Manama acted as a diplomatic surrogate for the Saudis and indeed the Emiratis. By using Manama's tentative engagement with Israelis as a trial balloon, Riyadh and Abu Dhabi could better gauge wider Arab reaction before deciding their next steps.[57]

Such instrumentalism of course should not obscure the real benefits that Bahrain believed could be achieved through a strategic dialogue with the Jewish state. In October 1994, the late Yossi Sarid, then serving as environment minister in the government of Yitzhak Rabin, made the first visit by an Israeli minister to Bahrain, made possible by the signing of the Oslo Accords the previous year. The Bahrainis made very clear, however, that closer ties would only follow once progress was made in talks with the PLO towards Palestinian statehood. The assassination of Rabin and the subsequent collapse of the Oslo process placed such hopes in abeyance but, despite proclamations of fidelity to the

Palestinian cause, senior members of the Bahraini royal family continued to meet with their Israeli counterparts on the margins of international events such as the World Economic Forum at Davos. During one such event in 2005, Sheikh Abdul Aziz bin Mubarak al-Khalifa, the Bahraini Under-secretary of State of Foreign Affairs, told the late Israeli President Shimon Peres that for every step Israel took towards the Palestinians, Bahrain would take two towards Israel.[58] These steps were never taken but the message was clear enough: Bahrain wanted dialogue. Certainly, Manama never exhibited the anti-Semitism that had so marked previous commentary towards Jews and Israel across the Gulf. The appointment in 2011 of Houda Ezra Ebrahim Nonoo as Bahrain's ambassador to Washington was therefore notable on two counts: not only was she the first female appointee from the Arab world to serve in this capacity, but she was also the first ever Jewish ambassador to serve from an Arab state.[59]

However, this was more than just token symbolism. While it demonstrated a modicum of social mobility among Bahrain's tiny Jewish population of thirty-six people, it also presaged the start of an incremental but calibrated strategy that increasingly saw Bahrain engage with a range of Jewish groups and influential Jewish leaders in the United States, most with close ties to Israel. By the beginning of 2017 this approach was brazen. King Hamad bin Isa al-Khalifa stunned the heads of the Simon

Wiesenthal Center in Los Angeles, Rabbis Marvin Hier and Abraham Cooper, during their visit to Bahrain when the monarch criticised the continued Arab economic boycott of Israel. That autumn, the Center played host to a multinational event that promoted religious tolerance, and where Nasser bin Hamad al-Khalifa, King Hamad's son, was in attendance. At the event, the Bahrain National Orchestra, which accompanied the prince on his trip to the West Coast of the United States, played '*Hatikva,*' the Israeli national anthem, alongside the American and Bahraini anthems, despite there being no official Israeli delegation at the event.[60]

Like Saudi Arabia, Bahrain had long opposed the JCPOA and continued to support the vocal opposition of Netanyahu to the deal, even after it was signed in the summer of 2015. Indeed, Israel's rejection of the deal offered a means by which Riyadh and Manama could both register their concerns and leverage influence in tandem with an actor they, more than most, knew carried political clout and bipartisan support on Capitol Hill. For Bahrain, this clout was amplified still further with the election of Donald Trump to the White House in November 2016, the incremental embrace of Israel and Israelis continuing apace. In May 2018, a Bahraini delegation participated in the Israeli leg of the Giro D'Italia bicycle race, and while reasserting its support for the Saudi-sponsored API, Bahrain welcomed the Israeli delegation to the forty-second UNESCO conference held in the capital Manama in June 2018. It led many to speculate whether Bahrain would be the first Gulf state to establish full diplomatic relations with Israel, despite the absence of any progress towards an agreement with the Palestinians.[61] In the wake of Netanyahu's surprise visit to Muscat in October 2018, Bahrain invited the Israeli economy and industry minister, Eli Cohen, to attend the annual Start-up Nations Ministerial Conference in Manama, a global event designed to foster global entrepreneurship across the hi-tech sector.[62] Bahrain, however, remained circumspect over the scope and scale of any burgeoning relationship with Israel.

Even so, and with concern over Iran very much to the fore, the June 2018 Twitter statement by the Bahraini Foreign Minister Khalid bin Ahmed al-Khalifa, that "Israel had the right to defend itself" against Iran, signalled an open alignment of strategic concern with the Jewish state.[63] He even noted that the relocation of the United States embassy to Jerusalem did not impact upon Palestinian claims to al-Quds, because it was located in the west of the city and away from the area claimed by Palestinians as their capital in the east. As a break from the emotive Arab consensus over the future of Jerusalem, it was a profound statement, but equally a sober acknowledgement among decision-makers in Manama that the road to Washington often runs through the corridors of power in Jerusalem. As if to emphasise the point, one unnamed Israeli official remained adamant that "Bahrain will be the first Gulf state to form [open diplomatic] ties with Israel."[64]

United Arab Emirates: Soft Power with a Hard Edge

Bahrain might well have been the first Gulf monarchy to establish formal diplomatic ties with Jerusalem. Yet its value to Israel remained as an entrée to the other, more powerful Gulf monarchies; of these, ties to the UAE became deeper and more developed, strategically and economically, than to any other monarchy in the Gulf. Again, shared views over Iran's growing regional reach coupled with the Emirati desire to harness Israel's undoubted technological prowess in cyber technologies to enhance its own state security apparatus, proved the drivers behind contacts first disclosed in 2010. Then the Israeli national daily newspaper, *Ha'aretz*, published a cache of diplomatic cables released by *Wikileaks* that detailed the warm relationship between former Israeli foreign minister and leader of the centrist Kadima party, Tzipi Livni, and her Emirati counterpart, Sheikh Abdullah bin Zayed. This was the case despite the absence of any formal diplomatic ties, low-level or otherwise, between the two states. Aside from shared suspicion over the regional designs of Tehran, a mutual loathing of the Muslim Brotherhood and its regional offshoots, including *Hamas*, underpinned this meeting of diplomatic minds.[65]

Later, in 2010, Israel's then Minister of Infrastructure Uzi Landau travelled to the Emirates to attend the International Renewable Energy Agency (IRENA) conference. Landau's attendance was the first visit by a serving Israeli minister to the country; however, two Israeli officials had visited the country just three months prior to his arrival to attend another IRENA conference.[66] A man whose hardline views towards the Palestinians brooked no compromise, it is notable that Landau's attendance paved the way for the establishment of a permanent Israeli mission at the agency by October 2015, a move that had been widely flagged. This established the first official Israeli representation in the UAE and garnered considerable coverage in the tightly controlled Emirati press. Israeli officials in turn were only too well aware of the sensitivity surrounding the mission and remained keen to ensure that its diplomatic footprint remained light.[67]

Accordingly, Rami Hatan, a relatively junior diplomat and the former director of the World Religious unit within the Israeli Ministry of Foreign Affairs, was appointed head of mission. Unlike the Israeli representation to MEDRC in Muscat, which had never been staffed on a regular basis, Hatan's posting to Dubai was permanent as he headed up the small Israeli mission to IRENA.[68] For some, it was a reasonable assumption to make that the IRENA mission represented something of a vanguard. Should ties between the UAE and Israel be placed on a formal footing, a more substantive mission could quickly be grafted on to the existing IRENA staff.[69] In 2016, the office hosted one expert in the field of renewable energies and one member of the Israeli security services.[70] While small, IRENA was a tangible expression of improved relations between the UAE and Israel which stretched back over a decade.[71]

This development followed several years of careful diplomatic manoeuvring and support Israel had given to the bid by the Emiratis to host the headquarters of IRENA, a bid which Jerusalem had supported over a rival German offer. Still, a price was exacted. Israeli officials stated—albeit anonymously—that a condition placed on the support they gave the UAE in 2009 was based on the guarantee of unrestricted Israeli participation in the project as well as the opening of a diplomatic mission within the UAE that would be formally accredited to the agency.[72] However, the UAE remained keen to scotch any rumours that Israeli participation in IRENA presaged the establishment of more formal diplomatic ties. Maryam al Falasi, the Director of Communications at the Ministry of Foreign Affairs, stated that:

> The International Renewable Energy Agency is an international, independent agency that works according to the laws, regulations and norms that govern the work of such organisations. Any agreement between IRENA and Israel has to date not signalled any change in the position of the UAE or its relations with Israel.

[The dealings of IRENA] do not under any circumstances cover any other activities, and do not involve any obligation upon the host country with regards to its diplomatic relations or any other relations.[73]

IRENA issued a parallel statement that coincided with the UAE government communication, outlining that,

[U]nder the agreement, which entered into force in October 2013, the UAE as a host country is responsible for the provision of facilities and services that ensure the proper functioning of the agency's work. Israel is a member of the agency. Under the agreement, the work of member missions is confined to the agency ... and bears no implication on the relations between the IRENA member and the host country.[74]

Neither government was willing to move these low-level ties beyond the public affirmation of shared membership of the IRENA, but this belied the warmth of an emerging relationship in which Israel's increasing use of hi-tech diplomacy began to leverage hard-power influence.[75] With its pro-Western orientation, a declared antipathy towards Hamas, and particularly its close relations with Saudi Arabia, the attraction of closer ties to the UAE was obvious.[76] If the Gulf monarchies had long looked at ties with Israel as a way to curry favour in Washington, Israel now increasingly regarded relations with the Emirates as underpinning ties to Riyadh. Claims that the UAE was given prior warning of Israel's

'Operation Protective Edge' in 2014, and that Abu Dhabi pledged to help reconstruction effort in Gaza if Hamas were eliminated, were vehemently denied by the Emiratis.[77] Even so, a clear pattern of increased regional accommodation based on shared security concerns was clearly discernible: an accommodation that saw Israeli concessions to the UAE now extend to the realm of US politics.

In December 2009, Washington and Abu Dhabi signed the '123' agreement for peaceful nuclear co-operation, an agreement that saw nuclear technology transferred to Abu Dhabi for the building of its first nuclear reactor. While the Emiratis agreed to forgo any nuclear fuel recycling capability, long regarded as integral to the establishment of a nuclear weapons programme, the development of any nuclear capacity by an Arab country had long been regarded as a security challenge by Israel. But in a sign that regional calculations in Jerusalem had shifted, mobilisation of opposition to the deal on Capitol Hill was conspicuous by its absence. US Congressional lawmakers approved the accord while pro-Israel lobby groups, including the powerful American Israel Public Affairs Committee, the American Jewish Committee and the Anti-Defamation League, refrained from raising any concerns. Although the agreement did not impact directly on relations between Israel and the UAE, the silence of the Israel lobby in Congress suggested that Jerusalem deliberately chose not to raise any objections. Given Israel's obvious sensitivity towards any deal involving nuclear research and development in the Middle East, Israel's studied silence on the issue was truly deafening. In 2017, reflecting more broadly on Israel's security ties to the UAE, one senior Emirati Air Force officer, Major-General Abdullah al-Hamshi, noted with unusual candour that the UAE and Israel were like "brothers with the United States as the older sibling, arbitrating over any differences between the two."[78] It was a telling statement.

It was in the realm of commerce and business, however, that bilateral ties truly flourished. Many Israeli businesses trade regularly with Dubai and Abu Dhabi via third counties, and visit the Emirates using foreign passports. It was even reported that Etihad, UAE's national airline company (as well as Qatar Airways) allowed Israeli passengers flying to East Asia to board their scheduled flights when travelling via Jordan, thereby benefitting from cheaper tickets.[79] It is hard to know the actual scale of these business dealings, not least because fidelity to the issue of Palestine, however symbolic, continued to place ideational constraints on the relationship. However, discreet edicts were issued by Abu Dhabi, designed specifically to remove obstacles to the flow of labour and capital where, previously, association with Israel would have proven an impediment. The UAE government came to an agreement with the United Kingdom to guarantee British nationals free entry and exit to the Gulf state regardless of the presence of either valid or expired Israeli visas or stamps.[80] This move towards greater freedom of movement was designed to help stimulate trade deals, given the increasing number of businesses in the UK with financial backing from the City of London engaging in high-value trade with Israel.[81]

The desire of the UAE to encourage such inward investment later saw the moratorium on Israeli visa stamps in passports extended to other European countries. Keen to tap in to a wider pool of talent that could help diversify its previous dependence on hydro-carbons as the mainstay of its economy, the UAE authorities announced in 2015 that "the existence of an Israeli stamp on a passport is not a reason to reject an appeal for entry to the UAE."[82] The relatively liberal stance taken by the UAE over this issue highlighted not just tolerance to an Israeli presence on Emirati soil, but a realisation that, in an increasingly knowledge-based, globalised economy, the absolute restrictions on Israel for those companies and individuals who enjoyed only a tangential relationship with the Jewish state made little sense.

That tolerance was of course tested. Mossad was believed to be behind the assassination of senior Hamas operative Mahmoud al-Mabhouh in a Dubai hotel on 19 January 2010.[83] Yet while the killing was met with public opprobrium in Abu Dhabi and an almost ritual condemnation across the region and much of Europe, such reactions were almost choreographed for domestic consumption: al-Mabhouh's alleged connections with Tehran and his role in acquiring Iranian arms for the Islamist movement in Gaza hardly earned him the gratitude of many of the Gulf monarchies. In as much as there can be diplomatic fall-out between states that have no official ties, it was relatively short-lived.[84]

Just two years later, Netanyahu met secretly with the UAE Foreign Minister, Sheikh Abdullah bin Zayed al-Nahyan, in the immediate aftermath of the Israeli premier's 2012 address to the UN where he again denounced Iran's nuclear programme and regional ambitions. While differences on the issue of Palestine were likely never to be resolved, bin Zayed "expressed his appreciation for Netanyahu's speech to the General Assembly, and the two agreed on a large number of issues concerning the question of a nuclear Iran."[85] It validated a defining element of the TSR: a recognition and acceptance that it guides actor(s) towards a particular type of action, and even acceptance of this action, while not precluding competition or co-operation in other realms.

It certainly had little bearing on a burgeoning military engagement in the realm of air power between Abu Dhabi and Jerusalem, an engagement that proved that, whatever the diplomatic embarrassment caused, both parties had moved on from the al-Mabhouh affair. From 2016 onwards, Israeli Air Force F16 'Sufa' jets flew alongside and trained with their Emirati counterparts in a series of air exercises in Europe and the United States, organised under the auspices of NATO. While the participation of the air forces of other nations helped 'dilute' the association with Israel, the fact that the UAE chose to participate in these war games, knowing full well that the IAF too would be present, was recognition of the warmth and increasing resilience of this discreet relationship.[86] Representing as it did a level of military association, let alone engagement that, just a decade before, would have been unprecedented, by 2018 these exercises had become the new norm, eliciting little more than a few lines in the Israeli national press. This exchange of expertise and experience even extended to discussion over the role and capabilities of the F-35 stealth fighter aircraft. One of the first recipients of what is widely considered to be the most capable strike aircraft in the world, Israel became the first state to deploy the F-35 operationally in May 2018. Two months later, it was reported that a delegation of UAE Air Force officers visited Israel to be briefed on its capabilities as the Emirates now looked to purchase their own squadron of F-35 jets.[87]

But it is in the realm of internal security that the UAE set out to harness Israel's undoubted expertise. In 2008 reports first surfaced that Israeli-owned (though not necessarily-based) companies were helping to train the security forces of an unnamed Gulf state, providing

advanced military technological knowhow, most notably in the areas of intelligence and surveillance.[88] It soon
emerged that the recipient of much of this training, and
with it the purchase of technology designed to bolster its
wider electronic surveillance assets, was the UAE.
ImageSat, a subsidiary of Israel Aerospace Industries,
reportedly supplied satellite reconnaissance services to
the United Arab Emirates, while the company Aero-
nautics won a contract to supply unmanned aerial vehicles (UAVs) or drones, again to the UAE.[89] Another
deal, reportedly concluded between the Swiss-registered
Israeli company Asia Global Technologies (AGT) and
the Emirate of Abu Dhabi (UAE), included the sale of
surveillance cameras, electronic fences and sensors to
monitor strategic infrastructure.[90] But particular interest
began to focus upon Israel's direct involvement in the
development of the UAE's Falcon Eye Surveillance system that

> [E]nables multiple governmental agencies to utilise a
> unified, cost-effective city platform for an abundance of
> crucial urban functions including crime prevention, traf-
> fic management, and emergency preparedness. The pro-
> ject infrastructure consists of high-definition sensors
> powered by advanced data processors and analytics, an
> integrated intelligence and investigation tools and mul-
> tiple tailored to various governmental agencies' use.[91]

Falcon Eye was the brainchild of Israeli hi-tech entrepreneur Mati Kochavi who, between 2007 and 2015

and through his Zurich-based subsidiary company AGT International, developed, installed and integrated thousands of high-resolution cameras, sensors and licence plate readers along the borders of the UAE and throughout its main conurbations. The total deal, worth an estimated $800 million, proved its worth in 2014 when the technology was used to track down the killer of an American schoolteacher, stabbed to death in a shopping mall in Abu Dhabi. So labour-intensive was the project to design, build and construct that special travel arrangements were devised to ensure that the project was delivered on time:

> Twice a week at the height of the project, a chartered Boeing 737, painted all white, took off from Tel Aviv's Ben Gurion Airport, touching down briefly in Cyprus or Jordan for political cover, and landed about three hours later in Abu Dhabi with dozens of Israeli engineers on board, many of them [just] out of the intelligence services. They lived and ate together—never in restaurants—carried transmitters and panic buttons at all times, and disguised their nationality and Hebrew names as best they could. They called Israel "C country"; Kochavi was known as "MK."[92]

The scope and scale of the Falcon Eye project likely remains the most lucrative trade deal signed between any Gulf state and an Israeli company at the time of writing, but others are following in its wake. Israeli high-tech companies have become world leaders in spyware, sometimes called 'Trojan horse programmes.' Innocuous text messages with links can be sent to mobile phones; if opened by the user, these effectively commandeer the phone, giving access to text messages, emails, infiltration of apps, even the ability to photograph and record conversations without the owner ever being aware. NSO, a company based in Herziliya, developed 'Pegasus,' described by *Forbes* magazine as the "world's most invasive mobile spy kit."[93]

Such technology is used by intelligence services and law-enforcement agencies countering, for example, terrorist networks and organised crime. Yet such surveillance capabilities also have a utility for autocratic regimes in monitoring dissident activities, both at home and abroad. Formal permission has to be given by Israel's Defence Exports Control Agency, part of the Israeli defence ministry, for such technology to be sold to overseas customers, but to who exactly and under what criteria such sales are condoned remain opaque. What has emerged is that Israeli-produced spyware has been sold to a range of autocratic regimes, including the UAE and Bahrain. Pegasus spyware was reportedly used to track and monitor the Emirati dissident and human rights activist Ahmed Mansoor, later sentenced to ten years in prison for publishing tweets critical of the regime on social media. It has even been alleged that Pegasus spyware was used to track and monitor over 150 members of the Qatari royal family. In a bid to win a contract from the UAE Supreme Council for National Security, one Israel company, Circles, intercepted the conversation of the editor of the Qatari based newspaper *Al-Arab* over a period of forty-eight hours. Similar technologies have also been sold to Bahrain that allow data gathering from social networks to be analysed in real time. In the case of Pegasus, because such spyware is deemed to be a weapon by Israel, its sale to the Emiratis could only have been authorised by the Israeli defence ministry.[94]

Such deals were perhaps best seen as the vanguard of Israel's own version of 'soft-power' diplomacy with hard-power impact that promised not just a financial return for the companies involved, but a wider security dividend for the Jewish state. However, not all Israelis involved in the cyber-security industry were comfortable with such sales. Aside from software being cloned by potential adversaries, the questionable human rights records of more autocratic customers raised questions as to the criteria being used to authorise sales.[95] But, as Dima Adamsky noted, "The cyber charm offensive has become one of the main endeavours in the Israeli struggle for international attractiveness."[96] It was a sentiment endorsed publicly by Netanyahu himself. Writing in *The Economist* at the beginning of 2018, the Israeli prime minister made no secret of the link between Israel's hi-tech sector and its ability to further its wider regional interests. He noted that two lessons could be drawn from what he referred to as Israel's economic miracle:

firstly, innovate or perish in an increasingly globalised market; secondly, "innovate to create alliances and advance peace." He went on to note that "Many Arab states now see Israel not as an enemy but as an indispensable ally in our battle against militant Islam. They also seek Israeli technology to help their economies. The potential normalisation with Arab states could help pave the way for peace with the Palestinians."[97]

Netanyahu was clearly outlining the contours of a new regional reality regarding some Arab Gulf monarchies. Whether they, in turn, fully appreciated reference to an implicit dependence on Israel's technological knowhow, let alone the barely concealed suggestion that the cart of Arab normalisation come before the horse of an Israeli–Palestinian peace deal, remains doubtful. Still, his statement highlighted a wider truth regarding economic ties and trading relations between Israel and the Gulf monarchies: that despite the thorny issue of Palestine and the Palestinians, such ties had become manifold in terms of their diversity, and manifest in terms of their wider political significance. The same week that the Israeli prime minister met Sultan Qabus in Muscat in October 2018, his minister for sport and culture Miri Regev, visited the UAE, accompanying an Israeli athlete competing in the World Judo Championships in Abu Dhabi, where the Israeli national anthem was played for the first time. Later, she was given a personal tour of Sheikh Zayed Grand Mosque, leading her to declare on social media, "We made history. The people of Israel live."[98]

Economic and Trade Relations with the Lower Gulf

It remains difficult to measure the actual trade levels between Israel and the monarchies of the Gulf with any accuracy. Because of the continuing stigma still attached to open trade deals with Israel, the volume of economic exchange has always been hidden behind front companies and third parties, making it hard to trace capital flows and the exchange of goods and services. But if the use of Israeli surveillance technologies by the Gulf monarchies is any guide, these economic ties look set to increase exponentially. The trajectory already exists: from 2003 to 2012 indirect trade with the Gulf monarchies represented Israel's third largest market in the Middle East, after the Palestinian Authority and Turkey.

While often conducted through third parties—there was a distinct preference for straw companies registered in Europe—annual trade in 2012 alone was reckoned to generate around $500 million.[99] Because of their sensitive nature, more recent figures have yet to be released by the Israeli government. Even so, the true volume of trade was likely to have been significantly higher because Israel benefited from additional Gulf market access, not only via the provision of goods and service through companies operating from Europe, but through goods delivered via third parties in the Middle East devoid of any Israeli insignia. Moreover, Saudi Arabia's accession to membership of the World Trade Organization (WTO) had been accepted on the basis that it would cease to uphold both the secondary and tertiary boycotts of Israeli goods and services. Although the compliance of international companies with the boycott had declined over the years, acceptance of this position by Saudi Arabia now encouraged investments by leading international car, food and electronics companies that had previously refrained from establishing commercial ties with Israeli companies. By 2016 it was estimated that the actual volume of Israeli indirect trade to the Gulf monarchies was close to $1 billion, with most of this going through European and other non-MENA states.[100]

Riyadh never formally stated its *de jure* acceptance of this particular condition of membership to the WTO, but the *de facto* impact on Israel's economy was profound.[101] Inward investment from global private investment in Israel's hi-tech industries—notably cyber security—and buttressed by collaborative innovation and research ventures, in areas ranging from nano technologies to car-navigation systems, came to define Israel as 'the start-up nation.' Much of this new-found wealth would have been denied to the Israelis if the secondary boycott had been upheld by the Gulf monarchies. When in 2017 the American technology giant Intel acquired the Israeli company Mobileye for $15.9 billion—a company that harnessed algorithms and artificial intelligence—to become a world leader in driverless technology, the deal was as much a reflection of the new regional reality as it was about Israel's undoubted prowess in hi-tech innovation.[102]

It was a view of Israel and its regional influence that Netanyahu expounded upon at every given global opportunity. Addressing the World Economic Forum in January 2016, for example, he set forth the virtues to be had from Israel playing a greater role in the regional economy, and the wider political benefits to be accrued from such exchanges across the Gulf monarchies. With a large defence and technology sector to nurture and sustain, Netanyahu deliberately promoted Israel's qualitative edge in the field of cyber defence in a speech clearly designed to link regional economic well-being with the threat posed by Iran to both Israel and the Gulf monarchies.[103] With 4.7 per cent of Israel's GDP being focused on the R&D sector, the greatest number of engineers as a proportion of the workforce in the Middle East and North Africa, and a new double taxation regime helping to address fears relating to the return on investments made, the focus of the conference turned to the geopolitical situation. Netanyahu argued that the economic security that Israel had achieved had held the potential to help wean the Gulf monarchies away from their dependence on fossil fuels as they now sought to diversify their economies and open up their public sectors for greater private investment.[104]

Netanyahu's comments were consistent with one of the key facets of the TSR outlined: that other modes and means of exchange can and do mark relations between erstwhile protagonists, and that over time this allows subtle and indeed not so subtle signals to be exchanged that can facilitate, incrementally, acceptance of a more open dialogue increasingly unencumbered by ideational constraint. As with the burgeoning nature of diplomatic ties, the modalities of increased economic exchange would likely remain discreet; but coupled with the renewed interest in resolving the region's security questions, this carried the potential to instigate broader collaboration over the coming years. At the very least, such sentiment underscored a wider Gulf-Arab acceptance of elite dialogue, an important variable, as noted in our framework, in legitimising a more substantive exchange of both political and strategic goods between regime actors. However, as important as such ties and sentiments had become to Jerusalem, their level and intensity were ultimately dependent on the position of Saudi Arabia and the extent to which Riyadh was willing to confront its own Wahhabi religious establishment— which had long regarded Israel as an apostasy—in its own efforts to construct a broader diplomatic and military front against Tehran.

3

MORE THAN THE SUM OF ITS PARTS?

ISRAELI–SAUDI RELATIONS

As the key actors in the evolution of the TSR, both Israel and Saudi Arabia have embraced not just the 'unwritten' and 'uncodified' of Klieman's TSR definition, but increasingly the more open if subtle signals between key actors, whose importance is more than just the symbolism of the act. Rather, as noted from the outset of this study, the TSR helps to engender over time a public acceptance of more open, even substantive exchange of strategic and political goods, thereby allowing the regime to change and adopt as ideational context dictates.

Certainly, from 2010 onwards, influential Saudis became more open in their dealings with Israel, an approach noteworthy for the absence of rancour that had hitherto marked any nuanced discussion of Israel. On the tenth anniversary of the 9/11 attacks, an article appeared in *The New York Times* in which the former

Saudi ambassador to London and Washington and one-time head of the Kingdom's General Intelligence Directorate, Prince Turki al-Faisal al-Saud, explained that the "2002 Arab Peace Plan must be the starting point for negotiations."[1] The Prince emphasised the Kingdom's renewed commitment to reach a comprehensive regional settlement, arguing that the API should be seen as the beginning rather than an absolute endpoint of any Israeli–Arab negotiations. The importance of the article was not just in declaring a Saudi position, influential as this was given the Kingdom's status as the protector of Islam's two most holiest sites. Rather, it lay in the fact that such a statement was made by a man considered close to the centre of Saudi decision-making and through an outlet designed to attract attention and comment in Israel as much as the United States. It also underscored Riyadh's claim to influence in the Sunni Arab world: only the Saudis could provide the Palestinian leadership with the political and religious legitimacy required to sign an agreement with Israel that addressed the core issues of refugees, borders and the status of East Jerusalem.

In retrospect, the interview laid the groundwork for a more public if still critical engagement with Israel. In March 2014, the Prince again used an interview with an international newspaper, *The Financial Times*, to acknowledge Israel's intelligence services as "[T]he most professional, although they've committed a lots of mistakes. But they do accomplish their missions."[2] Just two months later, in an event hosted in Brussels by the German Marshall Fund, the Saudi shared a platform, primarily to discuss the API, with the former head of Israeli military intelligence and—at the time of writing—Director of the Institute for National Security Studies, Major-General Amos Yadlin. Despite being outside their respective government decision-making circles (both men occupy leading positions in security think tanks), they retained some measure of influence over their respective administrations. The Saudi, scion of the late King Faisal, declined an open invitation from Yadlin to visit Jerusalem, the Israeli having invited him to pray at the Haram-al-Sharif and address the Knesset in Jerusalem. Many commentators described the reaction of al-Faisal as a "snub," but in reality the political limits placed on him were well known to both individuals and the circumscribed answer from the Saudi was to be expected.[3]

However, the importance of the meeting was to be found in its political symbolism rather than in any tangible progress made. Of great significance (and largely overlooked at the time) was the fact that the event was streamed live to a global audience on social media and the internet, breaking a long-held taboo that any Saudi, let alone one identified so closely with the ruling family, could ever appear in public with their erstwhile foe. While Crown Prince Turki continued to champion the

API as the basis for any wider engagement with Israel, his appearance was consistent with a discernible if low-key Saudi 'intellectual' approach towards Jerusalem that eschewed the crude stereotype and epithets of previous years.

This now embraced a more nuanced appreciation of the security dilemmas facing Jerusalem, and Israel's response modes. Brigadier-General Naef Bin Ahmed al-Saud, for example, wrote a detailed appreciation of the role played by social media in changing the security landscape across the region. Israel was mentioned by name, rather than sobriquet, with a recognition of the religious and social cleavages that distinguished Israeli society very much to the fore. But of particular note in his essay, published in the American military journal *Joint Force Quarterly*, was its thinly-veiled support for Israel's security response to those Turkish and other activists who in 2010 harnessed the global reach of social media to rally international support as they attempted to breach Israel's maritime blockade of the Gaza Strip. Drawing parallels with the decision of Riyadh to offer military support to the al-Khalifa regime in Bahrain, al-Saud noted that, "When foreigners [Iranians] aim to influence events under a particular nation's control, whether by social media or otherwise, that nation may take it upon itself to expel or repel such foreigners."[4]

The Brussels event was very much a portent of things to come. By 2015, official as well as semi-official contacts between high-ranking Israelis and Saudis had increased markedly, the frequency of such meetings reflecting shared concerns over one core issue: the regional ambitions of Iran. This paralleled a desire among several senior members of the al-Saud, albeit one that could not so easily be realised openly, of wishing to come to Israel. In 2015 for example, Prince al-Waleed bin Talal, perhaps rather presumptuously, announced his intention to visit for several days without specifying exactly when, to "[M]ark the new age of peace and fraternity," and "to open a direct dialogue with Israel to build amicable ties with our Israeli neighbours."[5]

However, the conundrum remained over who could or should take the next steps and move the relationship beyond a shared understanding of Iran's regional malfeasance. Both Riyadh and Jerusalem were with publics unwilling to entertain weakness in their leadership; this presented huge challenges for both governments in that any initiative could very easily be portrayed as a weakness by internal opposition, the practical manifestation of ideational constraint. In the case of Israel, it faced opposition by a powerful settler lobby which had long regarded any successful rapprochement with the wider Arab world, let alone the Palestinians, as a prelude to Israel being pressured to make substantial territorial concessions over the West Bank and Jerusalem.[6]

This challenge remained real for the Saudis too. Despite the state-controlled media, most Saudis remain sensitive to the issue of succession and any semi-overt links to Israel would undoubtedly inform the internal power struggles within the House of Saud. Moreover, the ideological struggle surrounding Islamic legitimacy between Saudi Arabia and Iran impacted on the power and status of the Kingdom across the region. Therefore, its ability both to confront what it regarded as Tehran's regional malfeasance, and reassert its hegemonic status—politically, religiously and economically—was seen as crucial to the survival and stability of the al-Saud dynasty. While its claim to be the custodian of the two holiest sites in Islam—Mecca and Medina—is by no means accepted by all across the Muslim world, the claim itself had long been regarded as underpinning the combination of piety and power on which the edifice of the Kingdom had come to rest.[7]

Even so, in early 2013 the secretary of state in the Obama Administration, John Kerry, welcomed the Arab League's proposal to revive peace talks between Israel and the Palestinians under the framework of the API, claiming that it represented "a very big step forward."[8] The Arab League's proposal, as presented by the Qatari foreign minister Sheik Hamad bin Jassem al-Thani, emphasised that peace between the Palestinians and Israelis was now "a strategic choice for the Arab states."[9] As for the Gulf monarchies, the API had always remained a far-reaching proposal in its scope and ambition, offering as it did the potential to extend both *de facto* and *de jure* recognition of Israel across the Arab and Muslim world.[10] The initiative, however, never received an official response from Israel. For Jerusalem, reference to a 'just and agreed-upon' solution to the Palestinian refugee problem and Syria's claim to sovereignty over the Golan Heights were highly problematic. The main sticking point, however, remained the emphasis placed by the initiative on a just resolution to the Palestinian refugee problem, the 'right of return' of refugees cutting to the core of demographic sensitivities regarding Israel's identity as a predominantly Jewish dispensation. More immediately though, the future of the Golan Heights was very much to the fore within Israel's national security concerns. From Jerusalem's perspective, the fragmentation of Syria as a unified state and the tragedy of its civil war only served to emphasise the immense strategic value of this mountain range, a view held right across Israel's political spectrum.[11]

It was, however, possible to discern two parallel processes connected to the initiative: on the one hand, the centre-left in Israel had long demanded a positive response to the API, with the Zionist Union, an amalgam of centre-left parties under its former leader Issac Herzog, proposing a regional conference at least based on its parameters.[12] On the other hand, Yair Lapid, leader of the centrist party Yesh Atid, and the decidedly hawkish defence minister Avigdor Lieberman, both suggested the need to 'wrap' the Israeli–Palestinian issue into a broader regional process, although both avoided direct reference to the API.[13] Netanyahu too repeatedly stated that the moderate Arab states no longer saw Israel as a threat but as an ally, suggesting that the API might at least provide the contours, if not the actual map, for directing both Israelis and Palestinians towards a final peace accord.[14]

Such sentiments aside, the API was already past its sell-by date after 2011, not least because of the weakness of the Arab League as a coherent regional institution, riven increasingly as it was by inter-Arab rivalries and factions. The journalist and regional affairs commentator Akiva Eldar claimed that the cancellation of the April 2016 Arab League summit in Marrakesh, where the initiative was due to have been discussed, symbolised the "erosion of the status of the Arab League since the Arab Spring" and in practice proved that the Arab Initiative was no longer relevant.[15] King of Morocco Muhammed VI reportedly cancelled the summit because of what he regarded as the façade of unity—a façade that, given the conflicts in Iraq, Syria, Yemen and Libya, could hardly disguise the deep rifts and divisions that now marked inter-Arab politics right across the Middle East and North Africa.[16]

Nowhere was this more apparent than among the Gulf monarchies. For Riyadh, the events that led to their own intervention in Bahrain, for example, were less an expression of the majority Shi'ite population demanding

greater political and social rights, and more the manifestation of Iranian meddling among their co-religionists
to further their regional ambitions. Such perceptions
informed their view of Tehran's nuclear programme with
the fear that its apogee would be realised in the establishment of Iran as the dominant hegemon throughout
the Gulf. According to a leaked diplomatic cable, it was
for this reason alone that in 2010 the late Saudi monarch, King Abdullah bin Abdulaziz al-Saud, urged
Washington to sever the head of the "Iranian snake."[17]
The advent of the Arab Uprisings, and with it the fragmentation of many of the old Republican autocracies
into their many sectarian and religious parts, served to
fuel the perception of Iran's malfeasance, and in turn
determined a more proactive Saudi policy across the
region. While this came to be realised in Riyadh's support for a range of non-state armed groups fighting both
the Islamic State (Daesh) and Iranian-sponsored proxies
in Syria, Iraq and Yemen, the Saudis began to openly
align their concerns over Iran's use of such forces, not
least the Houthis in Yemen, with the threat posed to
Israel by the Hezbollah in southern Lebanon.[18]

Alongside these ongoing conflicts, Riyadh also looked
to use its financial leverage to reinforce its fiat across the
region. In January 2016 it withheld $3 billion of aid to
the Lebanese army after Beirut refused to denounce the
storming of the Saudi embassy in Tehran.[19] This act of
diplomatic censure followed the execution of the Saudi

Shi'a cleric Nimr al Nimr (alongside over a dozen militants with alleged links to Al-Qaeda), whom Riyadh accused of sedition and conspiracy against the House of Saud. Further divisions were exposed after the decision of the Arab League, in the wake of strong representation from the GCC, to condemn Hezbollah as a terrorist organisation; Lebanon and Iraq opposed the decision outright while Algeria and Tunisia, mindful of their own domestic constituencies, adopted a somewhat diffident approach to the issue that only served to strain relations still further. In their totality, these events demonstrated that Riyadh was now prepared to use its diplomatic, economic and, in the case of Yemen, military clout to achieve its core regional interests. In March 2015, the Saudi-led military intervention into that blighted tribal state—an intervention approved by the ambitious Crown Prince Mohammed bin Salman and designed to curb the territorial advance of the pro-Iranian Houthi militia—surprised many observers by its scale and intensity.[20]

This regional competition with Tehran impacted too upon the theatre that is Palestinian politics. The Palestinian Authority (PA) rejected Iran's offer to donate around $7,000 to the family of every Palestinian killed in the so-called 'Al-Quds Intifada,' and $30,000 to every Palestinian family whose house had been destroyed by Israel, particularly in the Gaza Strip.[21] The PA saw this money as little more than financial support for its nemesis, Hamas, whose alliance and reliance upon Tehran had long informed opinion, both in Israel and the United States, that the movement remained beholden to Iran. The PA had long regarded the Iranian offer as little more than a thinly disguised, politicised version of almsgiving (*zakat*), a useful distillation of both piety and power that allowed continued Iranian interference in internal Palestinian affairs.[22] But Hamas, whose leadership left Damascus at the beginning of the Syrian civil war, remained torn between an Iran that had long supported 'resistance' activities and the position of the Gulf monarchies. By the end of 2011 it found itself sitting on an increasingly uncomfortable political fence, not least because the warming of ties between Cairo and Riyadh now threatened to isolate the organisation still further from a wider Arab constituency. While Hamas expressed its appreciation for the stance taken by Hezbollah against Israel, it remained deliberately opaque regarding the Arab League's designation of the Lebanese Shi'a movement as a terror organisation.

The PA now faced a dilemma over the shared understandings of the security landscape emerging between Israel and the Gulf Arab monarchies. It depended on 'normal' reciprocal relations with Israel, especially in the security and economic spheres, which involved daily interaction between the two sides. For this reason, the Palestinians proved less conservative on the question of practical normalisation than other Arab countries— even those that had signed peace agreements with Israel.

Yet, despite the Palestinians' relative flexibility, they looked to restrain any display of normalisation between Israel and the Arab states, particularly the Gulf monarchies and the Maghreb countries, hoping to retain this as leverage in negotiations with Israel over a permanent settlement. For Palestinian President Mahmoud Abbas, the API had established a clear sequential correlation between substantive progress on the establishment of a Palestinian state and the cultivation of normal relations between Arab states and Israel. This dichotomy highlighted the ongoing ideational block that prevented more open ties between Israel and the Gulf monarchies. Fidelity, however symbolic, to the Palestinian cause still determined the levels of more open engagement.

Yet, from Israel's perspective, the turmoil across the Arab Middle East and the fragmentation of Arab state solidarity created new opportunities for the renewal of a political process with the Palestinians, not perhaps on the basis of the API but along the lines of a more limited Saudi-led initiative. In the changing regional environment, Israel had much to gain from the renewal of a peace process, ideally one which allowed Jerusalem to pursue talks on a bilateral, as opposed to multilateral, basis. Such a bilateral approach was also meant to stymie international pressure, notably from the United States and the European Union, for Israel to negotiate with Syria over the future of the Golan. While mindful of Riyadh's need to shore up its own influence across the region, the hope remained that Saudi Arabia could leverage influence—diplomatic and economic—over the PA to be more forthcoming about renewing negotiations with Israel without imposing preconditions, most notably its insistence on a complete cessation of settlement construction in the occupied territories. The hoped-for outcome of such a process would advance a clear Israeli interest in marginalising Hamas and forcing the organisation to decide between Iran and Saudi Arabia, a choice between military 'opposition' and political isolation, or diplomacy and the advancement of a political solution, albeit one shaped around Israel's core interests.

Its own domestic concerns certainly caused Riyadh to rethink the context of its engagement with the whole issue of Palestine. Several reasons exist as to why Saudi Arabia remained keen to facilitate a peace agreement: aside from securing its position as a regional power, the tide of political change of a scale and type hitherto unknown now lapped at the shores of the Kingdom. Throughout 2015 and 2016, the steep fall in oil prices and latterly the power struggles within the palace over succession generated a set of exceptional challenges to political stability across Saudi Arabia. The grandsons of Ibn Saud, the founder of the Kingdom, may have begun to seize the reins of power, but not without continued unrest within the ruling family. The disputes centred on the growing power of Crown Prince Mohammed bin

Salman—the young, impetuous scion of the ailing monarch King Salman bin Abdulaziz al-Saud—at the expense of Crown Prince Muhammad bin Nayef, long regarded as the most experienced royal in the Saudi court in matters of national security.[23] Although the international media spotlight was focused on the Kingdom's foreign relations, notably its direct intervention in the Yemen against the Houthi, the internal power struggle within the ruling family as Mohammed bin Salman looked to consolidate his grip on power worried outside observers.[24]

At the same time, militants from Islamic State underscored the paucity of security across much of Saudi Arabia by launching a series of terrorist attacks against Shi'a citizens of the Kingdom, hoping that the ensuing carnage would both exacerbate sectarian tensions and help to inspire those Saudis disaffected with the al-Saud to challenge a regime whose claims to Islamic piety masked, as they saw it, an increasingly sclerotic political order. The initial territorial gains of Islamic State in Iraq and Syria, which bolstered the appeal of its ideology, undoubtedly proved attractive to many—mostly young Saudis already steeped in a strict Wahhabi-Salafi worldview that brooked no compromise. They appeared both willing and able to direct their rage before their own Shi'ite population, long regarded as apostates across much of society, and towards the House of Saud, particularly if it appeared conciliatory towards the Shi'a minority. The Saudi regime may have scored notable successes in its struggle against the threat posed by Al-Qaeda in the early 2000s, but the challenge posed by Islamic State—with its emphasis upon authenticity and legitimacy—was of an altogether different magnitude. For this 'religious blowback' Riyadh bore some responsibility: in view of the struggle with Iran, the regime had allowed senior Saudi clerics, the *ulema*, to spread virulently anti-Shi'a sentiment virtually unhindered in state-controlled mosques throughout the Kingdom, a simple if proven expedient to shore up public legitimacy for the regime in times of perceived crises.[25]

The depression in world energy markets between 2015 and 2017 compounded this wider turmoil.[26] With a bloated public sector, an ever-increasing population and a drastic decline in oil revenues that posed long-term threats to the rentier state model—the particular social contract that had so defined the political and social order of the Arab Gulf monarchies over five decades—Riyadh was now forced to re-evaluate the very basis of state–society relations. The April 2016 announcement of a new economic structure for the Kingdom—Vision 2030—by then Deputy Crown Prince Mohammed bin Salman, was designed to lessen Saudi dependence on that very social contract. With its goal of encouraging greater private-sector involvement in the provision of education and healthcare, as well as selling shares in the state-owned oil company Saudi

ARAMCO on world stock markets, Vision 2030 proposed a fundamental recasting of state–society relations throughout the Kingdom.[27] However, doubts were expressed that 2030 looked less like a vision and more like a pipe dream. Economists cast ever-increasing uncertainty over the ability of the Saudis to move away from oil dependence at a time when economic growth in the Kingdom proved sluggish. Moreover, the fallout from the brutal murder in October 2018 of Jamal Khashoggi while inside the Saudi consulate in Istanbul quickly reverberated beyond the diplomatic community. A man who had voiced support for the Muslim Brotherhood, and had come to criticise the concentration of power in the hands of the Crown Prince and his close associates, Khashoggi's bloody demise damaged business confidence as investors and entrepreneurs shied away from the Kingdom, wary of reputational damage if too closely associated with Mohammed bin Salman. Even the much-vaunted initial public offering of $100 billion in the state oil company Saudi ARAMCO, an offering designed to raise funds to encourage increased inward investment into the Saudi economy, was postponed indefinitely. Not only were legal issues raised over the viability of the share issue, but markets dictated price and Riyadh failed to realise the valuation it wanted.[28]

Saudi Arabia's activity in the global oil market was affected by a set of considerations, some of which were clearly contradictory. Its traditional strategy had always been to maximise long-term oil income from oil exports until its reserves were depleted, while concurrently developing alternative sources of income, the very basis of Vision 2030. However, this strategy did not support excessively high oil prices, as these only served to encourage investment in renewable energy supplies and technologies among oil-consumer states on which the Saudi economy depended. Equally, high-energy process reduced the incentives for the Saudis to develop their own renewable energy sector, notably in the field of solar power. It was a conundrum at the heart of Vision 2030 that economists warned could not easily be resolved.

These domestic travails only served to shed unwelcome light upon Riyadh's regional security posture, notably its prolonged engagement in the ongoing civil war in Yemen.[29] Although leading a regional coalition that enjoyed limited military success, notably the 'liberation' of Aden from Houthi control, the campaign remained mired in controversy: its military objectives had become increasingly opaque and the political and/or military mechanisms for ending the crises remained unclear as the Houthi rebels proved far more resilient than Riyadh ever expected.[30] After four years of the Saudi-led aerial campaign, 'Operation Decisive Storm,' the Houthi still controlled large swathes of north and central Yemen, including the port of Hodeidah and the capital Sana'a. The violence even reached deep into Saudi territory, where the Houthis acquired the ability—most likely from Iran—to fire surface-to-surface Scud missiles towards the Saudi capital and anti-ship missiles at Saudi naval vessels and merchant shipping, including some registered in the United States, patrolling off Yemen's Red Sea coast. Moreover, international criticism of the Saudi-led coalition mounted: aid agencies reported not just the tragic deaths of civilians hit by Saudi and Emirati air strikes in violation of International Humanitarian Law, but outbreaks of cholera and a widespread famine as food stocks rapidly diminished. Such was the level of civilian suffering that, by the spring of 2018, Yemen was widely seen as the world's most pressing humanitarian crisis.[31]

Even assuming that the coalition could eventually push the Houthis back to their stronghold in the mountains around Sa'da, the future of Yemen as a coherent state entity remained bleak. After almost six years of civil war, which tore apart the delicate political fabric of this tribal state, it became hard to visualise any political or military force capable of exercising effective sovereignty over Yemeni territory. By the end of 2018, Yemen had effectively become a patchwork of fiefdoms of competing regional and local forces, including jihadi organisations such as Al-Qaeda in the Arabian Peninsula, whose ability to blend its global ideology with local grievance amid a largely tribal landscape made it a particularly resilient foe.[32] If 'Decisive Storm' revealed anything, it exposed the limitations of Saudi Arabia to shape, let alone determine, the political order of Yemen through the use of military force. It was a hard lesson, but one the Saudi Crown Prince appeared unwilling to learn, fearful that open signs of Saudi retrenchment would only encourage Tehran's regional proxy still further.[33]

Yemen remained the cockpit in which Saudi-Iranian rivalry reached its bloody apogee, but in the eyes of many Saudis it highlighted a wider truth: that Tehran, basking in the success of a nuclear deal reached with the P5+1 in March 2015, felt emboldened to pursue a more expansive, indeed aggressive, regional policy. As already noted, this included continued accusations by Bahrain of brazen Iranian interference in the domestic politics of the Gulf monarchies. At the same time, the Obama Administration, much to the regret of Riyadh, continued to show worrying signs of military disengagement from the region. Dore Gold, former director general of Israel's foreign ministry, concurred with this analysis. On the eve of his appointment to this role in 2015 he noted that, in all likelihood, "The United States will not be the foremost country in the world in the coming years, for China will challenge it with its well-known strategic project: the Silk Road."[34]

Decision-makers in Israel now took careful note of the changes underway in the Kingdom, changes which if worked towards Israel's advantage had the potential to reshape the regional order in the Middle East and beyond in Israel's favour. Equally, the viability of the potential for developing co-operation between Jerusalem and Riyadh had to be carefully calibrated. The more internally vulnerable Saudi Arabia appeared, the less decision-makers in Riyadh—fearful that domestic unrest might coalesce around the issue of Palestine—would be able to align themselves with Israel's regional security agenda over Iran.

This was self-evident. Yet not everyone approved of Israel's growing alignment with the Gulf monarchies in general and Saudi Arabia in particular, questioning if the price of rapprochement with Israel's erstwhile foes was worth the wider reputational price to be paid in the court of international opinion. But, as the perceived gatekeeper to the Trump White House, Netanyahu had a powerful hand to play in this particular strategy. When harnessed to the 'soft power' of its comparative advantage in cyber security, dependency in the relationship was hardly symmetrical. Its expertise in technology, medicine, agriculture and of course security leveraged clear influence among the Gulf monarchies. Equally however, such ties had the potential to damage Israel's international reputation among Western, notably European, states where normative behaviour, not least in the realm of human rights, was held up as the benchmark in the conduct of foreign policy.[35]

Yet, as Netanyahu's response to the murder of the dissident Saudi journalist Jamal Khashoggi demonstrated, supporting the Saudi regime—and in particular shoring up the position of Crown Prince Mohammed bin Salman at the apex of the regime—was a core Israeli interest.[36] Therefore, while calling the brutal murder of the journalist 'horrendous', details of which had been drip-fed to the global media by a Turkish regime keen to amplify Riyadh's diplomatic discomfort, Netanyahu remained firm in his conviction that confronting Iran remained paramount: "[F]or the stability of the world, for the region and the world," he opined, it was imperative "that Saudi Arabia remain stable."[37] Netanyahu's staunch advocacy of the Crown Prince—who was believed by most, including the Central Intelligence Agency, to have authorised Khashoggi's removal—likely resonated in a White House where the conduct of Middle East policy had become almost a family affair, and where Saudi endorsement of a much-heralded peace plan believed to serve Israel's regional interests was being widely touted.[38]

By the beginning of 2019, the details of this peace plan had still to be disclosed. Critics pointed to a White House where foreign policy-making appeared to be either adrift or subject increasingly to the whims of a president keen to cut 'deals' but lacking in oversight or indeed understanding of the issues or detail involved. Beholden to an agenda that put 'America first', unilateralism became the hallmark of a Trump presidency that eschewed working through international institutions and global agreements, which for so long had been the framework of an international order that successive administrations in Washington had largely shaped.

Even for Israel, though, the Trump presidency proved to be something of a double-edged sword. To be sure, the May 2018 relocation of the United States embassy in Israel from Tel Aviv to Jerusalem proved the fulfilment of a campaign pledge made by Trump. It was seen as affirmation in Israel by its most powerful ally of its long-held claim to sovereignty over the entirety of the city, a claim never accepted by the majority of the international community. The subsequent demonstrations by Palestinians along the Gaza border, partly in response to the embassy, but also to mark *Nakhba* day and to proclaim their 'right of return,' soon turned violent: 110 Palestinians were killed by the IDF along the Gaza border. While a few had indeed tried to breach the fence, Israel's use of live fire against these protestors was condemned by much of the international community. Yet, amid the furore across much of Europe over the bloodshed as well as the embassy move, the fatalities and seeming usurpation of Palestinian claims to East Jerusalem elicited but the faintest of protests from Washington and most of the Gulf monarchies. Only Kuwait pushed for a United Nations investigation into the actions of Israel's security forces, calls subsequently blocked by the United States exercising its veto in the United Nations Security Council.[39] For Israel, President Trump appeared to be the gift that kept on giving.

The controversy of the embassy move aside, the muted response of Saudi Arabia, Bahrain and the UAE to these events was telling. That Gaza remained firmly under the control of Hamas largely explains their subdued response. Indeed, if a TSR is defined by the shared perception of threat—that mitigates excess competition or friction able to arise in other realms which might otherwise undermine the core aim of the regime—then its validity was certainly demonstrated over the ongoing events in Gaza.

Others, however, pointed to the close personal relationship between Crown Prince Mohammed bin Salman and President Trump's son-in-law, senior advisor and *de facto* Middle East envoy, Jared Kushner. For a man with little previous experience of diplomacy, Kushner's elevation to the White House was clearly the product of familial ties. From a Jewish Orthodox family and an avowed supporter of Israel, Kushner's father Charles was a long-time friend of Netanyahu. Like Trump, the Kushners had made their fortune in the real-estate business and had given large sums of money to various Israeli charities and causes, including donations to a *yeshiva* (religious seminary) in the West Bank settlement of Beit El.[40]

Through a Lebanese–American business associate with close ties to several Gulf investors, Jared Kushner was introduced to Yousef al-Otaiba, UAE ambassador in Washington who, in turn, eventually brokered a meeting between Kushner and the Crown Prince Mohammed bin Salman in New York in November 2016, soon after Trump's election victory. Despite initial scepticism towards Riyadh, Kushner was reportedly won over by a series of initiatives that included Saudi plans to establish an 'Arab NATO,' the purchase of $50 billion worth of US military equipment over four years and, alongside other Gulf monarchies, investments of over $300 billion in infrastructure projects across the United States. Perhaps more importantly, they provided a platform upon which Kushner and the Crown Prince built a personal relationship with direct access to both the President of the United States and Prime Minister of Israel.[41]

The international fallout over the Khashoggi affair tempered US–Saudi relations as the impetuous Crown Prince and his closest advisors were reined in by King Salman. By the beginning of 2019, it was clear that the latitude given to Mohammed bin Salman in determining Saudi foreign and security policy had been clipped, but not circumscribed. Indeed, Netanyahu's staunch defence of the young Prince as a necessary bulwark against Iran, yet whose removal might well usher in an era of instability in the Kingdom—thereby adversely impacting upon Israel's regional security interests—was almost prophetic in its timing.[42] With his penchant for conducting foreign policy via Twitter and against the advice of his own defence secretary, James Mattis, who promptly resigned, Trump's announcement that he would remove all US forces from Syria and Iraq following what he regarded as the defeat of Islamic State was met with ill-disguised concern in Israel and many of the Gulf monarchies. This was the other edge of the sword: regional retrenchment of US military forces that would allow Iran and her proxies to fill the subsequent vacuum.[43] While care should be taken to place the withdrawal of US troops in its regional context—most were present in a training and advisory capacity—their removal further underscored a persistent concern throughout Israel and the Gulf monarchies that Washington's commitment to their security, under the presidencies of Obama and now Trump, was increasingly less than the sum of its many parts.

Washington of course remained a regional actor in its own right, its military presence in and around the Gulf clearly formidable. Yet the perception of retrenchment now asked serious questions about the type of relationships both Jerusalem and Riyadh wished to pursue. In his treatment of the relationship, Elie Podeh noted that "Mutual Saudi–Israeli interests originally stemmed from the realist axiom of 'the enemy of my enemy is my friend.' Yet, new paths of cooperation were forged and new mutual interests explored."[44] Irrespective of the occupants of the White House, it seemed likely that at least some of the principles of the TSR had entrenched a normative understanding of those areas in which both Israel and Saudi Arabia, along with Bahrain, the UAE and perhaps Oman, could likely coalesce. Nowhere was this more apparent than in Israel's determination to scupper what many regarded as the most significant foreign policy achievement of the Obama Administration: the JCPOA.

4

ARMS SALES AND THE NUCLEAR QUESTION

On 8 May 2018, President Donald Trump announced to the world his intention to withdraw the United States from the Joint Comprehensive Plan of Action, thereby upholding a campaign pledge made while running for the White House. Seen by many as the flagship foreign policy achievement of the previous Obama Administration, the JCPOA—an agreement signed in July 2015 after painstaking negotiations between the five permanent members of the UN Security Council and Germany (P5+1), together with Iran—involved a clear quid pro quo: the lessening of economic sanctions against Tehran, including the release of Iranian assets overseas and the ability of European companies to trade freely with Iran, in return for an intrusive inspection regime designed to limit Iranian nuclear activity to low-level enrichment and research activities for a decade.[1]

While Trump's decision was met with dismay across much of Europe and among Democrats in the United

States, it was met with wholesale approbation in Jerusalem, Riyadh and Abu Dhabi. Long seen as a deal that emboldened, indeed rewarded, Iran for what they all regarded as its regional transgressions, Trump's repudiation of the JCPOA as a "bad deal" brought with it a promise to reimpose "the highest level economic sanctions" on Iran.[2] For Netanyahu in particular, it was a vindication of his tough, belligerent stance against the deal from the outset, a stance that had seen him cross the lines of bipartisanship in Israel's ties with the United States when he addressed a joint meeting of Congress in March 2015. Then, in a speech clearly aimed at US Secretary of State John Kerry, who was the most forceful advocate for the JCPOA in the Obama Administration, Netanyahu lambasted the negotiations as a "very bad deal," a phrase later to become Trump's mantra.[3]

To be sure, not everyone in Israel was against the agreement. While its provisions made no linkage between, for example, Iran's continued development of missile technologies and sanctions relief, former senior intelligence officials argued that the JCPOA provided a clear basis upon which Iran's nuclear programme, now much diminished in its practical manifestation, could be both monitored and checked.[4] It was a position shared in private by serving Israeli security officials who, in the two years since the deal was signed, had yet to find Tehran in violation of a single clause, despite Netanyahu claiming continued malfeasance on the part of Iran.

While the Israeli premier and his former defence minister, Avigdor Lieberman, believed that an American withdrawal from the agreement was decidedly in Israel interests, some senior security officials begged to differ. One report noted that:

> The senior ranks of the Israeli security establishment, intelligence community, and Foreign Ministry believe that even though the agreement is bad for Israel, American withdrawal from it would be even worse. The professional ranks of Israeli statecraft think that if America withdraws from the agreement, the other world powers will not follow through, and thus Iran will not become isolated nor face new international sanctions. Instead, the international community will be divided and the monitoring of Iran's nuclear program could suffer a setback.[5]

In light of the close association already existing between members of the Trump Administration and Binyamin Netanyahu, it would be easy to suggest that such ties proved decisive in pushing Washington's repudiation of the JCPOA. The evidence to date is circumspect and one should not dismiss lightly the belief held by both White House officials and respected figures in Israel that Iranian involvement in Syria, for example, had only increased in the wake of the deal. This argument was certainly put forcefully by senior Israeli officials. Former Defence Minister Moshe Ya'alon accused Iran of building an "international terror network" including "sleeper cells" that stockpile arms, gather intelligence and recruit operatives for potential strikes within strategic locations in Europe and the United States.[6] Moreover, while Iran may not have been in violation of the technical provisions of the deal, Netanyahu was clear that Iran remained in clear breach of its spirit and produced the evidence in a dramatic press conference to show it. On 30 April 2018, the Israeli premier announced to the world that the Israeli secret service, Mossad, had smuggled out from Iran some 55,000 documents and hundreds of CD Roms, material which provided further details of Iran's nuclear programme that appeared to have been kept from UN inspectors by being hidden in a series of innocuous warehouses in the suburbs of the Iranian capital. It was quite an astounding intelligence coup. While Western intelligence officials later claimed that the material added little to what was already known of Iran's past nuclear enterprise, the impact of Netanyahu's disclosure lay in its timing. Coming just a week before Trump announced Washington's withdraw from the JCPOA, it provided the president with much needed political cover given the controversy surrounding his decision.[7] For the Gulf monarchies, it burnished an enduring truth of the TSR: that close if discreet association with Israel helped amplify their core security concerns along the corridors of power in Washington.

Israel, the Gulf Monarchies and Arms Sales

When the JCPOA was signed in July 2015, Saudi Arabia, the UAE and Bahrain may have accepted its provisions as a *fait accompli*, but it was an acceptance shorn of diplomatic conviction precisely because it kept alive Iran's nuclear programme, whatever the international constraints and monitoring mechanisms put in place. Recognising these concerns, the United States now concluded a series of large arms deals with the Gulf monarchies in an attempt to offer their rulers some reassurance as they looked with increased trepidation over how a resurgent Iran might now act on the regional stage once the full weight of economic sanctions was lifted.

While publicly supportive of the deal, Saudi officials soon made clear their opposition. On 16 July 2015, just two days after the agreement had been signed with much fanfare in Vienna, Prince Bandar bin Sultan, former Saudi ambassador to the United States, noted in an opinion piece for the Saudi news site *Elaph* that the JCPOA would "wreak havoc on the region." He went on to argue that the deal was less secure than the nuclear deal struck between the United States and North Korea in 1994, a deal designed to freeze the construction and operation by the North Koreans of nuclear reactors suspected of being part of a covert nuclear weapons programme. The agreement broke down eight years later amid mutual recrimination between Washington and Pyongyang, but the lesson for Riyadh was clear: Washington and the parties to the agreement should not have negotiated with what the Saudis, their Gulf allies and of course Israel regarded as a rogue nation. As if to emphasise Riyadh's dismay, *Al Sharq al-Awsat*, the leading Saudi newspaper close to the ruling family, noted somewhat grimly that "the agreement would open the gates of evil in Middle East."[8]

Yet hope that such entreaties would influence the Obama Administration proved forlorn. Anxious to place clear water between the neo-conservative engagement with the Middle East that had marked the administration of George W. Bush, President Obama looked to avoid further foreign policy entanglement in a region that failed to bring strategic rewards for the United States, let alone stability for the region. This fed wider concerns held in both Jerusalem and Riyadh that under a president immersed in a Niebuhrian Realist tradition that emphasised the limits of power, Washington would look to revive diplomatic ties with Iran. Obama's pursuit of the JCPOA was the epitome of this approach, its sin of omission regarding missile technology in Jerusalem's eyes compounded by the fact that neither Israel nor Saudi Arabia had a public voice in the negotiations taking place between Tehran and the P5+1. It was this lack of voice that reportedly prompted both Israel and the Gulf monarchies to co-ordinate their diplomatic efforts behind the scenes in an attempt to exert pressure on Washington, London, Paris, Berlin and the EU to take a firm stance on the deal.[9]

Despite the best efforts of Netanyahu, including his highly charged speech before the US Congress in March 2015 that made the issue of Israel's security a partisan issue, the JCPOA was eventually signed in July. But having failed to scupper the Iran deal in Congress, were the Gulf monarchies—Saudi Arabia included—now convinced that Israel's influence in Washington was less than its many supposed parts? The answer was no: for Israel and the Gulf monarchies continued to share a malign view of Iranian influence throughout the region that placed Tehran at the epicentre of their regional security concerns. All shared the view that the JCPOA, as Ya'alon argued, only served to embolden Tehran's involvement in a series of proxy wars. Israeli coverage of the war in Yemen now invariably ascribed the success of the Houthi tribal militias—who captured the capital Sana'a in 2015 and went on to control large swathes of this fractured polity—to the support given by Iran. The fragmented nature of the Yemeni state and its multiple contested identities was rarely remarked upon in public policy statements. Moreover, Israeli press coverage of the Yemen civil war evinced little criticism over the conduct of a Saudi-led air campaign that, by the end of 2018, had yet to come close to returning Yemen's ousted president and Saudi supplicant, President Abdu Rabbu Mansour Hadi, to power in Sana'a.[10]

Such Israeli support, albeit implicit, for the actions of Riyadh and Abu Dhabi in Yemen, mirrored nonetheless the favourable coverage Netanyahu had enjoyed in the Arab Gulf media as he attempted to scupper the JCPOA. When the Israeli prime minister made his controversial speech before Congress in March 2015, a speech seen to be as partisan in its attack on the Obama Administration as it was against the conclusion of any deal with Iran, his words were applauded by many in the Gulf. While conceding that there was much that still divided Israel from the Arab world, Faisal Abbas, a respected journalist with Saudi-owned news channel *al-Arabiya*, wrote that irrespective of such differences "one must admit, Bibi did get it right, at least when it came to dealing with Iran."[11]

It was an open acknowledgement that Netanyahu's consistent public opposition to any agreement leaving Iran in possession of a viable nuclear breakout capability enjoyed Riyadh's affirmation, and confirmation too of a long-held view in Israel's diplomatic community that, because of the perceived leverage that Jerusalem could exercise in Washington, it was in effect doing the diplomatic bidding for the Gulf monarchies. It was a vocal expression of a core element of the TSR: the containment of Iran as a regional threat. Equally, the shared regional perception of an Obama White House preferring "leadership from behind" helped nurture and sustain a mutual acceptance "towards particular types of action," in this case joint political lobbying in Washington, as part of the evolving nature of the TSR.

However, such congruence was not initially realised in shared understandings over the best means to counter the challenge of Iran's nuclear programme. The likely response of the Gulf monarchies to a potential Israeli attack—for example against Iranian nuclear facilities, an attack much mooted in 2012—remained contingent on the perceived harm to their interests and regional standing.[12] The Gulf monarchies remained sensitive to the legacy of past conflicts, most notably the Iran-Iraq War and the First Gulf War of 1990–1. Of particular concern was that if Iran's nuclear facilities were targeted, Tehran would in turn drag the Gulf monarchies into a conflict by striking critical infrastructure and high-value targets in their territory such as oil-production sites or desalination facilities.

Moreover, in an era where social media now increasingly shaped popular perceptions of the news agenda, the Gulf monarchies remained sensitive to the shifts in wider public opinion and of course radical Islamist elements in their own countries. If the rulers appeared to have aided—even indirectly—an Israeli attack on Iranian nuclear sites, they feared domestic unrest could become widespread. When concerns over an Israeli attack on Iran's nuclear facilities were first raised internationally in 2007, Riyadh reportedly conveyed a message to Jerusalem that it would interdict any Israeli planes that crossed its airspace on the way to Iran.[13] All the states of the GCC continued to express, albeit reluctantly, support for a diplomatic solution to the nuclear crisis and a desire to participate more actively in the process (an implicit admission that they feared Washington was likely to negotiate with Iran at their expense).[14] They recognised Iran's determination, if not entitlement, to develop nuclear technology for peaceful purposes, but urged Tehran to co-operate fully with the international community and the inspection regime of the International Atomic Energy Agency.

The constraints on joint action, even permissive in the case of overflights, highlighted the limits of overt military collaboration between Saudi Arabia and Israel.[15] However, clandestine co-operation remained another issue. Senior officials from Israel's defence establishment had, in the past at least, established lines of communication with Gulf state members including Saudi Arabia.[16] In 2010, senior Israeli officials and their Gulf counterparts reportedly met on a number of occasions to discuss Iran, meetings that included talks between Mossad Director Meir Dagan and Saudi intelligence officials during a secret visit to the Kingdom.[17] Given the sensitivity of these contacts, it is perhaps not surprising that any reports of co-ordination aimed at countering Iran's nuclear programme were denied by both sides.[18]

Still, Israel dared to publicly hint that such co-operation, if not yet established, was a distinct possibility, and that the Saudi position had shifted. During his speech in October 2014 to mark the opening of the winter session of the Israeli Knesset, Prime Minister Netanyahu focused on the Iranian nuclear issue, saying,

> For the first time since the establishment of the State of Israel, a growing understanding is taking root in the Arab world, and it is not always said softly. This understanding, that Israel is not the enemy of Arabs and that we have a united front on many issues, might advance new possibilities in our region.[19]

No Gulf official publicly admitted to having such a united front with the Israelis, but the Saudi Prince and influential businessman Al-waleed bin Talal opined in an interview with *The Wall Street Journal* that "For the first time, Saudi Arabian and Israeli interests are almost parallel."[20] Another report on an Iranian news agency claimed that the former Saudi intelligence chief Bandar bin Sultan met with high-ranking Israeli officials in Geneva to discuss ways to promote mutual interests such as "containing Iran, and side-lining the Muslim Brotherhood."[21]

In its efforts to underpin Congressional support for the JCPOA, Washington now decided to sell advance weaponry to the Gulf monarchies and Israel, agreeing to supply its Gulf Arab allies with advanced weaponry such as the F-15SA fighter-bombers in addition to sophisticated missile defence systems such as the THAAD, capable of shooting down short, medium and intermediate ballistic missiles in their terminal phase. Both the qualitative and quantitative scale of these weapons sales brought only a muted response from Israel, and no opposition whatsoever from pro-Israel groups on Capitol Hill. It marked a clear shift in Israel's position: throughout the 1980s Jerusalem had, for example, mobilised such groups routinely to help block the sale of a massive arms package, one that had included Airborne Warning and Control Systems aircraft (AWACS) to Riyadh even though it was clear the whole package was geared primarily towards deterring Iran.

Times had now certainly changed. Jerusalem shifted its position as the scope of US arms sales to the Middle East increased by 103 per cent in the period 2013–17, compared to 2008–12. The figures were quite staggering. During this time, Saudi Arabia and the UAE, both among the five leading arms purchasers in the world, increased their weapons imports by 225 per cent and 51 per cent, respectively.[22] The scope of arms purchases by Saudi Arabia and the UAE exceeded those of all European NATO countries combined in the same period.[23] Moreover, a large part of their expenditure was directed at the purchase of offensive systems, both Western and non-Western. This included attack drones, surface-to-surface missiles (mainly short-range), GPS-guided munitions including bunker-busting ordnance, and air-launched Cruise missiles. While many were justifiably concerned at the prospect of a nuclear arms race in the Middle East—and the international community continued to focus on this issue—the region itself was part of a renewed conventional arms race, but with a different driver: fear of Iran, rather than Israel, combined with intra-regional competition among Gulf monarchies to acquire and maintain regional status and prestige. However, the quantity and quality of the weapons purchased raised concerns in Israel over maintaining its QME. For while the United States remained the preferred supplier, advance weaponry was now being purchased from countries over which Israel had little influence or leverage.[24]

Saudi Arabia and the UAE in particular now increased their security ties with China and Russia. Beijing and Moscow imposed fewer restrictions than Washington on the export of advanced weapon systems. While intended to strengthen security relations between customer and supplier, such purchases sent a political message: they put pressure on the United States to be more forthcoming over the sale of their own systems, notably the F35 Stealth Fighter to Riyadh and Abu Dhabi. To be sure, the acquisition of weapons from different sources created logistical difficulties: the need for suitable spare parts, specialised training, and a specific maintenance setup placed a burden on militaries whose ability to incorporate such technologies had hitherto been overly reliant on Western defence contractors. However, varied procurement was meant to lessen dependence on the United States and reinforce the ability of these countries to pursue a more independent policy. Some of the deals with China and Russia included technology transfer and joint-production agreements. For example, China—which had supplied unmanned aerial vehicles or 'drones' to Jordan, Iraq, Algeria, the UAE and Saudi Arabia—now agreed to establish a plant in Saudi Arabia to manufacture attack variants of these drones under franchise.[25]

This procurement process was driven by the fear of Iran but also by the ongoing standoff between Qatar and Saudi Arabia. Riyadh had tried to accelerate its acquisition of the United States THAAD air defence system (already operated by UAE), but in 2017 it signed a memorandum of understanding with Moscow to purchase the Russian S400 system, which included Russia's consent to transfer technology. The Saudis had a particular interest in closer ties with Russia as part of their plan to develop a domestic arms industry under the framework of "Vision 2030."[26] Against the background of the rivalry between Doha and Riyadh, Qatar now acquired its own inventory of Chinese SY-400 surface-to-surface missiles.[27]

The weapon systems now reaching some of the Gulf monarchies either matched or in some cases proved more advanced than those in Israel's arsenal. For the Gulf monarchies, they remained their main insurance against Iran, enabling them to assist and if necessary to integrate operationally with any possible United States action against Tehran, as well as to bolster defences against any Iranian response. The interest shown by Saudi Arabia and the UAE in acquiring the F-35 advanced fighter, a plane that became operational with the IAF in 2018, was testament to their continued qualitative ambition.[28]

Although Jerusalem was fully aware that such weapons were mainly geared towards meeting the Iranian threat, it brought a series of political dilemmas to the fore that cut to the core of Israel's enduring security concerns. While increased arms sales to Saudi Arabia and other Gulf monarchies had been the sweetener that President Obama added to the bitter pill of the JCPOA, the Trump Administration now saw such arms sales as largely transactional, driven by the need to compete with other suppliers (above all Russia and China) as much as any need to contain the perceived Iranian threat. Certainly, Israel did not want to undermine ties with a Trump White House whose diplomatic support for the Jewish state—as evidenced by the relocation of the US embassy from Tel Aviv to Jerusalem—was palpable, but whose emphasis on "bringing the jobs back to America" was a key driver in his foreign policy. In addition, the security co-operation between Israel and the Gulf monarchies (as well as with Egypt and Jordan) even under the constraints of the TSR was tangible, and Jerusalem had no wish to scupper the progress made by opposing US arms sales.

In light of these developing ties and the drive to create a bloc against Iran, Israel chose to soften its stance regarding the export of advanced arms to these countries. In part, given its own sale of advanced security systems to some Gulf monarchies, notably the UAE, it could not do otherwise. Even so, the extent to which the Israeli government could influence the mercurial President Trump over the scope and scale of weapons systems in order to retain its QME remained a pressing concern, but one that had to be balanced against how any opposition to a particular weapons system might harm the developing relations between Israel and its fraternal enemies. And, for many Israelis, fraternal enemies they did remain. Although the Arab Gulf monarchies had never been involved in direct military conflict with Israel, the possibility that the weapons now purchased could be turned on Israel at some future point could not be ignored. Fine political judgements now had to be exercised in determining when to raise concerns in Washington over the sale of high-end weapons platforms that might undermine Israel's QME in a range of military technologies.

While far from constituting a formal military alliance, and while sensitive to the need to ensure its qualitative advantage in weapons systems, the TSR that had emerged allowed Israel to recognise that the defence needs of the Gulf monarchies were both real, pressing and in its own interest. This was recognised too by the Gulf monarchies: by refusing to exercise its undoubted influence on Capitol Hill, Israel was signalling the emergence of a strategic concordance. Indeed, the analysis suggests something more profound in Israeli strategic thinking: that by not opposing these arms sales, Israel regarded the Saudis, Emiratis and Bahrainis as forming an alternative 'front line' in the continuing standoff with Iran.

Yet while the development of Iran's nuclear programme continued to dominate debate regarding the scope and scale of Israel's ties with the Gulf, Tehran's continued development of a ballistic missile programme—something not covered by the provisions of the JCPOA—highlighted the wider sensitivities surrounding both Iranian military telemetry and, of course, the desire to weaponise such rockets with a nuclear warhead. In this regard, Iran rather forced the hand of Israel, pushing Jerusalem out of strategic need towards the Arab fold. With a range of 2,000 km, these missiles were likely calibrated to strike targets across much of the Middle East, but remained of insufficient range to threaten territory in Western Europe. This direct threat to Israel and the Gulf monarchies, coupled with a reluctance of the P5+1 to allow the JCPOA to embrace Iran's missile programmes, provided the very urgent push for a new security regime to emerge across the region, one configured to deter Iran but continually shaped in large part by perceptions of Washington's regional retrenchment.

With these regional conditions to the fore, the possibility that leaders of the Gulf monarchies might involve Israel as an essential partner in any future regional defence regime were far from fanciful. Evidence of the emerging confluence of strategic interests between Saudi Arabia, Bahrain, the UAE and Israel dating back to 2005 could be found in leaked US diplomatic cables, which exposed how Gulf concerns over Iran—notably in the UAE and Bahrain—had been forcefully expressed in Washington.[29] By 2018 and in light of the widely held view that Washington's commitment to the security of its Middle East allies was lessening, the symbiotic nature of the TSR, not least in the field of public and 'soft' diplomacy outlined, increasingly became a defining feature of Israel's relations with the Gulf monarchies. However, while the struggle against the JCPOA highlighted the shared interests that had brought Israel and the Gulf monarchies closer together, it also brought to the fore debates over Emirati and Saudi nuclear ambitions, whose scope and scale placed them clearly at odds with existential concerns in Israel over regional nuclear proliferation.

The UAE and Saudi Arabia: Opening the Nuclear Pandora's Box?

In August 2016, it was announced that a bloc of Arab states, led by Egypt, would break from past practice and refrain from seeking a resolution at the annual IAEA general conference, demanding oversight of Israel's nuclear facilities.[30] It was a subtle if notable expression that pressing concerns over Syria, as well as Iran, trumped more longstanding Arab demands that Jerusalem open up its nuclear facilities for inspection. Its longstanding policy of nuclear ambiguity notwithstanding, Israel had long been suspected of possessing nuclear weapons and the wherewithal to deliver them by land, sea and air, a nuclear triad that had both first- and second-strike capabilities—the very essence of an effective deterrent posture that marked superpower competition during the Cold War. However, such strategic opacity never disguised Israel's determination to prevent the spread of nuclear technology, let alone nuclear weapons across the Middle East. In turn, this issue now posed important questions over the extent to which—the levels of co-operation established with Riyadh and Abu Dhabi notwithstanding—Jerusalem was willing to accommodate their nuclear ambitions. For, just as the alliance with Israel could help amplify their collective voice in Washington, so Jerusalem could muffle their nuclear demands in those selfsame corridors of power. If the ideational constraints of Palestine proved the main impediment to more open relations, the issue of nuclear ambition asked equally pertinent questions over the scope of these ties.[31]

In March 2018, the UAE announced that it had completed construction of the first of four nuclear power stations it had first commissioned from South Korea in 2008. With the expectation that this reactor would become operational by 2019 or 2020 at the latest, Abu Dhabi was destined to be the first Arab state to have developed a viable civilian nuclear programme. Throughout its development, the Emiratis remained completely transparent over the scope and scale of their programme. Already signatories to the Non-Proliferation Treaty (NPT), they also signed the '123' nuclear co-operation agreement with the United States, voluntarily foregoing any attempt to enrich uranium or the reprocessing of spent fuel for the production of plutonium, thereby adhering to the so-called 'Gold Standard.'[32] The UAE did indeed have a strong case for developing nuclear power: the reactors would likely supply a quarter of its energy needs by 2025, reduce its carbon footprint, and help develop employment opportunities as the UAE looked to lessen its dependence upon expatriate expertise. Moreover, despite a price tag of $20 billion that involved heavy government subsidies, the programme enjoyed wide approbation among Emiratis, with one opinion poll suggesting that over eighty per cent supported the programme.[33]

Saudi Arabia also looked to embrace a nuclear future. The development of a nuclear energy programme was integral to Crown Prince Mohammed bin Salman's grandiose plan, Vision 2030, to lessen the Kingdom's dependence on hydro-carbons which increasingly came to be consumed by a growing population long used to cheap energy. While the plans of the Saudi Crown

Prince to sell off a small stake of Saudi ARAMCO had already begun to unravel before the Khashoggi affair, this did not alter the fundamental need for the Kingdom to diversify its energy supplies if the bulk of its oil was to be sold overseas. Riyadh's plans were certainly ambitious: up to sixteen nuclear reactors had been earmarked for construction. Most observers believed, however, that the sheer cost involved for an increasingly stagnant economy would curb this number.[34]

Even so, the desire to develop a nuclear programme and attendant research facilities could not be divorced from the fractious regional security complex. While the Saudis welcomed President Trump's repudiation of the JCPOA, it had, by common consent, still been an agreement that curbed Iranian enrichment activity. While it remained unclear whether a renewed US-sponsored sanctions regime would prompt Tehran to walk away from the provisions of the agreement in their entirety, the signs were not good. Equally, Riyadh made it clear that should the Iranians decide to do so, Saudi Arabia would look to develop its own indigenous nuclear weapons capability, unlocking the Pandora's box of nuclear proliferation as the logic of the security dilemma took hold across the Gulf.

Since it launched its nuclear programme in 2009, the UAE had been definite that its scope and trajectory remained geared towards civilian use only. Still, observers could only be impressed by its 'fast track nuclear programme' designed to ensure energy security for an ever-expanding population. The UAE hoped that its four commissioned nuclear reactors would be supplying a quarter of its energy needs, having signed co-operation agreements with Argentina, Canada, France, Japan, Russia and most notably South Korea, for the transfer of technology, nuclear materials and the construction of facilities. The cost of the reactor built at Barakah, capable of producing 1.3 GW, was reckoned to be around $20 billion, a staggering amount but one that Emiratis appeared willing to bear.[35] While subjective, one poll conducted by the UAE government in 2018 put public support for nuclear energy development at eighty-two per cent, with eighty-nine per cent supportive of building a civilian nuclear infrastructure.[36] The costs involved in the programme were explained by the fact that the Emiratis were building their programme from scratch.

While the longer-term aim was to train a cadre of UAE nationals capable of running and controlling the programme—the 'Emiratisation of nuclearisation'—it would likely be a generation before this occurred. Some saw this dependence on foreign expertise as underpinning the agreements the UAE had already signed ensuring complete operational transparency. This included the so-called '123' nuclear co-operation agreement with the United States, the threshold set as the "Gold Standard" under the Nuclear Non-Proliferation Act (formerly the Atomic Energy Act), which linked US nuclear assistance to third parties with strict non-proliferation criteria. Given that the production of nuclear weapons requires access to facilities able to enrich uranium, or the ability to produce plutonium to a weapon's-grade level, the Emiratis remained well within the bounds of their civilian programme.

While much of the modern world might regard nuclear power as outdated, for modernising powers in the Gulf region nuclear power remained an aspirational goal. Much of this was laid out in the Nuclear White Paper (NWP) published by the UAE government in 2008.[37] This emphasised a "green driver" behind the embrace of nuclear energy: the Emirati desire to reduce its carbon footprint. But this "green" rationale only partly explained the Emirati drive for "clean" energy. Gas and oil might well be conserved for more profitable export markets, while surplus electricity could be sold to Gulf neighbours should a proper grid distribution system be established across the region.[38] But, as noted, the start-up costs were vast, not least when compared to renewables, and there was little firm expectation that a return on this investment would ever be realised. Yet, as Mari Luomi argued, the Emirati programme was in large part being driven by prestige. More accurately, it remained an ambitious project on the part of Abu Dhabi alone, despite the regulatory structures and co-operation agreements with project partners having been reached at the wider federal level of the Emirates.[39]

However, while having to buy in the expertise to develop the programme, the UAE saw the acquisition of nuclear power as a key indicator of its developing technical prowess and growing regional influence, a necessary ingredient in the pursuit of modernity. This came at a time of increased commercial tensions between Abu Dhabi and Doha over the wholesale price to be paid for gas from Qatari fields that had previously supplied Emirati power stations. In 2008–9, the more distant northern Emirates and Sharjah suffered power shortages, a key factor in pushing Abu Dhabi towards the nuclear option with its promise of energy security.[40] This also suggested a rider to the argument put forward by Scott Sagan over a decade before: he argued that the acquisition of nuclear weapons would enhance stateness, prestige and identity of the actor involved. The development of a viable civilian nuclear energy programme carried equal weight.[41]

That Abu Dhabi fast-tracked its programme was, however, the product of a unique quid pro quo arrangement. Memoranda of understanding were signed with several international partners, notably France, the United States and South Korea, who devised the programme while Abu Dhabi's willingness to forgo any enrichment process and abide fully by the provisions of the NPT set new standards for nuclear transparency. Indeed, in 2009 the UAE became the first state in the world with civil nuclear aspirations to outlaw domestic enrichment and reprocessing. This in turn allowed unfettered access to US nuclear technology and know-how. Others suggested that the Obama Administration actually pushed the Emiratis into adopting this position, hoping that this would act as an example, not least to Iran, over what the United States deemed permissible in the nuclear realm.

Still, the UAE leveraged its nuclear programme to influence and shape existing defence relationships. The period after 2009 saw increased arms sales and training agreements reached with both France and the United States, the French having already opened a military base in Abu Dhabi in 2008. Controversially, the nuclear deal struck with Seoul contained hidden clauses requiring the South Koreans to provide military support to the UAE if requested. For example, from 2011 South Korean special forces began training their Emirati counterparts.[42] These defence relations constituted an important facet of the Emirati sense of prestige since, as Luomi noted, prestige had long been associated with actors that lack established power. In the case of the UAE, the prestige to be derived from its nuclear programme enjoyed widespread public support, a condition of their relatively new-found stateness that bound a largely homogeneous population to the well-being of the state as energy security was enhanced.

While it is a stretch to link the nuclear programme to the UAE's more assertive regional role—notably its military involvement in the Yemen civil war alongside the Saudis, as well as conducting air strikes with NATO and Arab partners in Libya, Iraq and Syria—it nonetheless informed how Abu Dhabi now viewed that role.[43] In particular, the signing of the JCPOA in 2015 saw senior government officials drop hints that it might revisit the provisions of the '123' nuclear agreement with the United States, precisely because its provisions allowed for limited Iranian enrichment, something denied to the UAE. The UAE ambassador to Washington, Yousef al-Otaiba, reportedly told one American senator that "your worst enemy has been given this right to enrich and this is a right that your friends are also going to want, and we won't be the only country."[44]

Now, with the JCPOA all but moribund and Iran threatening to walk away from its provisions, the warnings of al-Otaiba had particular resonance. Of course, the UAE still did not possess enough trained personnel to develop its own indigenous enrichment capability. But given the animus between Abu Dhabi and Tehran, and the UAE's willingness to engage Iran's regional influence both directly and through proxies, scrutiny over its nuclear programme only increased. While it had yet to move off the 'Gold Standard,' the UAE certainly entertained the possibility in various guises. In July 2009, Crown Prince Sheikh Mohammed bin Zayed al-Nahyan had asked his country to be placed under Washington's nuclear umbrella. A year later, al-Otaiba reportedly called for an all-out attack by the United States on Iran's nuclear facilities should circumstance in the Gulf dictate, rather than face the future prospect of a Tehran armed with nuclear weapons.[45] Longer-term, movement off the 'Gold Standard' together with the attendant dangers of regional proliferation appeared more pronounced as the UAE considered its nuclear future.

Saudi interest in developing a nuclear programme can be traced back to 1978, although it was only in 2006 that Riyadh, at the annual summit of the GCC, declared its intent to build sixteen nuclear reactors. The justifications given were familiar: energy diversification and security; a fast-growing demographic; the need to expand the production of desalinated water supplies; and a desire to cut domestic consumption of carbon-based fuel. Still, its road to developing a nuclear programme was slow. Like the UAE, the Saudis lacked a sufficient technical base on which to build their programme, although the establishment of the King Abdullah City for Atomic and Renewable Energy in 2010 was a clear declaration of intent. Still, the development of a nuclear programme remained intrinsically linked to Riyadh's broader construct of security, designed to enhance its regional prestige and power while reinforcing societal solidarity. As already noted, the reach of its civilian nuclear ambition was likely beyond Saudi Arabia's material grasp: the price tag of \$100 billion probably underestimated the start-up and initial running costs involved, while Saudi Arabia also lacked the skills base to run and sustain such a programme. Nevertheless, with at least two reactors destined to be operational by 2020 or 2022, the direction of travel was clear.[46] Moreover, the importance of nuclear energy to wider societal security across Saudi Arabia in a post-rentier era could not be dismissed lightly. Cheap, plentiful energy remained a cornerstone of a social order still beholden to autocratic modes and methods of control.

Nuclear energy proved attractive to Saudi Arabia for other reasons too, not least in the realm of water desalination. Most of the kingdom's drinking water was desalinated, and in the long term the use of nuclear energy to fuel the desalination process would be cheaper than oil. Moreover, Saudi Arabia regularly issued statements and information regarding its increasing energy needs, apparently as a means of justifying development of a nuclear programme and emphasising its non-military attributes.[47] The demand stemmed from a variety of factors beyond the projected population growth: the need to expand the industrial sector; high energy consumption caused by airconditioning, particularly during the summer months; and the need to roll back subsidised energy prices. The implications of the failure to develop these sources were serious. According to a report by the British think tank, The Royal Institute for International Affairs, Saudi Arabia would soon become an oil importer if it failed to diversify its energy supplies.[48]

Yet if Saudi Arabia's civil nuclear ambitions were relatively transparent, concern remained that, driven by its regional rivalry with Iran, military redundancy would be built into its programme. Certainly, nascent militarisation of its programme could be identified from comments made by, among others, the former head of Saudi intelligence, Turki al-Faisal, in 2014, through to Mohammed bin Salman. During his visit to the United States in spring 2018, the Crown Prince stated as much during an interview with 60 Minutes, the influential current affairs programme broadcast by CBS. Asked about his country's nuclear ambitions, the likely heir to the Saudi throne was characteristically blunt: Saudi Arabia was not actively seeking to acquire nuclear weapons but "If Iran developed a nuclear bomb, we will follow suit as soon as possible."[49] For, while Saudi Arabia continued to support the idea of the Middle East as a Nuclear Weapons Free Zone, and indeed remained a signatory to the NPT with international oversight of its limited nuclear research facilities, it refused to forgo developing its own enrichment capability or adhere to the 123 agreement, a prerequisite if it was to access US nuclear technology and knowhow.

At the beginning of 2019, it remained unclear whether Saudi, Emirati and Israeli opposition to the JCPOA would generate the unintended consequence of pushing Iran towards producing highly enriched uranium, an act that would have profound consequences for Gulf security and inter-Arab politics. It should not be forgotten, however, that Saudi Arabia opposed the

JCPOA precisely because it allowed Iran to produce low-enriched uranium. While the safeguards surrounding the JCPOA have been well aired, prestige and paranoia informed Riyadh's position. As noted, Saudi endorsement of the agreement in 2015 lacked any enthusiasm of the convert, the regional aggression of Iran taken as a given and unlikely to be constrained by the Obama Administration's flagship foreign-policy achievement. Its repudiation by President Trump was therefore welcomed in Riyadh, Abu Dhabi and Jerusalem; while the rest of the signatories to the agreement continued to endorse its provisions, it was, to all intents, moribund.

Whether Tehran would indeed forgo its adherence remained to be seen. Given the reimposition of sanctions, the leadership of the Islamic Republic perhaps had little to lose at a time when economic distress was becoming increasingly widespread across Iran. Only the fear of inviting US military attack acted as constraint; that and perhaps a wider belief that, on this issue at least, world opinion was largely sympathetic to the Iranian position. However, sympathy alone could not rescue the Iranian economy, and voices within Iran advocating a resumption of its nuclear programme to demonstrate its sovereignty and power looked likely to grow. The Saudis were only too well aware of this: Riyadh's drive for a viable nuclear programme served the purpose of accentuating its domestic and regional prestige, wrapped in the argument of sovereign choice, the very rationale long pushed by Iran in justifying its own programme. The irony was telling.

There was of course an element of opacity (and not a little hubris) regarding the Saudi position. Riyadh never explicitly stated that it would develop nuclear weapons, although it reserved the option of developing such a capability. Riyadh certainly had ready access to the raw materials to do so: it could, for example, mine its own uranium for the enrichment cycle, giving it a privileged position in terms of fuel self-sufficiency. However, it faced two practical constraints: a lack of in-house expertise to 'go it alone' and a reluctance in Washington to transfer or sell nuclear technology to a third party without absolute safeguards being in place, notably the prevention of enrichment.

Yet while the Obama Administration was clear in its insistence that the sale and transfer of nuclear technology could only take place under the "Gold Standard," the international nuclear marketplace dictates choice. Like the UAE, the Saudis signed MOUs with a range of states including China and Russia, whose safeguards over the sale and exchange of nuclear technology were decidedly more lax. Moreover, the US nuclear industry was desperate for new contracts at a time when American companies, notably Westinghouse Electric, were struggling. The threat to US companies securing such deals was real. In 2016 Beijing initialled a deal with Riyadh worth $2.4 billion to build a facility in Saudi Arabia for the manufacture of nuclear-related technologies.[50]

Much depends on the nature of US–Saudi relations and the type of future security guarantees offered to Riyadh. On coming to office, the Trump Administration signalled it might well relax the rules surrounding the '123' agreement if it helped secure contracts for US companies. This would require wider Congressional approval and was not a given.[51] Indeed, the warnings from some experts were stark; writing in *Foreign Policy* in the spring of 2018, Victor Galinsky and Henry Sokoloski argued:

> Saudi Arabia is neither a stable state nor a benign actor in the Middle East that deserves US coddling. The truth is that the Saudis have been the main purveyors of the fundamentalist religious doctrines that have spread the seeds of terrorism throughout the Arab world. Given that Saudi Arabia is now engaged with Iran in a struggle for regional dominance, Riyadh's resistance to restrictions on uranium enrichment and plutonium extraction amounts to a public declaration that the kingdom wants to keep the nuclear weapons option open.[52]

Should the Saudis decide to develop their own enrichment facility, the UAE appears set to follow, delivering a fatal blow to the JCPOA and its own "Gold Standard." By 2018, however, the insistence by Riyadh that it had a 'right to enrich' had yet to be realised in any practical steps taken towards this end. Yet Saudi statements did contribute to the incremental militarisation of the issue, necessary to prepare the wider public that, should the ideological conflict with Iran so demand, the Kingdom would revise its current programme to embrace the development of a nuclear weapons capability. The issue therefore was not about whether the Saudis could enrich. After all, this remained a technical matter for an episteme that the Saudis could pay for. Rather, the logic of the security dilemma across the Gulf increasingly demanded that Saudi Arabia had to develop and maintain a weapons-grade enrichment capacity. Its refusal to sign the Additional Protocol to the NPT, that enforces stricter safeguards over the use of nuclear material and technologies, certainly suggested as much.

The extent to which Riyadh might realise its ambition remained contingent nonetheless on the Trump Administration. With his self-declared penchant for 'cutting deals' and under pressure to push a much-needed trade agreement to bolster a struggling nuclear industry, the prospect of landing large contracts for United States companies in the development of a Saudi nuclear programme had electoral as well as financial appeal. As noted, however, sufficient concerns were raised over selling technology to a regime that many, like Galinsky and Sokoloski above, regarded as neither "stable" nor "benign." Republicans and Democrats alike raised serious concerns about fuelling a nuclear arms race across the region, concerns that, behind closed doors, had allegedly been raised by Netanyahu himself with the Trump Administration. Mark Meadows, a Republican from North Carolina, spoke for many across both Houses of Congress when he opined: "[W]hen terrorist organisations have demonstrated an interest in obtaining nuclear fissile material, and when our ally Israel and other states in the region have long standing tensions, our government must be cautious and informed about the implications of a nuclear transfer to any state in the Middle East."[53]

Much of course depended on the extent to which Trump was willing to accede to Netanyahu's wishes or be swayed by his own nuclear lobby. Up until the end of 2018 it appeared that the latter was in the ascendant, although the widespread revulsion across the aisle at the murder of Jamal Khashoggi put any immediate agreement on the political back-burner.[54] Whether Saudi Arabia was in fact willing to avail itself of other suppliers less hamstrung by normative concerns remained to be seen, although with its new-found influence across the Middle East, and the respect garnered by its actions in Syria, Russia appeared well placed to exploit Washington's unease. Equally, by the end of 2018, the extent to which a new round of United States sanctions might push Iran to abandon the JCPOA—despite the urging of the other P5 members, plus Germany, to remain beholden to its protocols—remained unclear. But, as Zvi Bar'el noted, Netanyahu had every chance of being the victim of his own success in thwarting the JCPOA and "facing two nuclear powers instead of one: Iran, which declared it will restart its nuclear programme if the agreement is violated, and Saudi Arabia, which would want to acquire nuclear weapons too as a deterrent against an Iran freed from the bonds of its nuclear agreement."[55]

Israel actually had a clear interest in ensuring that Riyadh worked with Washington, if only because by doing so the United States would gain closer access to the Saudi nuclear project. The United States places a greater emphasis on safety and can supervise what goes on in the realm of nuclear development, thereby exercising leverage over Riyadh within the wider sphere of its relationship with the US. This could serve to decrease Saudi motivation to covertly develop an uranium capability with Chinese or Russian assistance, if only because of the unwanted global attention, not least from the IAEA, that doing so would attract. As a signatory of the NPT, Saudi Arabia would experience difficulties in disguising a nuclear programme with military redundancy; at the very least, it would be subject to the same level of inspections imposed on other countries, as well as possible sanctions if ever suspected of weaponising its programme.

Energy minister, Yuval Steinitz, articulated Israel's position clearly enough when he claimed he had full confidence that the United States would not relax nonproliferation standards in any nuclear-power deal agreed with Saudi Arabia. Any effort by Riyadh to pressure Washington to relax the "Gold Standard" over uranium enrichment or the reprocessing of nuclear fuel would, he implied, be countered by Israel on Capitol Hill. "Once you allow one country to enrich uranium or reprocess fuel," Steinitz concluded, "it will be extremely difficult to tell other countries in this vicinity or elsewhere in the world not to do so."[56]

However, Israel's opposition was informed by a wider regional security logic. If authorisation was given for Saudi uranium enrichment, this might result in a regional spiral in which states such as Egypt and Turkey would also claim this 'right.' Negotiations between the United States and Jordan on this very issue were halted due to Jordan's refusal to renounce the right to enrich uranium in its territory, and any agreement with Saudi Arabia would have implications for its neighbour to the north. Moreover, the UAE would regard itself as no longer obligated to abide by the "Gold Standard," and the US would then encounter difficulties justifying the imposition of additional restrictions on Iran's nuclear programme. Framing these debates was concern in Washington over the future political stability of the Kingdom: the Khashoggi affair and the alleged involvement of Crown Prince Mohammed bin Salman served to highlight anxiety that political stability in the Kingdom was being sacrificed to the whims of a young potentate impatient for change and willing to ride roughshod over long-established rules governing the dispensation of power across the Kingdom.

Some commentators suggested that this was actually an opportunity for Israel to gain diplomatic leverage over Saudi Arabia by helping unlock Riyadh's nuclear impasse with Washington. In return, Israel would gain formal recognition from key Gulf monarchies before negotiating with the Palestinians from a clear position of strength.[57] While not beyond the realm of possibility, such a scenario appeared unlikely. The Khashoggi affair cast a pall on relations between Washington and Riyadh, while, despite his very public advocacy for the Crown Prince, Netanyahu's embrace of the young Saudi ruler never extended to undermining a core tenet of Israeli strategic thinking: the Begin Doctrine. Named after the late Israeli Prime Minister Menachem Begin, it codified Israel's determination to prevent any Arab state from developing a nuclear weapons capability. It led Israel to bomb the Iraqi nuclear reactor at Osirak outside Baghdad in 1981 and the Syrian nuclear facility under construction at al-Kibar on the banks of the Euphrates in 2007.[58] This should come as little surprise; as noted throughout this study, the nature of the TSR allows for co-operation in some areas while not denying ongoing competition (and coercion) in others, where core security interests dictate. The broader issue is the extent to which the TSR actually mitigates the more damaging potential of such competition.

The driver behind Israel's opposition to Iran's nuclear programme had always been the primordial fear of weapons of mass destruction in the hands of a clerical regime so utterly opposed to Zionism and the very idea of a Jewish state. Certainly, Netanyahu continually placed great weight on this existential challenge on the global stage to justify Israel's hard-line opposition both to any programme and the JCPOA. Yet an equally pressing rationale was always present: that the acquisition of such a capability and the impact on the regional balance of power would allow Iran to gain influence, directly and through its proxies, across the region as mutual deterrence was achieved. If Israel wished to remain the regional hegemon, undermining the JCPOA with the support of key Gulf partners was only one half of its wider regional strategy. By the summer of 2015, confronting its nemesis and its proxies in Syria amid the malady of the Syrian civil war turned out to be the other.

5

LIMITS OF COLLUSION

THE SYRIAN CIVIL WAR

Clichés are often glib, but they capture truths. Invoking the seasons, the political shift from 'Arab spring' to 'Arab winter' became one of them. The hopes engendered by mass protests in 2010/11 against long-time autocrats in Tunisia, Egypt and Yemen soon gave way to a level of internecine violence that was shocking in its scale, intensity and brutality. This was much more than the Arab Cold War that marked the ideological standoff between Arab nationalist regimes led by Egyptian President Gamal Abdul Nasser and the dynastic orders that coalesced around Saudi Arabia in the 1960s. By the autumn of 2011, Syria and Iraq had emerged as cockpits of Sunni–Shi'ite sectarian violence as state and non-state actors, supported by Saudi Arabia and Iran respectively, engaged in a pitiless struggle over the husks of both states. By 2018, deaths caused in the Syrian civil war alone had long surpassed those killed in all Arab–Israeli wars combined, up to and including the 2006 Lebanon war and the various bouts of violence between Israel and Hamas in Gaza.[1]

But the Syrian civil war also acted as a cracked mirror on the international community, reflecting a distorted image of Western engagement in a war where there were seemingly few good choices and where decision-making in the capitals of North America and Europe was framed by the bitter experience of the largely Anglo-American invasion and occupation of Iraq a decade previously. The portents for direct Western intervention in the conflict were therefore never good: the Obama Administration allowed itself to be outmanoeuvred by Moscow following President Vladimir Putin's decision to project military force to shore up the regime of his client, Bashar al-Assad. Not only was this intervention crucial in ensuring Assad's immediate survival and eventually changing the fortunes of a bitter internecine conflict in favour of Damascus, but it also served to highlight the apparent impotence of a Washington reluctant to back words with deeds and extend explicit security guarantees to its erstwhile Gulf Arab allies.[2]

Both Israel and Saudi Arabia took note, but it was Netanyahu who gave a powerful voice to wider regional concerns. At the 2016 World Economic Forum in Davos, the Israeli premier used this gathering of the global political and economic elite to articulate the dangers of American retrenchment from the Middle East. He did so by referencing what he regarded as Israel's own experience of ceding territory:

> [W]hat we've seen is that when you have Western forces withdraw in the Middle East anywhere, then immediately, what comes in is militant Islam. It happened to us in Lebanon—we went out, Iran walked in with its proxy Hezbollah; it happened to us in Gaza—we walked out, Iran walked in with Islamic Jihad and with Hamas. And of course people in Israel who want a solution, as I do, between us and the Palestinians, say well, we don't want to govern the Palestinians, but we don't want the territories that are handed over to them to be used as territories, as a launching ground for militant Islamic attacks, as happened before in Lebanon and in Gaza.[3]

By making these previously endogenous issues of Palestinian security an exogenous issue tied to current fears of radicalisation and further regional collapse shared by all regional powers, Netanyahu sought to lessen the pressure faced by Israel to make tangible concessions in the so-called 'intractable conflict.' For their part the Gulf monarchies remained determined to avoid any further reduction in regional security. Their resources were already stretched: the Houthi rebellion and the outbreak of civil war in Yemen, the need to shore up financially the struggling regime of President Abdel Fattah al-Sisi in Cairo, as well the ongoing conflicts in Iraq and Syria presented Saudi Arabia and its Gulf allies with a range of complex security challenges they now struggled to meet. These challenges, coupled with increased estrangement between Qatar on the one side, and Saudi Arabia, the UAE and Bahrain on the other, saw the issue of Palestine pushed to the margins of regional debate, with demands for the restitution of Palestine and Palestinian national rights no longer the touchstone of Arab unity.

It was not surprising that Israel and the Gulf monarchies found themselves sharing common ground regarding shared perceptions of the core regional threat: Iran. It led one Washington official to comment that if "[h]e covered the face of top officials he met during recent trips to Riyadh, Abu Dhabi and Tel Aviv, and listened to their perceptions on the issues and future of the Middle East, he would not be able to differentiate between Saudi, Emirati, and Israeli."[4] Of course, in 2015 the shared concern was still opposition to the nuclear agreement and the view, real or otherwise, that this not only left Iran with a breakout capability to develop a nuclear weapon, but encouraged and indeed rewarded Iranian intrigue across the Middle East. For Netanyahu and many Israelis, it delivered the feared 'Shi'a crescent' from Tehran, via Baghdad and Damascus, to Beirut.[5]

Senior Israeli officials certainly boasted of their contacts with the Gulf monarchies. In April 2014, former Foreign Minister and later Defence Minister Avigdor

Lieberman revealed that he had been party to secret talks, with a view to establishing diplomatic ties with several Arab nations that up until then had been overtly hostile to the Jewish state. The shared perception of threat over Iran's nuclear programme—as well as the growth of radical Islamist groups of varying hues—created, Lieberman argued, common regional interests. He added,

> For the first time, there is an understanding there that the real threat is not Israel, the Jews or Zionism. It is Iran, global Jihad, and Al Qaeda ... There are contacts, there are talks, but we are very close to the stage in which within a year or eighteen months it will no longer be a secret, it will be conducted openly.[6]

However, a spokesperson for the Saudi Arabian foreign ministry was quick to dismiss Lieberman's remarks, insisting that no talks had taken place with Israel at any level.[7]

Lieberman might well have been guilty of verbal hyperbole. As noted, whatever the true nature of Gulf attitudes towards the Palestinians as people, ideational fidelity towards the cause of Palestine remained an emotional loadstone not easily shifted from the path towards closer ties with Israel.[8] Still, as Yousef al-Otaiba, the UAE ambassador to Washington, declared: "The US and the regional allies cannot find a solution to Syria, stabilise Egypt, and halt the Iranian threat without the other; there is simply no way around working together to resolve these issues."[9] Israel was never mentioned by name, but the reference to the "regional ally" alluded to the need to involve Jerusalem, whose attitude and position on many of the issues in the Middle East, from the fall of the Mubarak regime to the increased influence of Iran and Hezbollah in the Syrian civil war, coincided with that of the Gulf monarchies on key issues: Islamic State, the changing face of Iran's geopolitical status, and wider regional uncertainty in the aftermath of the Arab Spring. While opposition to the JCPOA provided the most fertile ground for co-operation, the civil war in Syria offered a practical litmus test of how parties to the TSR were able to pool interests and resources as Israel looked to roll back Tehran's regional gains.

Israel and the Syrian Civil War

It remains somewhat surprising to many observers that, given its challenge to the Arab state system throughout the Middle East, Israel never regarded Daesh or Islamic State as a direct security challenge resulting from the chaos of state fragmentation in Iraq and civil war in Syria. This is not to suggest, of course, that the group did not pose a security threat to Israel; its ideological antipathy towards the very idea of a Jewish dispensation in land regarded by its adherents as an Islamic *waqf* (endowment to Muslims) was and remains real. Rather, the capacity of Islamic State to physically threaten the sovereignty of the

Jewish state was always limited. Lacking air power, long-range missiles and the technical ability to develop delivery systems harnessed to conventional or non-conventional weapons, the tyranny of distance meant that Israel was never a realistic strategic—as opposed to terrorist—target for Islamic State militants.

To be sure, outright hostility to Jews (let alone Israelis) informed the ideology of Islamic State from the outset. Threats against Israel including its imminent annihilation punctuated propaganda, most especially through its English language magazine *Dabiq*.[10] In October 2015 Islamic State released a sixteen-minute video in fluent Hebrew that threatened to attack Israel "for the crimes ... committed against the Palestinian people." Islamic State went on to announce that they "will enter the al-Aqsa mosque as conquerors, using our cars as bombs to strike the Jewish ramparts ... soon there will not be a single Jew left in Jerusalem. We will move to eradicate the disease of the Jewish people worldwide."[11]

Inflated rhetoric aside, Islamic State likely had a healthy regard for the capabilities of the IDF, wary of its long experience in guerrilla warfare and counterterrorism and of course its aerial ability to strike over distance. As one of the few Western journalists allowed access inside Islamic State, the German journalist Jürgen Todenhöfer certainly sensed this during discussions with Islamic State officials who appeared remarkably candid in their assessment of Israel's martial prowess: "[T]hey know the Israelis are very tough as far as fighting against guerrillas and terrorists ... the IDF are a real danger."[12] The anti-Israel diatribe therefore represented no more than a largely rhetorical device, claiming fidelity to the cause of Palestine while at the same time disguising the clear limitations in its ability to target Israel directly, or in mobilising the wider Muslim *umma* (community of believers) to take up the struggle against the Jewish state. For Israel, the real security challenge presented by Islamic State was one by default: the destabilising impact caused by its advances in Syria upon neighbouring Jordan as it struggled to cope with massive refugee flows. The need to ensure close security co-operation with the Hashemite Kingdom, including the exchange of intelligence, become a core Israeli interest.[13]

Still, at the start of the Syrian civil war in 2011, Jerusalem maintained what could be considered a studied neutrality towards the conflict, refusing to be drawn into the ground fighting but adopting a measured response to the various security challenges it faced, notably in the Golan Heights. While Israel may have preferred to see regime change in Damascus, former Israeli ambassador to the United States and expert on Syria Professor Itamar Rabinovich also noted the keenly felt concerns in Jerusalem over any likely successor to the Assad regime. Israel, he argued, would have few diplomatic cards to play with his successor.[14] For example, would a new regime, perhaps of a militant Sunni character with close links to Al-Qaeda affiliates, abide by rules of the game that in the absence of a formal peace treaty had still prevented war between Jerusalem and Damascus for four decades? Accordingly, the measures taken by Israel at the start of the conflict, as the Syrian state began to fragment, were all largely defensive. The border fence was strengthened and IDF reinforcements deployed to deny terrorist infiltration.[15] Those strikes carried out by the Israeli Air Force, deep inside Syria, were designed to prevent chemical-weapon storage depots falling into the hands of jihadi groups at a time when IDF military intelligence firmly believed that the fall of Assad was only a matter of time.[16] Perhaps more visible was the open commitment of IDF medical units to provide assistance to wounded fighters from Syrian opposition groups recovered along the border, acts of humanitarian assistance Israel was keen to publicise to a global audience.[17]

While such acts were widely applauded, they were driven in part by a quid pro quo understanding: humanitarian assistance in exchange for assurances over the safety of the Syrian Druze community. Israel feared that should this community be threatened, Jerusalem would come under extreme pressure from its own Druze citizens to intervene directly on Syrian territory to protect their co-religionists. While fraught with great risk, the IDF did strike targets across the Syrian Golan in response to mortar rounds and rockets landing inside Israeli territory.[18] Such retaliatory strikes were carefully calibrated to send a message. One particular Israeli strike in January 2015 in Syria killed General Mohammed Allahdadi of the Iranian Revolutionary Guard Corps (IRGC) and with him Jihad Mugniyeh, son of Imad Mugniyeh, who, until his assassination in Damascus in 2008, was regarded as the most senior military commander within Hezbollah.[19]

It remains unclear whether good intelligence or mere happenstance resulted in these deaths. It was nevertheless a severe blow to Tehran and Damascus as well as Hezbollah, a blow whose significance was as much symbolic as it was operational.[20] Whatever rationale lay behind the presence of a senior member of the IRGC on the Golan, for Jerusalem it was evidence of how the fate of the Assad regime was now irrevocably entwined with the fortunes of Hezbollah and Iran. Such path dependencies saw Syria attempting to transfer increasingly sophisticated missile systems to the Lebanese Shi'a movement, systems which allegedly would have given Hezbollah a shore-to-ship capability that could hit Israeli vessels and gas platforms in the eastern Mediterranean, as well as other missile systems targeting strategic sites across the length and breadth of the country. A series of air strikes of varying intensity along the Syrian-Lebanese border in 2013, designed to interdict and destroy such weapons reaching the Lebanese militia, were widely attributed to Israel which remained mindful of their wider strategic utility in any future confrontation.[21] Such strikes were soon to intensify in both their scope and reach, but beyond the ritual firebrand speeches from Sheikh Hassan Nasrallah, the initial response of Hezbollah to such strikes remained muted. At a time when its commitment to the war in Syria required ever greater investment in men and material, the Lebanese Shi'a movement was hardly in a position to prosecute a two-front war, least of all against the strongest military power in the region.[22]

These aerial attacks against Hezbollah certainly enjoyed support in Riyadh and contrasted sharply with the increased dismay felt by Israel and Saudi Arabia over the unwillingness of the Obama Administration to use force against the regime in Damascus. This followed from the proven use of nerve agents by Syrian forces against civilians in the Damascus suburb of Ghouta on 21 August 2013, and despite a previous commitment—Obama's infamous red line having been crossed—to do so. The dismay in Jerusalem was compounded by the fact that Unit 8200, Israel's main signals intelligence unit, allegedly passed on to Washington the transcript of an intercepted phonecall from a Syrian Army unit, the 155th Brigade, widely held responsible for the atrocity.[23] But Washington now used the refusal of the British parliament to back strikes by the Royal Air Force against Syrian military facilities to obfuscate their own red lines. While the international pressure on Assad now forced him to co-operate with a Russian plan—to have his stockpile of chemical weapons removed and destroyed under UN inspectors—this was scant compensation for the Gulf monarchies, who felt that a moment of reckoning had been missed. In November 2013 and in protest at this failure of collective Western nerve, the Saudis refused to take up their designated seat on the United Nations Security Council.[24]

The later use of chlorine gas and other nerve agents by Damascus, to clear rebels from Syria's main conurbations in the spring of 2018, merely underscored for Jerusalem the paucity of efforts by the international community to disarm Syria of its chemical-weapons capabilities. More than anything else, it both justified and reinforced Israel's determination to maintain freedom of military action, unencumbered by fidelity to international norms and formalised rules of engagement that so constrained the action of Western powers. Equally, however, Jerusalem's whole approach to the Syrian civil war was an exemplar of *realpolitik*.

Israel never became part of the formal military coalition against Islamic State targets, for example in Syria. Indeed, the very idea of an overt Israeli military presence alongside participating Arab air forces as part of 'Operation Inherent Resolve' was politically untenable. Once, when pressed to define Israel's preferred outcome from the civil war, Netanyahu spoke for many Israelis when he opined: "My rule is simple, you know? When both your enemies are fighting each other, don't strengthen either one. Weaken both. And that's more or less what we try to do."[25] Clearly, Jerusalem believed in the advantages to be had in a war of attrition that was degrading, both in men and material, their Shi'a nemesis on the one hand and the various Sunni militias on the other who, rhetoric aside, had yet to present a direct threat to the Jewish state.

Still, even a limited Iranian military presence close to Israel's northern border remained a red line for Jerusalem, one that Lieberman made clear Israel was not prepared to see crossed without consequences. In the spring of 2018, during the course of an interview with the London-based Saudi news agency *Elaph*, he made clear that he would "not sit idly by while I watch Iran try to transfer advance weapons close to the Golan Heights," before going on to claim that, if Tel Aviv were attacked with such weapons, strikes on Tehran would follow.[26] The use of *Elaph* to reach out to a wider Saudi and Gulf audience was no coincidence. Indeed, it followed in the wake of a similar interview in autumn 2017 given by the former Chief of Staff Lieutenant-General Gadi Eisenkott, an interview seen by many as preparing Saudis for bringing the Israeli–Saudi dialogue firmly into the open by its emphasis upon shared security interests.[27]

Others warned, however, that Israeli–Saudi security interests in Lebanon and Syria were not necessarily aligned. Shared concerns over Iran's military presence aside, warnings that Saudi political manoeuvring in the Lebanese political arena was designed to precipitate a clash between Israel and Hezbollah were voiced. When, during a visit to Riyadh in November 2017, the Lebanese Prime Minister Saad Hariri announced his intention to resign on Saudi state television, claiming that the malfeasance of Hezbollah and its allies in Lebanese politics had pushed him towards this decision, few believed this act of politicide had not been orchestrated behind the scenes by Mohammed bin Salman, anxious to create a crisis of governance in Lebanon that would be laid at the door of Hezbollah. Former United States ambassador to Israel, Dan Shapiro, believed that should such a scenario be played out, Riyadh hoped it would "lead Hezbollah to seek an accelerated confrontation with Israel as a means of unifying Lebanese support for their dominance."[28]

Hariri's resignation had clearly been extracted under duress: once he returned to Beirut, it was promptly withdrawn, thereby averting a constitutional crisis that might well have tipped Lebanon back into another bout of internecine violence. Even so, it was a salutary lesson for Israel that it, and it alone, would choose how and where it would strike at its nemesis in Lebanon and Syria.[29] For, even though a balance of deterrence had largely conditioned the actions of the IDF and Hezbollah since the war of 2006, the intervention of Moscow on the side clear of Bashar al-Assad in the summer of 2015 now saw Damascus take an incrementally more proactive role in transferring weapons systems to Hezbollah, including advanced surface-to-surface and surface-to-air missiles, while allowing the increased presence of Iranian military units, notably the IRGC, on Syrian soil.[30]

Until 2017, the Israeli use of air power had largely, although not exclusively, been targeted at Syrian chemical-weapons facilities.[31] Now, faced with a steep change in both the quality and quantity of weapons deliveries, Israel increased the scale and tempo of air operations against Syrian, Iranian and Hezbollah targets across Syria. Attacks on military compounds close to airports, including Damascus, were a particular priority. Israel suspected that Iranian civilian freight aircraft were being used to transport weapons to such sites before onward delivery to Hezbollah. While Israel had maintained a studied silence surrounding allegations of its involvement in previous attacks, for the first time it publicly acknowledged responsibility for a series of multiple air strikes on Hezbollah targets inside Syria on the night of 17 March 2017.[32]

Several reasons explain this new-found openness on the part of Jerusalem. Most obviously, these strikes were not just about the physical denial of military aid to Hezbollah, but a clear warning to both Damascus and Tehran that Israel could not tolerate Iran gaining a permanent foothold so close to its borders. Equally,

Netanyahu believed a permissive regional environment now operated in Israel's favour. With Trump in office plus very close family friendships that, at the very least, acted as conduit between Jerusalem and Riyadh, few objections were raised to Israeli actions in the capitals of the Gulf. If anything, these strikes were met with the approval of Gulf rulers and burnished Israel's credibility. If the Obama Administration had been hesitant in its dealings with Syria, Israel's increasingly robust response presented the polar opposite. It was a view that carried weight in Tehran. With both Israel and Saudi Arabia keen to make plain Iran's regional ambitions before the annual gathering of leading diplomats and politicians at the Munich Security conference in March 2017, an Iranian foreign ministry spokesman, Bahram Qassemi, noted that both states were "hand in glove" across the Middle East.[33]

Hand in glove they may have been, but Israel's increasing assertiveness over the skies of Syria was initially abetted, if not helped, by Russia. Netanyahu in particular enjoyed good relations with Vladimir Putin, a relationship that now witnessed a strategic paradox being played out: Russia rebuilt and enhanced the air-defence systems of Syria while continuing to offer substantial military aid to Damascus and its proxy allies. At the same time, a 'hotline' was established between the IDF and Russian forces in Syria that effectively regulated the airspace over Syria, *de facto* recognition that

Israel would continue to strike those self-same allies Moscow was equipping and training.[34] As if to underscore the twisted logic of these arrangements, Israel disclosed that up to the beginning of 2017 it had conducted over a hundred air strikes in Lebanon and Syria since the start of the Syrian civil war, most of which were delivered by line-of-sight weaponry, rather than stand-off missiles guided remotely to their targets.[35]

This was demonstrated most clearly on the night of 9 May 2018. A day after Washington announced its withdrawal from the JCPOA, the clash between Israel and Iran reached a new level of intensity. After Iranian forces—thought to be members of the Al-Quds force of the IRGC—fired twenty rockets against IDF positions in the Golan Heights, Israel responded by launching extensive strikes against a range of Iranian targets across Syria in an operation called 'House of Cards.' It was a deliberate attempt to up the ante, demonstrating an intelligence superiority and military prowess designed to intimidate, degrade and deter Tehran (and Damascus) from establishing bases anywhere close to Israel's northern borders.[36]

Of course, this did not mitigate entirely the risk of direct clashes between the IDF and Syrian forces, nor between the Israeli Air Force and their Russian counterparts. The downing of an Israeli Air Force F16I by Syrian air defences in February 2018, and perhaps more worryingly the destruction of a Russian Air Force

Ilyushin reconnaissance plane off the coast of Syria in September—an act initially blamed on the Israel Air Force whose jets had been operating in close proximity—highlighted the febrile nature of these ad hoc security arrangements.[37] The tempo of Israeli air sorties conducted over Syria between the beginning of 2017 and the autumn of 2018 was more than double that of the previous five years. At the same time, the willingness of Syria to be more aggressive in defending its airspace, and the use of a drone—flown remotely by the IRGC into northern Israel before being shot down—underscored the fact that, despite its military sway, Moscow had only finite leverage over the actions of Damascus and Tehran.[38]

Yet beyond ensuring the survival of Bashar al-Assad and drawing its own red lines accordingly, this was a situation that Russia appeared to accept, though it remained fraught with danger. The increased presence of Iranian military personnel and assets in Syria from 2016 onwards was seen by some as the direct consequence of the JCPOA. More likely, however, it stemmed from Russia's timely intervention in a civil war that by the end of 2017 had clearly begun to swing in Assad's favour. Even before this shift, though, prominent Israeli security officials had begun to argue that Israeli intervention in the war now had to move beyond humanitarian assistance to refugees and the wounded fighters along its border with Syria. Amos Yadlin, for example, argued that moral rectitude and strategic imperative made this necessary: not only were the deaths of over 400,000 people and Damascus's continued use of chemical weapons morally indefensible; but, strategically, what he referred to as the Tehran-Assad-Nasrallah alliance, had garnered little practical opposition from across the region when compared to the Western and regional forces assembled to confront Islamic State. He opined:

> Israel must develop a multi-faceted strategy on this matter. A basic condition for this is the creation of a local alliance, even an unofficial one, with Sunni powers such as Saudi Arabia, the Gulf monarchies, Turkey, Jordan, and Egypt. ... The Sunni nations of the Middle East have shared interests with Israel as far as combating the radical axis is concerned.[39]

Indeed, the protection of refugees along the northern border—Israel's own form of R2P (responsibility to protect)—was consistent with more pronounced clandestine activity to further Israeli national security interests.[40] Rumours had long circulated that Israel had in fact been supplying weapons, money and tactical intelligence to Syrian opposition groups, operating under the umbrella of the Free Syrian Army in and around the Golan Heights and the southern Syrian town of Deraa. While Israel refused to confirm these reports, such actions had a clear strategic logic to them as Jerusalem looked to ensure that pro-Iranian militias were denied territory and the ability to manoeuvre on the Syrian side of the

Golan Heights.[41] At the same time, Netanyahu sought assurances from Moscow that it would pressure Damascus to keep Iran and its various Shi'ite militias at least eighty km from the Israeli–Syrian border.[42] Netanyahu certainly believed he had a *modus vivendi* with Russia. Following a meeting with President Putin in Moscow in January 2018, the Israeli premier declared publicly that the Russians "fully understand our position and the seriousness with which we view such threats … The Russian Army is on our border and we have managed to preserve our interests and freedom to act [by] coordinating expectations."[43]

However, as the downing of the Ilyushin reconnaissance aircraft demonstrated, such understandings were strained. Moscow's ability to do Israel's bidding over the activities of Hezbollah and Iran remained circumscribed. The eighty-km buffer was never a realistic option given the proximity of Damascus to the Golan Heights. It was also an unacceptable demand over Syrian territorial sovereignty that Assad could never accept. The "tens of kilometres" later reported proved a more realistic expectation. Therefore, what now emerged was what Yadlin referred to as "Israel's war between wars," a dedicated effort to use its superior air power and intelligence capabilities to degrade Iranian, Syrian and Hezbollah military assets, notably in the realm of missile technology, regarded by Israel as a potent strategic threat. It was a threat that Netanyahu outlined to the international community during his annual speech to the United Nations in New York on 27 September 2018. In a striking, if somewhat theatrical, speech, he produced aerial reconnaissance photographs which he claimed were Hezbollah missile-storage facilities in the very heart of Beirut, close to the Rafik Hariri International Airport.[44] While these particular targets had still escaped the attention of the Israeli Air Force by the end of 2018—direct attacks on the Lebanese capital remained a red line that Israel could not easily cross—Eisenkott later disclosed in a parting interview, before handing over to his successor in early 2019, that Israel had struck thousands of Iranian targets inside Syria, strikes that had prevented Iran from realising its "grandiose vision" but for which Israel rarely publicly claimed credit.[45]

There is little doubt that Israel inflicted real damage on Iran, Syria and its various militia allies. Indeed, when coupled with the discovery and destruction by the IDF of six attack tunnels dug by Hezbollah under the border fence with Israel in preparation for any new war, the IDF chalked up notable operational successes in this 'war between wars.' Yet while Israel's use of air power was impressive, it could not change the wider political and strategic equation in Syria that by the end of 2018 saw Assad very much in the ascendant. Indeed, this reality was understood in Jerusalem by that summer and was reflected in five key points that now determined Israel's approach to events in Syria: (1) to degrade and deny missile systems held by Iran, Syria and Hezbollah, targeted at Israel; (2) the removal of all pro-Iranian forces from Syria; (3) restoration of the 1974 separation of forces agreement on the Golan Heights and restoration of the status quo ante that had held for thirty-seven years following the end of the October 1973 war; (4) Israel's freedom of action "against any party that acts against us from Syrian territory," including Iran, Islamic State and Hezbollah; (5) agreement with Moscow (and acceptance in Washington) that Assad would remain in power and that Israel would not attempt to unseat him.[46] It was an outlook that in no small measure came to be shared by two of Israel's erstwhile Gulf partners: Bahrain and the UAE.

Increasingly, many Arab states had begun to reassess their demands for the removal of Assad and the emergence of a new political dispensation in Syria as a precondition for re-establishing diplomatic ties. A pragmatic approach yet to be shared by most Western states, it understood that, backed by Russia and Iran, the Syrian president would likely remain in power. Their long-held antipathies aside, reality now determined engagement. It was an approach that reflected lessons learned from Iraq: there, refusal to engage with a largely Shi'a government had allowed Tehran to fill the void. On 27 December 2018, the UAE reopened its embassy in Damascus, with Bahrain quickly announcing its intention to follow suit. While Saudi Arabia had yet to tread in their wake, the Emirati and Bahraini decision was driven by *realpolitik*, the belief being that such ties (and reopening) to the Sunni Gulf might, over time, lessen Assad's dependence upon Iran. Given his reliance on military support from Tehran, however, this remained a distant hope.

It reflected, too, the limitations of relying on proxies to fight regional wars. The Gulf monarchies had largely failed to exercise any operational influence over the scope and direction of the Syrian civil war, their supplies of money and weapons to increasingly disparate rebel groups leveraging little military influence or political gains. If anything, it underscored their helplessness: despite the vast amounts of treasure expended on opposition groups of various ideological hues in six years of conflict, the future of Arab Syria was being determined by three non-Arab powers: Turkey, Iran and Russia.[47] This was a remarkable reversal of fortune and highlighted the limits of what could be achieved by those party to a TSR unable (or unwilling) to nail their interests publicly to the same mast. While the emergence of Islamic State—both physically and in terms of wider societal appeal—presented a more immediate challenge to the Gulf monarchies, it had been the removal of the Assad regime, long seen in Riyadh, Manama and Abu Dhabi as a supplicant of Tehran, that remained a particular strategic challenge, one where their interests closely aligned with those of Israel.

While visiting Israel in March 2014, this synergy of interest had been remarked upon by the former US Chairman of the Joint Chiefs of Staff, General Martin E. Dempsey. During the course of a discussion with his IDF counterparts, he suggested "[A]n outreach to other partners who may not have been partners in the past ... what I mean is the Gulf monarchies in particular, who heretofore may not have been open-minded to the potential for co-operation with Israel, in any way."[48] He suggested, in oblique terms, that future collaboration might embrace intelligence sharing, shared expertise in counter-terrorism and involvement in co-ordinated diplomatic efforts to resolve the Syrian civil war.

How well briefed Dempsey had been over the variated ties between Israel and the Gulf monarchies when he made his comments remains unclear. This could be seen as Washington's endorsement of a new regional order it saw already emerging. Equally, with an Obama Administration keen to lessen its strategic footprint across the Middle East, encouraging a rapprochement between Israel and the Gulf monarchies had a clear political logic. But, like Israel, the Gulf monarchies proved reluctant to take on a more direct role in the Syrian civil war beyond limited air strikes and aid sent to proxy forces. Up until 2013, the Saudis remained hopeful that military intervention by Washington of a scale and intensity able to shift the internal balance of power away from Damascus would be forthcoming.[49] Riyadh had championed the Syrian National Coalition, a loose alliance of anti-Assad groups whose antipathy towards the regime in Damascus was more often than not matched by intense internal rivalries that did little to advance their own increasingly viperous cause. Equally, the Saudis were careful to calibrate their support for these opposition groups, just enough to allow the Syrian opposition forces small victories to sap the strength of Damascus and its proxy allies, but ultimately remaining beholden to Riyadh and its wider regional agenda. Yet although it may have been a tactic that worked well for the Saudis in the past—the Yemen civil war in the 1960s being the most telling example—such aid now proved insufficient to help these various opposition groups gain operational advantage on the battlefield, let alone hold their own against Assad's forces.[50]

However, faced with a marked reluctance on the part of Washington to place 'boots on the ground,' the Gulf monarchies shied away from committing troops to the fray in Syria. Indeed, with the Saudi military struggling to impose its will in Yemen, the appetite in Riyadh to engage more widely in the region's conflicts was soon diminished. Instead, support for war by proxy remained the preferred method of countering Iran's drive for regional hegemony. In Israel, the conflict in Yemen that had seen surface-to-surface missiles launched by the Houthi towards the Saudi capital elicited sympathy in Israel given the similar threat it faced across its northern border from Hezbollah's formidable arsenal of missiles.[51] This experience, more than anything else, particularly chimed with the Saudis and Emiratis. At the very least, the Gulf monarchies now understood Jerusalem's often harsh response to both Hezbollah and Hamas, enemies whose ability to deploy missiles and mortars of varying ranges and lethality had only increased exponentially.

CONCLUSION

REVEALED INTERESTS, HIDDEN PARTNERSHIPS

In December 2018 and before a conference organised by the Jerusalem Institute for Strategic Studies, Yair Golan, a former IDF deputy chief of staff, poured metaphorical cold water on those in Israel advocating closer ties with the Gulf monarchies: "We should," he noted, "be very very careful regarding the Gulf monarchies." While Golan agreed that "common interests" were apparent, he warned that "we [Israelis] rely on a completely different set of values and we should not overemphasise this relationship."[1] It was a reminder to Israel's decision-makers that whatever their immediate worth, the ties established with the Gulf monarchies were likely to be of limited duration (if not value), and certainly not ones that could be enhanced by shared norms or longer-term interests.

Golan certainly had a point. The Arab world has never been a paragon of co-operation and unity; since 2011, state fragmentation, religious division and sectarian cleavage further undermined the Arab state system.

Where once the Arab world could at least coalesce around the symbolism of Palestine, it is now increasingly seen by some as a source of vexation, a problem to be managed rather than solved amid the wider bloodshed across Syria, Iraq and Yemen. The regional mosaic hardly conformed to a coherent pattern of intra-Arab or indeed Islamic coherence despite its varied parts. The continued stand-off between Qatar, supported by Turkey on the one hand, and Saudi Arabia, Egypt, the UAE and Bahrain on the other, proved resistant to any resolution. The continued "embrace" by Doha for the Muslim Brotherhood and its regional offshoots seemingly placed it beyond the collective Saudi-Emirati-Egyptian pale.[2] Add to this the alliance of Syria, Iran and Hezbollah—a triumvirate that for many Arabs oversaw a Shi'a ascendancy from Tehran to Beirut—and the faultlines of the Middle East hardly provide firm ground on which to build diplomatic engagement, let alone intra-Arab reconciliation.

The approach of Saudi Arabia, Bahrain, Qatar, the United Arab Emirates and Oman towards Israel has been shaped by this context with its seemingly contradictory demands: sensitivity to their status and position in the Arab world; wary of a perceptible if diminishing public animus towards Jerusalem; the continued need to co-opt their respective *ulema* (Muslim clerical establishments); demonstrations of political and economic munificence towards the Palestinian cause, but ultimately maintaining a relationship with Israel as a necessary bulwark against the ambitions of their main rival, Iran. While acknowledging the increased volume of these contacts, not all Israelis remained convinced that such ties constitute a regime, let alone one defined by tacit consent of the parties involved. Efraim Halevy, a man who enjoyed a long and distinguished career in Mossad, including a central role in brokering the peace treaty with Jordan in 1994, remained unconvinced. For him, such a regime involves mutual security obligations, not just interests: the Gulf monarchies did not want to be exposed to accusations of being "in bed" with Israel, while Jerusalem could not "extend its commitments to the security of others beyond its capabilities."[3]

Of course, there is weight to this argument. Military power and the ability to project this power, either through word or deed, has long informed alliance theories. Halevy is surely correct to suggest that a TSR, if restricted by definition to its military component, hardly defines Israel's relations with the Gulf monarchies, let alone Saudi Arabia. But the construct of the TSR developed in this volume is more than just the manifestation of military power. Indeed, the use by Aaron Klieman to describe the condition of Jordanian–Israeli relations nearly three decades ago embraced forms of engagement beyond understandings of hard power. The six defining features of the TSR that have emerged between Israel and the Gulf monarchies since 2011 have followed this tradition. As noted from the outset, the 'modes and means' of the TSR embrace diplomatic support and, increasingly, economic engagement in areas where mutual interests converge. The response of Israel and Saudi Arabia to the JCPOA is the most obvious example; the willingness of Jerusalem to condone some advanced weapons sales to the Gulf monarchies, through its political silence on Capitol Hill, is another. Equally, Israel's particular use of 'soft power', not least in the realm of cyber security, was at the forefront of establishing economic ties with several Gulf monarchies, notably the UAE. While Netanyahu can be accused of pushing the value of these ties too far and too fast into the public limelight for his own internal political purposes, he was surely correct when he highlighted the role played by the hi-tech sector in radically recasting Israel's regional ties.

To be sure, the Gulf monarchies always recognised Israel's military power and its close ties with the United States (as well as its influence in Congress) as key drivers in their relationships with Jerusalem, drivers that they sought to mobilise against Iran. Recognising this reality underpinned the process of covert normalisation that has taken various forms, as this book has argued. However, "normal relations"—the Saudis' preferred phrase— always remained a distant hope in the absence of any tangible Israeli–Palestinian peace process. Undoubtedly, the Gulf states continued to perceive the Israeli– Palestinian conflict as a source of regional instability, ripe for exploitation by Iran and its proxies, notably Hamas and Hezbollah. Yet they always remained doubtful over Israel's willingness to countenance a meaningful territorial accommodation with the Palestinians. While holding to the promise of the API as providing a framework for at least discussing the issue of borders, refugees and the status of East Jerusalem, continued expansion of settlement construction in the West Bank and around East Jerusalem were acts hardly designed to demonstrate Israel's good faith in reaching an accommodation.[4]

For its part, Israel remained cautious about the prospects of true normalisation with countries such as Saudi Arabia, whose dismissal of Israel's right to exist for over six decades was for so long a staple of its foreign policy. It was an approach born of bitter experience. Jerusalem remained underwhelmed by the relatively limited diplomatic returns derived from its previous peace agreements with Egypt and Jordan. It had certainly accrued strategic gains, not least in removing a formidable Arab conventional military threat from its eastern and southern borders. However, there was no pressing imperative, domestic or international, for the 'painful compromises' over territory that most Israelis believed would be required under the API, but whose benefits most believed would be scant.

It should also be noted that, given the scope and nature of Israel's ties with the Gulf monarchies, all parties actually had little real incentive to embrace full normalisation. Of course, the TSR might not allow for the full military and diplomatic weight of the "Fraternal Enemies" to be exercised in shaping the regional dispensation of power, but that was never its primary purpose. Rather it was a framework that allowed the Gulf monarchies—notably the Saudis, Bahrainis, Emiratis and recently (albeit more visibly) the Omanis—to enjoy the advantages of dealing with Israel without having to pay the price in terms of a febrile domestic base or wider regional challenges to their legitimacy. Even so, the Arab street has become more accepting of the reality of increased contact with Israel, notably through co-ordinated public events streamed live on social media. This was another key element of the TSR, and an increasingly important one as these events helped mediate public engagement with elite decision-makers in otherwise autocratic societies.

Yet Israel too derived similar advantages. While external security issues have long dominated political discourse in Israel, its own internal divisions over the future of the West Bank, the wider settlement project and the increasing religiosity that has come to mark much of Israeli society, are acute.[5] While these splits have long been seen as containing the seeds of civil strife, the assassination in 1995 of Yitzhak Rabin by a young Jewish zealot over the issue of land for peace was a potent reminder of the febrile nature of political discourse across much of Israel. While most Israelis expect the majority of settlements—most situated close to the 1948 Green Line—to be incorporated within Israel proper in any settlement with the Palestinians, the very idea that land promised by God to the Jewish people could ever be shared remains anathema to many right-wing religious Israelis. In short, ideational constraints mean that, for Israel and the Gulf monarchies, semi-covert normalisation serves the shared purpose of regional security while ensuring domestic stability.[6]

Much of this covert normalisation has of course been underpinned by 'soft-public' engagement. At the forefront of the effort to improve relations between Israel and the Gulf Arabs have been private individuals with strong links to their relevant governments, as well as influential think tanks that are closely aligned with the ruling elite. The individuals—including former ministers, military officials and security experts—have pioneered the development of back-door channels between the erstwhile protagonists. As opposed to governments, such people can make public overtures that help lay the foundations for closer relationships at open forums or invited events that garner widespread media attention. One such notable event hosted by the Washington-based Council on Foreign Relations in June 2015 brought together Dore Gold, then serving as Director General of the Israeli Foreign Ministry, and Saudi General Anwar Eshki. While ostensibly unofficial, these events helped facilitate private conversations between individuals closely connected to elite decision-making circles in their respective realms. Whatever the nature of discussions between the two men conducted behind closed doors, the symbolism of such events was not lost on Israelis, Saudis or indeed a wider public across the Middle East. Beyond the usual platitudes over the need to work towards regional peace, both recognised that common concerns meant "Israelis and Saudis could work together."[7]

Their engagement was not unique. Having broken the mould by engaging with Amos Yadlin before an invited audience in Brussels in 2014, Prince Turki al-Faisal gave a repeat performance, this time alongside Efraim Halevy in New York in October 2017, an event organised by the pro-Israel think tank Israel Policy Forum. The symbolism of the venue, the Temple Emanu-El synagogue in Manhattan, proved as significant as the actual opinions expressed by the distinguished panellists. It was the first time the Saudi had spoken publicly in a Jewish place of worship, where he continued to extol the virtues of the API, emphasised the need to confront Iran, and impressed upon Israelis and Arabs the need for both to make concessions for peace. The rewards, he claimed, would be immense:

> Imagine, ladies and gentlemen, if the Arabs and Israelis got together on scientific development; imagine if we got together on developing water resources which is need for both of us; medical research and accomplish-

ments, business activities and so on. All of this is in front of us if only we can reach peace between our peoples and our governments. And we're denying ourselves this because we are sitting back and denying ourselves the peace ... I've always said to my Jewish audiences in the past and I'll say it again today, with Jewish money and Arab brains we can go far![8]

The tongue-in-cheek remark aside, Prince Turki had been clear that as far as he knew "as a private citizen," there had been no "under the table" discussion with Israel. Indeed, he let it be known that in Riyadh there had been private irritation at Netanyahu issuing proclamations that "hinted" at a strong relationship, something that the Saudi was clear could only come about on the basis of progressing the API. Of course, the truth may be so precious that, to paraphrase Winston Churchill, it remains an enigma wrapped in a riddle and surrounded by the bodyguard of ambiguity. Ambiguity has, however, occasionally dropped its guard. In 2013, the Israeli state budget released online inadvertently revealed, after a careful examination of its audit, that a representative diplomatic mission had been opened in a Gulf state.[9] That Gulf state was the United Arab Emirates.

Tensions between the Gulf monarchies and Iran remain the key element connecting them to Israel and it would be difficult to imagine the same level of co-operation—not least, for example, in Israel's attitudes towards arms sales—if they did not share a deep-seated fear of

Tehran's increasing regional footprint. Even so, once signed, the Israelis noted Riyadh's official acceptance of the JCPOA, the Saudis claiming it was a "preliminary step towards a comprehensive solution to the Iranian nuclear program," before adding the proviso that it should lead to "the removal of weapons of mass destruction, especially nuclear weapons, from the Middle East." For Jerusalem it suggested that pressure for Israel to be more forthcoming on its own nuclear programme would not likely abate in the wider court of Arab opinion. In response to the JCPOA, Jerusalem declared that it would continue to seek "enhanced preparedness for pre-emptive strikes against countries with no joint border with Israel." This was a clear warning that it reserved the right to launch preventive strikes against Iran's nuclear facilities and also, perhaps, against any other state that looked to develop a nuclear weapons capability.[10]

It was affirmation of the continued currency of the Begin Doctrine, as the 2007 strike on the Syrian al-Kibar reactor demonstrated.[11] When existential challenges focused collective minds in Jerusalem, time and distance proved no obstacle to Israel's ability to act. It is a point worth noting. Fraternal enemies they may be, but revelations that Saudi Arabia might have a functioning ballistic missile programme located at the military base of al-Dawadmi, 150 miles west of Riyadh, clearly raised questions in Israel concerning the scope of the Kingdom's nuclear programme. Given its known technical limitations, it has been suggested that Saudi Arabia might have relied upon Chinese technology, confirming Riyadh's increasing willingness to operate beyond the constraints of the United States.[12] Analysis would suggest that this is a Saudi step towards building up its deterrent capability against Iran, but even so it highlighted the limits of the TSR: it may manage relations in one realm, but it cannot prevent competition in others.

This is just one area, albeit a strategically highly significant one, where actor expectations both converge as well as diverge. Nevertheless, the broader point about the TSR as it has emerged between Israel and the Gulf monarchies still stands: it has mitigated excess competition so that the core aim of the regime, containing Iran, is realised. To be sure, not all are convinced that the Iranian threat is as real as has been portrayed. A faltering economy, increasing social unrest and a new round of sanctions compounding further the sense of economic anomie suggest a regime struggling to enforce its regional fiat or consolidate gains made.[13] However, this remains a minority view. Gawdat Bahgat pointed out that while all-out war between Iran and Israel is unlikely, Netanyahu's strategy, supported by the Gulf monarchies, was to "increase military and economic pressure on Iran in Syria and elsewhere" in order to promote "regime change" in Tehran."[14]

Against the backdrop of the Syrian crisis and the broader upheaval of the Arab Spring, all parties in the

TSR shared a similar strategic outlook concerning a host of threat scenarios presented by Iran, Hezbollah, Al-Qaeda and other Sunni jihadi groups. However, despite shared commitments to fighting regional extremist groups and a common perception of the Arab Spring as a source of "instability," no Gulf dynastic regime had, by the end of 2018, proved willing to establish formal diplomatic ties with Israel. However, as noted, this was never the substance of the TSR. Rather, it allowed Israel access to key Gulf decision-makers without having to pay a price in the currency of concession to the Palestinians. Indeed, the TSR allowed the relationship to largely circumvent the issue of Palestine to the domestic benefit of all parties. Diplomatic recognition was never an end in itself, despite the more inflated hopes of some Israeli politicians. As Moshe Ya'alon noted, "Historically the Arab countries had used the 'Palestinian issue' as a political weapon against Israel. Now they are in the 'same boat' with Israel, they have no need for that weapon. In fact, now they need Israel."[15]

Nevertheless, all this has been framed by growing concern in Israel and the capitals of the Gulf monarchies over Washington's retrenchment from the region. Though it was a process widely seen to have begun under the Obama Administration, the Trump Administration did little to assuage fears. A moribund peace process; the drawdown of US forces from Iraq, Afghanistan and Syria; the increasing independence from Middle Eastern oil combined with public statements regarding a pivot towards Asia: these all suggested that Washington's influence and interest in the Middle East had begun to diminish even before Trump entered the White House. Collectively they were taken as signs of superpower retrenchment, if not outright retreat. Though the Gulf monarchies had lauded Trump's hard-line stance against Iran on entering the White House, their initial optimism somewhat waned after two years. As one Gulf Arab diplomat noted, much beyond the mantra of America first, "We have no idea what he's [Trump] trying to achieve—and I suspect that neither does he."[16] Standing tough on Iran and abandoning the JCPOA might have earned the president regional plaudits, but his seemingly precipitous decision to withdraw all US forces from Syria, on the basis that Islamic State had been defeated, created a lacunae that experts in Washington forecast would quickly be filled by Iran and its proxies. As if to emphasise the point, Trump's defence secretary James Mattis resigned in protest, while others, including pro-Israel lobby groups in Washington, warned of the consequences of abandoning regional allies such as the Kurdish militias.[17]

We should, of course, be wary regarding the actual level of United States retrenchment. At the time of writing it still has bases and access to military facilities across the Gulf region, notably in Bahrain, Oman, Kuwait, the UAE and Qatar. While its own dependence on Middle

East oil might have diminished, ensuring the well-being of the global economy still necessitates a strong US air and naval presence across the Gulf. The TSR developed in this study has, the authors argue, allowed Israel to amplify the diplomatic voices of the Gulf monarchies, individually and collectively, along the corridors of power in Washington; indeed it was a mainstay of the burgeoning relationships that developed. However, since the Obama Administration the American pivot away from the region has raised wider concerns that Israel's traction in Washington might be waning, thereby lessening the value of the TSR.

For now, the jury remains out, but it should be remembered that the TSR is a framework—not a linear process—to meet a defined end. Its purpose remains the containment of Iran, and to this extent its underlying principles, albeit unwritten, remain the basis for cooperation. Irrespective of strategic introspection in Washington, Israel remains the region's strongest military power and, as demonstrated increasingly in Syria, one willing to take the fight to Iran where necessary. In targeting its nemesis in such a way, it has served the interests of Riyadh and Abu Dhabi in particular. Equally, Israel has been willing to furnish at least some of their security needs: ties to the Emiratis are perhaps the most notable, both in the realm of military training and in the provision of cyber technologies. Israel's use of its own version of soft power, an important facet of the TSR, has been used to remarkable effect. There might not be a normative confluence to the TSR that underpins more open security regimes, but its hard ties, soft-power impact and shared diplomatic interests do still bind.

At the same time, Israeli policy-makers seem to believe that the Jewish state would not benefit from a multilateral approach to the Gulf monarchies, even one that could be institutionalised covertly. This reflects a continuity in Israel's attitude towards peace negotiations and a continued preference for bilateral relations. Multilateral engagement where the collective weight of Arab opinion can be brought to bear have always been anathema to Israel. Equally, there is a normative argument against building too close an alliance between the Gulf monarchies and Israel. Despite Riyadh's important role in the global oil market, Saudi Arabia's domestic behaviour alone should probably disqualify the country as a close ally of Israel. As noted by Yair Golan, would it be wise for Israel to continue to build bridges with Saudi Arabia given the international condemnation from traditional allies over the Khashoggi affair and the Kingdom's air campaign in Yemen? Can Israel justify improving relations with Saudi Arabia when the latter remains so clearly involved in human rights violations?[18] Ultimately, however, *realpolitik* determines Israeli policy: the immediate need to secure the region from further political atrophy trumps the pursuit of a normative-driven regional engagement that can never leverage long-term influence, let alone tangible gains. The shared interest of Israel and the Gulf monarchies (of Saudi Arabia, the UAE and Bahrain) in reducing the power of radical forces across the region has, to all intents and purposes, pushed meaningful engagement on an Israel-Palestine peace process to the sidelines. Indeed, for Jerusalem, what are the tangible gains to be had? In March 2016, outlining the reality of Israel's diplomatic position, Netanyahu opined that the Jewish state had "ties with 161 countries. The one who is isolated is not Israel, but those countries that don't have ties with Israel, and the list is getting smaller all the time."[19]

As if to prove the point, the Israeli premier announced in January 2019 the resumption of diplomatic ties with Chad, a largely Muslim state, forty-seven years after the last Israeli ambassador was asked to leave N'Djamena. It was an event Netanyahu linked clearly to Israel's ties with the Gulf monarchies when he declared, "First you penetrate the Arab world, and that helps you to penetrate the Muslim countries. The big difference is that you have a clear process of normalisation with the Arab world, though it is not complete and not formal, and with that you go to the [non-Arab] Muslim world."[20]

Still, the logic of classical realism would suggest that at the very least, a formal alliance between Israel and at least three of the Gulf monarchies, conditioned by a shared view of Iran as a malign regional actor, would likely emerge. That it has failed to do so speaks volumes for the continued hold that Palestine continues to exercise over the collective Arab conscience.[21] Of course, closer relations between Jerusalem and the Gulf monarchies in particular have the potential to breathe new life in the moribund Israel-Palestine peace process. More broadly, Abu Dhabi and Riyadh in particular could assist, for example, the financing of joint Israeli–Palestinian projects. This could provide the additional benefit of diplomatic legitimacy to the Jewish state while bolstering the financial stability of any future Palestinian state, although much of course depends on Hamas. This, in turn, could result in a more productive Israeli attitude towards the territorial concessions long seen as the basis of any enduring peace agreement, although internal opposition in Israel to such concessions on ideological grounds alone remains powerful.

These economic incentives appeared to underpin the much-trumpeted "deal of the century" being proposed by Jared Kushner, described by one commentator as President Trump's "Metternich."[22] An initiative designed to break the impasse between Israel and the Palestinian Authority, carefully leaked details of the plan in the spring of 2019 suggested that Israel's continued control (and perhaps annexation of the key settlement blocs in the West Bank) would be traded for massive inward investment in areas under the control of the Palestinians, coupled with enhanced autonomy. These provisions were to be discussed at a specially convened conference in

Bahrain, scheduled for the end of June 2019, with the UAE and Saudi Arabia confirming their participation.[23] While it confirmed the closeness of ties between these three Gulf monarchies and the Trump Administration, and was likely aimed at cementing still further regional opposition against Iran, it nonetheless appeared to fall far short of embracing full Palestinian statehood. It led most informed commentators, including the former Israeli deputy foreign minister in the Rabin government, Yossi Beilin, to conclude that at best the initiative was premature, and at worst stillborn. Few believed that the supposed beneficiaries, the Palestinians themselves, would trade their national rights for economic betterment.[24]

Israeli policy-makers, however, seem to believe that the Jewish state has little to gain from such a holistic approach. By contrast, the loose institutional framework of the TSR has allowed the Gulf monarchies to calibrate the level and intensity of ties with Jerusalem, an arrangement favoured by Israel but with a recognition that Riyadh holds the whip hand. It may also reflect a continuity in Jerusalem's attitude towards peace, one in which it has demonstrated a continued preference for conducting bilateral negotiations. Of course, the improved relations and the benefits that may accrue from such ties remain contingent upon inter-Arab relations, internal GCC politics and progress being made in Israeli–Palestinian negotiations.[25] An attempt to force such relations from the shadows would undermine much of what has been achieved thus far; the opprobrium of the Arab street still conditions state behaviour. Even so, there is a wide range of policy options between full diplomatic relations and a total lack of contact, and the actors involved have taken advantage of this. Israelis in particular recognise this, and in public forums remain keen to highlight the shared interests between Jerusalem and what Major-General Herzi Halevy, a former head of Israeli military intelligence, referred to as "pragmatic Sunni countries."[26]

The six defining elements of the TSR outlined in this study and that frame the relations between Israel and the Gulf monarchies span a range of activities, but ultimately recognise that hard security determines the level of engagement. They recognise too that internal constraints on all sides determine the type and intensity of external engagement, a conceptual observation that challenges a purely realist account of regional power politics devoid of ideational content. In this regard there is also a realisation that amid the upheaval and fragmentation of much of the Middle East, state-based interests still matter and the interests of Jerusalem and Riyadh in this instance perhaps matter most. Geographical proximity has never been an issue and nor has the varied nature of ties between Israel and Gulf monarchies, precisely because Riyadh's dominance of the Gulf security relations has largely determined the level of engagement with Israel. For now, the scope and intensity of the ties established relate primarily to Iran. Yet if the view holds that Washington's diplomatic and military footprint among these erstwhile regional protagonists has become increasingly faint, the TSR that has emerged between Israel and the Gulf monarchies might well become a template for understanding shifts in alliances and regional security systems, across the wider Middle East, North Africa and beyond.

NOTES

INTRODUCTION: FRAMEWORK FOR ANALYSIS

1. 'Full Text: Prime Minister Benjamin Netanyahu's 2018 UN General Assembly Speech', *Ha'aretz*, 27 September 2018.
2. Binyamin Netanyahu, 'Innovation Nation', *The Economist: The World in 2018*, December 2017, p. 90.
3. See for example Ariel I. Ahram and Ellen Lust, 'The Decline and Fall of the Arab State', *Survival*, vol. 58 no. 2 (2016), pp. 7–34; Amichai Magen (ed.), *The Crisis of Governance in the Middle East: Implications for Democracy, Development and Security*, Tel Aviv: IDC Herziliya/Konrad-Adenauer Stiftung, 2013, pp. 21–9.
4. On Israel's ties with Morocco, see Yossi Alpher, *Periphery: Israel's Search for Middle East Allies*, London: Rowman & Littlefield, 2015, pp. 25–8. On Israel's ties with Jordan, see Joseph Nevo, *King Hussein and the Evolution of Jordan's Perception of a Political Settlement with Israel*, Brighton: Sussex Academic Press, 2006. On the role of Mossad in brokering the peace treaty with Israel, see Efraim Halevy, 'The real story behind the Israeli–Jordanian peace deal', *Ha'aretz*, 4 April 2018.

5. Martin Kramer, 'Israel and the Post-American Middle East', *Foreign Affairs*, vol. 95 no. 4 (2016), p. 52.

6. Glenn E. Perry, 'Israeli involvement in Inter-Arab Politics', *International Journal of Islamic and Arab Studies*, vol. 1 no. 1 (1984), p. 16.

7. Barak David, 'Wikileaks Blows Cover of Israel's Covert Ties', *Ha'aretz* [in English], 29 November 2010; Yoel Guzansky, *The Arab Gulf Monarchies and Reform in the Middle East*, Basingstoke: Palgrave-Macmillan, 2015, p. 129; 'Address by FM Livni to the 8th Doha Forum on Democracy, Development and Free Trade', Israel Ministry of Foreign Affairs, 14 April 2008, https://mfa.gov.il/MFA/PressRoom/2008/Pages/Address%20by%20FM%20Livni%20to%20the%20Doha%20Con-ference%2014-Apr-2008.aspx, last accessed 5 July 2019.

8. Morten Valbjørn and André Bank, 'The New Arab Cold War: Rediscovering the Arab dimension of Middle East regional politics', *Review of International Studies*, vol. 38 no. 1 (2012), p. 15; Amos Harel and Avi Issacharoff, *34 Days: Israel, Hezbollah and the War in Lebanon*, Basingstoke: Palgrave-Macmillan, 2008, pp. 102–4.

9. On security communities and security complexes, see Barry Buzan and Ole Wæver, *Regions and Powers: The Structure of International Security*, Cambridge: Cambridge University Press, 2003, pp. 42–4.

10. On protest movements and their role in challenging state dispensations across the Middle East, see John Chalcraft, *Popular Politics in the Making of the Modern Middle East*, Cambridge: Cambridge University Press, 2016; Charles Tripp, *The Power and the People: Paths of Resistance in the Middle East*, Cambridge: Cambridge University Press,

2013. On state fragmentation in the Arab world, see Kobi Michael and Yoel Guzansky, *The Arab World on the Road to State Failure*, Tel Aviv: Institute for National Security Studies, 2017.

11. Charles Lipson, 'Are Security Regimes Possible? Historical Cases and Modern Issues', in Efraim Inbar (ed.), *Regional Security Regimes: Israel and Its Neighbors*, New York: SUNY Press, 1995, pp. 3–33.

12. See for example Stephen Krasner, *International Regimes*, New York: Cornell University Press, 1983.

13. See Robert Jervis, 'From Balance to Concert: A Study of the Concert of International Security Cooperation', in Kenneth Oye (ed.), *Co-operation under Anarchy*, Princeton, N.J.: Princeton University Press, 1985, pp. 58–79.

14. The Damascus Declaration followed on from previous attempts in the 1980s at developing a collective Gulf security structure, known as Peninsula Shield. See Yoel Guzansky, 'Defence Cooperation in the Arabian Gulf: The Peninsula Shield Force put to the Test', *Middle Eastern Studies*, vol. 50 no. 4 (2014), pp. 640–54.

15. Janice Gross Stein, 'Detection and Defection: Security Regimes and the Management of International Conflict', *International Journal*, vol. 40 no. 4 (1985), pp. 604–18.

16. Efraim Inbar and Shmuel Sandler, 'The changing Israeli strategic equation: Toward a Security Regime', *Review of International Studies*, vol. 21 no. 1 (1995), p. 41.

17. Aharon Klieman, 'The Israel-Jordan Tacit Security Regime', in Efraim Inbar (ed.), *Regional Security Regimes: Israel and its Neighbours*, New York: State University of New York Press, 1995, p. 127.

18. Ibid., p. 129.
19. Ibid., p. 130.
20. Ibid., p. 130.
21. Barak Ravid, 'Saudi foreign minister rejects Netanyahu's demand to "update" Arab Peace Initiative', *Ha'aretz*, 3 June 2016; 'Israeli official praises Saudi king for stance on Iran, economy', *Yediot Aharanot*, 16 June 2016.
22. Yoel Guzansky and Clive Jones, 'Israel's Relations with the Gulf Monarchies: Towards the Emergence of a Tacit Security Regime?', *Contemporary Security Policy*, vol. 38 no. 3 (2017), pp. 398–419.
23. Ian Black, 'Just Below the Surface: Israel, the Arab Gulf States and the Limits of Cooperation', LSE Middle East Centre Report, March 2019, pp. 1–37, http://eprints.lse.ac.uk/100313/, last accessed 5 July 2019.
24. For a full account of Israel's array of clandestine alliances, see Clive Jones and Tore T. Petersen (eds), *Israel's Clandestine Diplomacies*, London: Hurst, 2013.
25. On Israeli–Iranian relations, see Dalia Dassa Kaye, Alireza Nader and Parisa Roshan, *Israel and Iran: A Dangerous Rivalry*, Santa Monica: RAND/National Defense Research Institute, 2011, pp. 19–37; Ronen Bergman, *The Secret War with Iran: The 30-Year Covert Struggle for Control of a Rogue State*, Oxford: One World, 2008; Trita Parsi, *Treacherous Alliance: The Secret Dealings of Iran, Israel, and the U.S*, Yale: Yale University Press, 2007. Israeli security officials, as opposed to their political masters, often stress the rational nature of the Iranian regime. It is precisely because they are rational and recognise Israel's strength militarily that such officials believed that deterrence works against Iran. See the comments of the

former director of Mossad, Efraim Halevy, in Bergman, *The Secret War*, p. 270.

26. Jeffrey Goldberg, 'Saudi Crown Prince: Iran's Supreme Leader "Makes Hitler Look Good"', *The Atlantic*, 2 April 2018, https://www.theatlantic.com/international/archive/2018/04/mohammed-bin-salman-iran-israel/557036/, last accessed 5 July 2019.

27. '"Palestinians must make peace or shut up" Saudi Crown Prince said to tell US Jews', *The Times of Israel*, 29 April 2018.

28. Author interview with Lieutenant-General (Res) Moshe Ya'alon, Tel Aviv, 21 March 2018.

29. Goldberg, op. cit.

30. Noa Landau and Reuters, 'Netanyahu: Events at Istanbul consulate "horrendous", but Saudi stability must be maintained', *Ha'aretz*, 2 November 2018.

31. 'Saudi lobbyist in US urges "collaborative alliance" with Israel', *The Times of Israel*, 12 October 2016.

1. ISRAEL'S RELATIONS WITH THE GULF
MONARCHIES: HISTORY AND CONTEXT

1. Yossi Alpher, *Periphery: Israel's Search for Middle East Allies*, London: Rowman & Littlefield, 2015, pp. 38–9. One former senior Mossad officer was sent even to Oman in the mid-1970s to offer advice to Sultan Qabus and his close advisors on how best to prosecute their war against communist-backed insurgents in the Dhofar region. Private information disclosed to the authors. See also Clive Jones, *Britain and the Yemen Civil War, 1962–1965*, Brighton: Sussex Academic Press, 2010, pp. 146–51; this book gave the first authoritative account of Israeli clandestine involve-

ment in the Yemen civil war. See also Asher Orkaby, 'The 1964 Israeli airlift to Yemen and the expansion of weapons diplomacy', *Diplomacy and Statecraft*, vol. 26 no. 4 (2016), p. 667.

2. The Gulf, which is mainly known as the "Persian Gulf" and is sometimes called the "Arab Gulf," is called in this study by its neutral name, "the Gulf." The dispute between the Arab Gulf monarchies and Iran over the name is more semantic. The UN was even asked to address this issue, and it established a committee of experts which chose the name "Persian Gulf," claiming that this was for geographic, historical and legal reasons. See United Nations Group of Experts on Geographical Names, Working Paper No. 61, *Historical, Geographical and Legal Validity of the Name: Persian Gulf*, Vienna, 2006.

3. Elisheva Rosman-Stollman, 'Balancing Acts: The Gulf Monarchies and Israel', *Middle Eastern Studies*, vol. 40 no. 4 (2004), p. 204.

4. Michael Kahanov, *Saudi Arabia and the Conflict in Palestine*, Jerusalem: Carmel, 2012, pp. 201–11.

5. David Holden and Richard Johns, *The House of Saud: The Rise and Rule of the Most Powerful Dynasty in the Arab World*, New York: Holt, Rinehart, and Winston, 1981, pp. 252–338.

6. Nadav Safran, *Saudi Arabia: The Ceaseless Quest for Security*, Cambridge, MA: The Belknap Press of Harvard University Press, 1985, pp. 68–156.

7. Joseph Kostiner, 'Saudi Arabia and the Arab–Israeli Peace Process: The Fluctuation of Regional Coordination', *British Journal of Middle Eastern Studies*, vol. 36 no. 3 (2009), pp. 417–29.

8. Saad el Shazly, *The Arab Military Option*, San Francisco: American Mideast Research, 1986, pp. 177–80.

9. Joseph Kostiner, 'The Roots of the Arab Peace Plan and its Reversals', in Ephraim Lavie (ed.), *Israel and the Arab Peace Initiative*, Tel Aviv: Tel Aviv University Press, 2010, pp. 97–8.

10. Kostiner, 'Saudi Arabia and the Arab–Israeli Peace Process', pp. 417–29.

11. Elie Podeh, 'From Fahd to 'Abdallah: The Origins of the Saudi Peace Initiatives and their Impact on the Arab System and Israel', Harry S. Truman Research Institute for the Advancement of Peace, Gitelson Peace Publications, Hebrew University of Jerusalem, July 2003, pp. 5–7.

12. Joseph Kostiner, *The Marginal Peace: The Attitudes of Persian Arabian Gulf Monarchies Towards Israel and the Peace Process*, Tel Aviv: Tel Aviv University Press, 2008, pp. 24–5.

13. Ibid., pp. 26–7.

14. Ibid., pp. 32–3.

15. Gilles Kepel, *The Prophet and the Pharaoh: Muslim Extremism in Egypt*, London: Al-Saqi Books, 1985, pp. 210–24.

16. Elie Podeh, *Chances for Peace: Missed Opportunities in the Arab–Israeli Conflict*, Austin TX: University of Texas Press, 2015, pp. 157–68.

17. Yezid Sayigh, *Armed Struggle and the Search for State: The Palestinian National Movement, 1949–1993*, Oxford: Oxford University Press, 1999, pp. 638–59.

18. Clive Jones, *Soviet Jewish Aliyah: Impact and Implications for Israel and the Middle East*, London: Frank Cass, 1996, pp. 92–3.

19. Rory Miller, *Desert Kingdoms to Global Powers: The Rise of the Arab Gulf*, London: Yale University Press, 2016, p. 97.

20. Nimrod Goren, 'When Bahrain once welcomed Israelis', *Ha'aretz*, 22 December 2015.

21. Uzi Rabi, 'Qatar's Relations with Israel: Challenging Arab and Gulf Norms', *Middle East Journal*, vol. 63 no. 3 (2009), pp. 451–2.

22. 'The Shia Crescendo: Shia militias are proliferating across the Middle East', *The Economist*, 28 March 2015.

23. Amos Harel and Avi Issacharoff, *34 Days: Israel, Hezbollah and the War in Lebanon*, Basingstoke: Palgrave-Macmillan, 2008, p. 102.

24. Joseph Kostiner, 'Coping with Regional Challenges: A case study of Crown Prince Abdullah's Peace Initiative', in Paul Aarts and Gerd Nonneman (eds), *Saudi Arabia in the Balance*, London: Hurst, 2005, pp. 353–4.

25. Podeh, *Chances for Peace*, p. 305.

26. Kostiner, 'Saudi Arabia and the Arab–Israeli peace process', p. 424.

27. Joshua Teitelbaum, *The Arab Peace Initiative: A Primer and Future Prospects*, Jerusalem: Jerusalem Centre for Public Affairs, 2009, http://www.jcpa.org/text/Arab-Peace-Initiative.pdf, last accessed 4 July 2019, pp. 15–18.

28. 'U/S Burns meeting at Israel's MFA on Lebanon, NATO, the Vatican, Moderate Arab States and India', WikiLeaks, 24 August 2007, http://wikileaks.org/plusd/cables/07TELAVIV2576_a.html, last accessed 5 July 2019.

29. Ehud Eiran, 'Israel's Response to the JCPOA', in Payam Mohseni (ed.),*Tipping the Balance? Implications of the*

Iran Nuclear Deal on Israeli Security, Cambridge, MA: Harvard Kennedy School/Belfer Center for Science and International Affairs, 2015, p. 63.

30. On Israel's initial reaction to the Arab uprisings, see Clive Jones and Beverley Milton-Edwards, 'Missing the "devils" we knew? Israel and Political Islam amid the Arab Awakening', *International Affairs*, vol. 89 no. 2 (2013), pp. 399–415.

31. Itamar Rabinovich and Itai Brun, 'Israel and the Arab Turmoil', The Hoover Institution, Stanford University, 10 October 2017, https://www.hoover.org/research/israel-and-arab-turmoil-0, last accessed 5 July 2019.

32. Mamoun Fandy, 'No Longer an Arab–Israeli conflict', *Asharq Al-Awsat*, 11 August 2014, https://eng-archive.aawsat.com/mamoun-fandy-ph-d/opinion/opinion-no-longer-an-arab-israeli-conflict, last accessed 5 July 2019.

2. ISRAEL AND THE LOWER GULF: SMALL-STATE DIPLOMACY

1. Shaikh Salman bin Hamad al-Khalifa, 'The Arab Peace Initiative for Israel and the Palestinians', *The Washington Post*, 16 July 2009.

2. Yossi Melman, 'Ha'aretz Wikileaks exclusive: Bahrain king boasted of intelligence ties with Israel', *Ha'aretz*, 8 April 2011; Becca Wasser, 'Israel and the Gulf States', IISS Voices, *International Institute for Strategic Studies*, 22 August 2013.

3. 'Kuwaiti Writer to Muslims: Stop Cursing Jews and Christians in The Friday Sermons', *MEMRI*, 5 April 2016, https://www.memri.org/reports/kuwaiti-writer-muslims-stop-cursing-jews-and-christians-friday-sermons, last accessed 5 July 2019.

4. Jad Mouawad, 'Kuwait Airways Drops Flights to Avoid Israeli Passengers', *The New York Times*, 15 January 2016.

5. Maayan Grosiman, 'Kuwait pushes to expel Knesset from international parliamentary group', *The Jerusalem Post*, 13 April 2016.

6. Asda'a Burson-Martseller, 'Inside the hearts and minds of Arab youth', Arab Youth Survey, 13 April 2016, https://www.arabyouthsurvey.com/pdf/whitepaper/en/2016-AYS-White-Paper.pdf, last accessed 5 July 2019.

7. Yoel Guzansky, 'The Foreign-Policy Tools of Small Powers: Strategic Hedging in the Persian Gulf', *Middle East Policy*, vol. 22 no. 1 (2015), pp. 112–22.

8. While the rebels (*adoo*) in Dhofar (1964–76) received support from the People's Democratic Republic of South Yemen, the Soviet Union, East Germany, Cuba and various Palestinian organisations, most support came from the People's Republic of China. Political and military support for Sultan Qabus came primarily from the United Kingdom with support from Jordan and Iran. Israel's covert advice and support to the sultan remained largely hidden from the British. Author interview with a senior official in the Omani Foreign Service, Muscat, 11 April 2011.

9. Private information disclosed to the authors.

10. Jeremy Jones and Nicholas Ridout, *Oman, Culture and Diplomacy*, Edinburgh: Edinburgh University Press, 2012, pp. 211–23.

11. See for example Tore T. Petersen, *Anglo-American Policy toward the Persian Gulf, 1978–1985*, Brighton: Sussex Academic Press, 2015, pp. 107–23.

12. Uzi Rabi, 'Oman and the Arab–Israeli conflict: The reflec-

tion of a pragmatic foreign policy', *Israel Affairs*, vol. 11 no. 3 (2005), p. 550.

13. Ibid., pp. 535–51.

14. Ronen Bergman, 'Oman is Israel's link to the Middle East', *Yediot Aharanot*, 28 October 2018.

15. The architect behind this meeting was the same Mossad officer who had brokered Israel's covert military and intelligence support to the Omani government two decades previously. Private information disclosed to the authors.

16. Rabi, op. cit., pp. 535–51.

17. Raphael Ahren, 'Israel and the Gulf monarchies: It's complicated', *The Times of Israel*, 9 August 2013; Jones and Ridout, op. cit., pp. 237–8.

18. MEDRC's operations are overseen by the Secretary General of Oman's Foreign Ministry, and the organisation's executive council is composed of senior officials from all the member countries, which include Israel, the Palestinian Authority, Jordan, Oman, Qatar, the US, Spain, the Netherlands, Japan and South Korea. Currently, the organisation is holding membership talks with the UAE, Iraq and China. One of the co-authors, Yoel Guzansky, was a guest of the centre in April 2011.

19. Uzi Rabi, 'Qatar's Relations with Israel: Challenging Arab and Gulf Norms', *Middle East Journal*, vol. 63 no. 3 (2009), pp. 444–7.

20. Jones and Ridout, op. cit., pp. 246–8; Jim Krane, 'Israeli Deputy PM visits Qatar', *The Washington Post*, 29 January 2007.

21. Barak Ravid, 'Top Israeli Diplomat holds Secret Talks in Oman', *Ha'aretz*, 24 November 2009.

22. On Oman's regional role, see Sigurd Neubauer, 'Oman:

The Gulf's Go-between', *The Arab Gulf Institute in Washington*, Issue Paper no. 1, 5 February 2016, http://www.agsiw.org/oman-the-gulfs-go-between/, last accessed 5 July 2019.

23. Zvi Bar'el, 'The Sultan's new friend: Just why did Netanyahu visit Oman', *Ha'aretz*, 28 October 2018.

24. Mehul Srivastava and Simeon Kerr, 'Netanyahu seeks to bolster Israeli ties with Gulf nations', *Financial Times*, 29 October 2018.

25. Bergman, op. cit.

26. Nicholas Redman, 'Oman: Small State, big Voice', 30 October 2018, https://www.iiss.org/blogs/analysis/2018/10/oman-alawi-speech, last accessed 5 July 2019.

27. Andrew F. Cooper and Bessma Momani, 'Qatar and Expanded Contours of Small State Diplomacy, The International Spectator', *Italian Journal of International Affairs*, vol. 46 no. 3 (2011), pp. 113–28.

28. David B. Roberts, 'Understanding Qatar's Foreign Policy Objectives', *Mediterranean Politics*, vol. 17 no. 2 (2012), pp. 232–9.

29. Cooper and Momani, op. cit., pp. 113–28.

30. Rabi, op. cit, pp. 444–7. Israel's need for imported gas has now all but vanished following the discovery of massive gas fields off its Mediterranean coast. See Alan Craig and Clive Jones, *Discovery of Israel's Gas Fields and their Geopolitical Implications—The Emirates Occasional Papers No. 81*, Abu Dhabi: ECSSR, 2013, p. 74.

31. Barak Ravid, 'Israel Rejects Qatar Bid to Restore Diplomatic Ties', *Ha'aretz*, 18 May 2010.

32. For a detailed account of the Hariri assassination, see

Nicholas Blandford, *Killing Mr Lebanon: The Assassination of Rafik Hariri and its Impact on the Middle East*, London: I.B. Tauris, 2009.

33. Ravid, op. cit.

34. Rabi, op. cit., pp. 443–59.

35. 'Israel to sever ties with Qatar', *Agence France Presse*, 26 August 2011, http://www.dailystar.com.lb//News/Middle-East/2011/Aug-26/147209-israel-to-sever-ties-with-qatar.ashx, last accessed 5 July 2019.

36. Jodi Rudoren, 'Qatar's Emir Visists Gaza, Pledging $400 Million to *Hamas*,' *The New York Times*, 24 October 2010.

37. 'Report: Netanyahu and Abbas met secretly in Jordan prior to Gaza ceasefire', *The Jerusalem Post*, 28 August 2014.

38. One of the authors, Yoel Guzansky, was present in the hall during the emir's speech.

39. Lina Khatib, 'Qatar's foreign policy: The limits of pragmatism', *International Affairs*, vol. 89 no. 2 (2013), pp. 417–31.

40. Ibid., pp. 417–31.

41. Ibid.

42. Barbara Opall-Rome and Awad Mustafa, 'Israel's Angst over Qatar Sale could End Boeing's F-15 Line', *Defense News*, 28 February 2016, http://www.defensenews.com/story/defense/air-space/air-force/2016/02/28/israels-angst-over-qatar-sale-could-end-boeings-f-15-line/80895346/, last accessed 5 July 2019.

43. Khatib, op. cit., pp. 417–31.

44. Cinzia Bianco and Gareth Stansfield, 'The Intra-GCC Crises: Mapping GCC fragmentation after 2011', *International Affairs*, vol. 94 no. 3 (2018), pp. 615–16.

45. On a visit to Doha in November 2018, an official told one of the authors that an attack by Saudi-led forces had been a distinct possibility in the spring of that year. The presence of US forces in Qatar and sharp words from Washington had proved enough to stay Riyadh's hand.

46. Hassan Hassan, 'Qatar won the Saudi Blockade', *Foreign Policy*, 4 June 2018, https://foreignpolicy.com/2018/06/04/qatar-won-the-saudi-blockade/, last accessed 5 July 2019.

47. Bianco and Stansfield, op. cit., p. 623.

48. Elhanan Miller, 'Israel singles out Qatar as key Hamas terror sponsor', *The Times of Israel*, 23 July 2014. For a discussion of Qatar's alleged ties to the Muslim Brotherhood, see Neubauer, op. cit. Others argue that Qatari support of the Muslim Brotherhood is not just a reflection of foreign policy preference but also a legacy of the role played by Egyptian exiles in the educational bureaucratic development of the state. See David Roberts, 'Qatar and the Muslim Brotherhood: Pragmatism or Preference?', *Middle East Policy Council*, vol. 21 no. 3, Fall 2017, https://www.mepc.org/qatar-and-muslim-brotherhood-pragmatism-or-preference, last accessed 5 July 2019.

49. Ibid.

50. Ibid.

51. 'Israeli Embassy in U.S.: We oppose Qatar's outreach to pro-Israel U.S Jews', *Ha'aretz*, 31 January 2018.

52. Zvi Bar'el, 'The Qatar dilemma: When even a supporter of terrorism can be an Israeli ally', *Ha'aretz*, 22 August 2018.

53. Yoel Guzansky and Kobi Michael, 'Israel's Qatari Dilemma', *INSS Insight*, no. 1034, 14 March 2018,

http://www.inss.org.il/publication/israels-qatari-dilem ma/?offset=13&posts=114&subject=263, last accessed 5 July 2019.

54. Raphael Ahren, 'Bahraini princess had life-saving surgery in Israel, deputy minister says', *The Times of Israel*, 8 February 2016.

55. Jane Kinninmont, 'Bahrain', in Christopher Davidson (ed.), *Power and Politics in the Persian Monarchies*, London: Hurst, 2011, pp. 54–62.

56. Rory Miller, *Desert Kingdoms to Global Powers: The Rise of the Arab Gulf*, London: Yale University Press, 2016, pp. 204–16.

57. Amir Tibon, 'The tiny Gulf state beating its neighbours in race for warmer ties with Israel', *Ha'aretz*, 1 July 2018.

58. 'Bahrain: Message to the Arab League', WikiLeaks, 16 March 2005, at http://wikileaks.org/plusd/cables/ 05MANAMA397_a.html, last accessed 5 July 2019.

59. Natasha Mozgovoya, 'Meet Houda Ezra Ibrahim Nonoo, Bahrain's Jewish U.S. Ambassador', *Ha'aretz*, 14 March 2011.

60. 'Two US rabbis say Bahrain's king wants Arab boycott of Israel to end', *Ha'aretz*, 22 September 2017; 'Bahraini prince makes unusual visit to "pro-Israel" L.A. museum', *Ha'aretz*, 18 September 2017.

61. Moran Zaga, 'Are ties between Israel and Bahrain warming?', *The Jerusalem Post*, 1 August 2018.

62. 'Economy minister Cohen invited to conference in Bahrain', *Yediot Aharanot*, 11 November 2018.

63. Tibon, op. cit.

64. Philip Podosky, 'Official to i24NEWS: "Bahrain will be first Gulf state to form ties with Israel"', *i24 News*, 20 June

2018, https://www.i24news.tv/en/news/israel/diplomacy-defense/177564-180620-bahrain-doesn-t-view-israel-as-enemy-will-be-first-gulf-state-to-establish-ties, last accessed 5 July 2019.

65. Barak David, 'Wikileaks Blows Cover of Israel's Covert Ties', *Ha'aretz*, 29 November 2010; Yoel Guzansky, *The Arab Gulf Monarchies and Reform in the Middle East*, p. 129.

66. Ron Friedman, 'First visit by Israeli minister to UAE', *The Jerusalem Post*, 18 January 2010.

67. Barak Rabid, 'Exclusive: Israel to Open First Diplomatic Mission in Abu Dhabi', *Ha'aretz*, 27 November 2015.

68. Ibid.

69. Simon Henderson, 'Israel's Gulf Breakthrough', *The Washington Institute Policy Brief*, 30 November 2015, http://www.washingtoninstitute.org/policy-analysis/view/israels-gulf-breakthrough, last accessed 5 July 2019.

70. Hagar Shezaf and Rori Donaghy, 'Israel eyes improved ties with Gulf monarchies after "foothold" gained in the UAE', *Middle East Eye*, 18 January 2016, http://www.middleeasteye.net/news/israel-eyes-improved-gulf-states-relationship-ties-flourish-uae-895004700, last accessed 5 July 2019.

71. Henderson, op. cit.

72. Ravid, 'Exclusive: Israel to Open First Diplomatic Mission in Abu Dhabi', op. cit.

73. Ali Younes, 'Israel to open office for renewable energy in Abu Dhabi', *Al Jazeera English*, 27 November 2015, http://www.aljazeera.com/news/2015/11/israel-open-office-renewable-energy-abu-dhabi-151127184424647.html, last accessed 5 July 2019.

74. 'Israeli Delegation Discusses Cooperation with IRENA on Advancement of Renewable Energy', IRENA Press Office, 27 November 2015, https://www.irena.org/news-room/pressreleases/2015/Nov/Israeli-Delegation-Discusses-Cooperation-with-IRENA-on-Advancement-of-Renewable-Energy, last accessed 5 July 2019.

75. John Reed, 'Israel Inc: A nation's calling card helps it defy isolation', *The Financial Times*, 7 June 2017.

76. David Pollock, 'New Poll Shows Majority of Saudis, Kuwaitis, Emiratis Reject ISIS, Back Two-State Solution with Israel', at http://www.washingtoninstitute.org/policy-analysis/view/new-poll-shows-majority-of-saudis-kuwaitis-emiratis-reject-isis-back-two-st, last accessed 5 July 2019.

77. 'UAE "offered" to fund Israel's Gaza offensive', Doha Desk, *The Peninsula Qatar*, http://thepeninsulaqatar.com/news/qatar/292061/uae-offered-to-fund-israel-s-gaza-offensive, last accessed 24 February 2016.

78. 'UAE and Israel are like "brothers" says senior general', *Middle East Monitor*, 17 November 2017, https://www.middleeastmonitor.com/20171117-uae-and-israel-are-like-brothers-says-senior-general/, last accessed 5 July 2019.

79. Yori Yanover, 'Israelis risk flying through enemy countries to save buck', *The Jewish Press*, 1 March 2012, http://www.jewishpress.com/news/breaking-news/to-save-a-buck-israelis-risk-flying-through-enemy-countries/2012/03/01/, last accessed 5 July 2019.

80. One of the authors can personally attest to this, having flown regularly to the Gulf with an Israeli stamp in his passport.

81. 'Doing business in Israel: Israel trade and export guide', UK Government Trade and Investment Report, 27 May 2015, https://www.gov.uk/government/publications/exporting-to-israel/exporting-to-israel, last accessed 5 July 2019.

82. FAQs, UAE Embassy in the Netherlands, 2015, http://www.uae-embassy.ae/Embassies/nl/faq's/5148, last accessed 24 February 2018.

83. See Dan Raviv and Yossi Melman, *Spies Against Armageddon*, New York: Levant Books, 2012, pp. 302–8.

84. Just prior to the assassination of al-Mabhouh, the former Israeli minister for National Infrastructure Uzi Landau had attended a meeting of the Abu Dhabi-based International Renewable Energy Agency (IRENA), a visit that quickly drew harsh criticism of the UAE from Iran. See 'Iran leader slams UAE over visit by Israeli minister', *Ha'aretz*, 23 January 2010.

85. The meeting took place on 28 September 2012, in the Loews Regency Hotel, New York. See Barak Ravid, 'Exclusive: Netanyahu secretly met with UAE foreign minister in 2012 in New York', *Ha'aretz*, 21 July 2017.

86. See Amos Harel, 'Israeli pilots trained in US with Pakistani, UAE air forces', *Ha'aretz*, 1 September 2016; Gili Cohen, 'Israeli Air Force holds joint exercise with United Arab Emirates, US and Italy', *Ha'aretz*, 29 March 2017; 'Israel and UAE fly together in annual joint exercise in Greece', *Ha'aretz*, 22 March 2018.

87. 'Exclusive: Israel hosted UAE military delegation to review F-35s, sources say', *i24News*, 4 July 2018, https://i24news.tv/en/news/israel/178686–180704-sources-tell-i24news—israel-hosted-uae-military-delegation-to-review-f-35s, last accessed 5 July 2019.

88. Yossi Melman, 'Should Retired IDF Officers Do Business in Arab States or Not?', *Ha'aretz*, 18 September 2008.

89. 'UAE buying arms from Israel', *Middle East Monitor*, 5 February 2018, https://www.middleeastmonitor.com/20180205-uae-buying-arms-from-israel/, last accessed 5 July 2019.

90. 'Emirates "has security links with Israel"', *UPI*, 27 January 2012, http://www.upi.com/Business_News/Security-Industry/2012/01/27/Emirates-has-security-links-with-Israel/73471327687767/, last accessed 5 July 2019.

91. Jonathan Ferziger and Peter Waldman, 'How Do Israel's Tech Firms Do Business in Saudi Arabia? Very Quietly', *Bloomberg News Online*, 2 February 2017, https://www.bloomberg.com/news/features/2017–02–02/how-do-israel-s-tech-firms-do-business-in-saudi-arabia-very-quietly, last accessed 5 July 2019.

92. Rori Donaghy, 'Falcon Eye: The Israeli-installed mass civil surveillance system of Abu Dhabi', *Middle East Eye*, 28 February 2015, http://www.middleeasteye.net/news/uae-israel-surveillance-2104952769, last accessed 5 July 2019.

93. Hagar Shezaf and Jonathan Jacobson, 'Revealed: Israel's cyber-spy industry helps world dictators hunt dissidents and gays', *Ha'aretz*, 20 October 2018.

94. Ibid. See also David D. Kirkpatrick and Azam Ahmed, 'Hacking a Prince, an Emir and a Journalist to Impress a Client', *The New York Times*, 31 August 2018; Mehul Srivastava, 'Computer vision: How Israel's secret soldiers drive its tech success', *The Financial Times*, 20 November 2018.

95. Ronen Bergman, 'Israeli-made spyware made it to the Arab world', *Yediot Aharanot*, 8 September 2016.

96. See Dmitry Adamsky, 'The Israeli Odyssey toward its National Cyber Security Strategy', *The Washington Quarterly*, vol. 40 no. 2 (2017), p. 124.

97. Binyamin Netanyahu, 'Innovation Nation: The World in 2018', *The Economist*, December 2017.

98. 'Israeli culture minister visits Abu Dhabi's Sheikh Zayed mosque', *The National* (UAE), 29 October 2018, https://www.thenational.ae/uae/government/israeli-cultural-minister-visits-abu-dhabi-s-sheikh-zayed-grand-mosque-1.785540, last accessed 5 July 2019.

99. Yitzhak Gal, 'Israeli Trade with Middle East Markets in 2011', *Middle East Economy, Moshe Dayan Center for Middle East and African Studies*, vol. 22 no. 1 (2012).

100. 'Assessing Israel's Trade with its Arab Neighbours', Report for the Tony Blair Institute for Global Change/ Middle East, 14 August 2018, http://institute.global/insight/middle-east/assessing-israels-trade-its-arab-neighbours, last accessed 5 July 2019.

101. Michael Freund, 'Congressman raps Saudis for anti-Israel boycott', *The Jerusalem Post*, 15 September 2011.

102. John Reed, 'Amnon Shashua, Israel's hands-off tech entrepreneur', *The Financial Times*, 17 March 2017.

103. 'PM Netanyahu at the WEF event hosted by Fareed Zakaria (CNN)', 21 January 2016, http://mfa.gov.il/MFA/PressRoom/2016/Pages/PM-Netanyahu-at-the-WEF-event-hosted-by-Fareed-Zakaria-21-Jan-2016.aspx, last accessed 5 July 2019.

104. Itay Zetelny, 'The Israeli Hi-Tech Industry', EY Report, Tel Aviv, January 2014, https://ec.europa.eu/assets/jrc/events/20140120-tto-circle/jrc-20140120-tto-circle-zetelny.pdf, last accessed 5 July 2019.

3. MORE THAN THE SUM OF ITS PARTS? ISRAELI–SAUDI RELATIONS

1. Turki al-Faisal, 'Veto a State, Lose an Ally', *The New York Times*, 12 September 2011.

2. Edward Luce, 'Lunch with the FT: Prince Turki al-Faisal', *The Financial Times*, 14 March 2014.

3. 'Israel and the Middle East: Seeking Common Ground: A Conversation with HRH Prince Turki bin Faisail Al Saud and General Amos Yadlin', The German Marshall Fund of the United States, Brussels, 26 May 2014, https://www.youtube.com/watch?v=TOHmgzbh7XA, last accessed 5 July 2019; 'Saudi royal snubs invite to Jerusalem by Israeli ex-intel boss', *The Jerusalem Post*, 26 May 2014. Yoel Guzansky accompanied Yadlin to this meeting and was present during the debate chaired by David Ignatius of *The Washington Post*.

4. Naef Bin Ahmed al-Saud, 'The Evolution of Saudi Security and Enforcement on Communication', *Joint Force Quarterly*, vol. 65, 2nd Quarter (2012), pp. 39–43; Amir Oren, 'For Saudi Arabia, Israel is turning from foe to friend', *Ha'aretz*, 15 April 2012.

5. Aziz Allilou, 'Saudi Arabia's Al-Waleed Bin Talal to Pay Official Visit to Israel', *Morocco World News*, 5 July 2015, http://www.moroccoworldnews.com/2015/07/162534/saudi-arabias-al-waleed-bin-talal-to-pay-official-visit-to-israel/, last accessed 5 July 2019.

6. Despite their relatively small numbers, the challenge of right-wing religious nationalism in Israel is regarded by some as one of the most profound security challenges facing the state of Israel, not least because of a refusal to countenance territorial compromise over land they consider to

be part of God's covenant to the Jewish people. See Motti Inbari, *Messianic Religious Zionism Confronts Israeli Territorial Compromises*, Cambridge: Cambridge University Press, 2012, pp. 107–50.

7. Anoush Ehteshami, 'Saudi Arabia as a Resurgent Regional Power', *The International Spectator: Italian Journal of International Affairs*, vol. 53 no. 5 (2018), p. 83.

8. 'Kerry calls new Arab League peace stance "big step forward", *Reuters*, 30 April 2013, http://www.reuters.com/article/us-palestinians-israel-usa-idUSBRE93T16Z20130430, last accessed 5 July 2019.

9. Steven Lee Myers and Jodi Rudoren, 'Kerry Calls Arab League Plan to Revive Talks With Israel a "Big Step"', *The New York Times*, 1 May 2013.

10. 'Beirut Declaration on Saudi Peace Initiative-28-Mar-2002', Israeli Ministry of Foreign Affairs, 28 March 2002, http://www.mfa.gov.il/mfa/foreignpolicy/peace/guide/pages/beirut%20declaration%20on%20saudi%20peace%20initiative%20-%2028-.aspx, last accessed 5 July 2019.

11. Ibid.

12. Raphael Ahren, 'Why is Israel so afraid of the Arab Peace Initiative?', *The Times of Israel*, 8 June 2013.

13. Barak Ravid, 'Lieberman to Kerry: Palestinian Peace Hopeless, but Mideast Ripe for Regional Deal', *Ha'aretz*, 26 June 2014; 'To save Israel, Lapid pitches "separation" from Palestinians', *Times of Israel*, 25 June 2016.

14. Raphael Ahren, 'Time for Arab states to publicize their Israel ties, Netanyahu says', *The Times of Israel*, 14 February 2016.

15. Akiva Eldar, 'Why cancelled Arab League summit should

worry Israelis', 3 March 2016, http://www.al-monitor.
com/pulse/originals/2016/03/marrakesh-arab-league-
summit-arab-peace-initiative-netanyahu.html#ixzz450
ob1eUv, last accessed 5 July 2019.

16. 'Morocco "cancels" Arab League summit: Useless and
hypocritical', *The New Arab*, 20 February 2016, https://
www.alaraby.co.uk/english/news/2016/2/20/morocco-
cancels-arab-league-summit-useless-and-hypocritical, last
accessed 5 July 2019.

17. 'U.S. Embassy cables: Saudi King urges U.S. strike on Iran',
The Guardian, 28 November 2010.

18. Ron Ben-Yishai, 'Saudi Arabia's war of independence',
Yediot Aharanot, 17 December 2015.

19. Erika Solomon and Simeon Kerr, 'Saudi Arabia turns the
screw on Lebanon's economy', *The Financial Times*,
8 March 2016.

20. Daniel Byman, 'Yemen's Disastrous War', *Survival*, vol. 60
no. 5 (2018), pp. 141–58.

21. Ahmad Melhem, 'Why is the Palestinian Authority angry
over Iran's offer of aid?', *Al-Monitor*, 9 March 2016,
http://www.al-monitor.com/pulse/originals/2016/03/
iran-aid-palestinian-victims-intifada-anger-pa.html, last
accessed 5 July 2019. The 'al-Quds' intifada referred to a
series of knife attacks as well as the use of vehicles against
Israeli civilians and security personnel in the winter of
2015–16.

22. Jack Moore, 'Iran ceases financial aid to Hamas in Gaza
official claims', *Newsweek Magazine*, 28 July 2015, http://
europe.newsweek.com/iran-ceases-financial-aid-hamas-
gaza-official-claims-330889, last accessed 5 July 2019.

23. Simeon Kerr, 'Mohammed bin Nayef, Saudi strong man
in a power struggle', *The Financial Times*, 8 January 2016.

24. Andy Critchlow, 'The power struggle behind the Saudi night of the long knives', *The Daily Telegraph*, 11 November 2017; Ehteshami, 'Saudi Arabia as a Resurgent Regional Power', pp. 88–92.

25. Yoel Guzansky, 'The Islamic State vs the Saudi State', in Yoram Schweitzer and Omer Eliav (eds), *The Islamic State: How Viable Is It?*, Tel Aviv: INSS, 2016, pp. 173–9.

26. Clifford Krauss, 'Oil Prices: What's Behind the Drop? Simple Economics', *The New York Times*, 13 January 2015.

27. Yoel Guzansky and Erez Striem, 'Saudi Arabia: A Build-up of Internal and External Challenges', INSS *Insight*, no: 768, November 2015, https://www.inss.org.il/publication/saudi-arabia-a-buildup-of-internal-and-external-challenges/, last accessed 5 July 2019.

28. Simeon Kerr and Anjli Raval, 'Khashoggi death condemns Saudi megaplan to backburner', *The Financial Times*, 12 December 2018.

29. For the background to Saudi Arabia's intervention in the Yemen, see Ginny Hill, *Yemen Endures: Civil War, Saudi Adventurism and the Future of Arabia*, Hurst: London, 2017, p. 391.

30. Anthony H. Cordesman, 'The War in Yemen: Hard Choices in a Hard War', Center for Strategic and International Studies Report, 9 May 2017, pp. 1–7, https://www.csis.org/analysis/war-yemen-hard-choices-hard-war, last accessed 5 July 2019.

31. Bel Trew, 'Millions starve as Saudi bombs tear Yemen apart', *The Times*, 27 October 2016; Nasser al-Sakkaf and Andrew England, 'Caught in the Crossfire', *The Financial Times*, 12 January 2018; Byman, 'Yemen's Disastrous War', pp. 143–8.

32. Peter Salisbury, *Yemen: National Chaos, Local Order*, London: Royal Institute for International Affairs, 2017, pp. 9–23; Elizabeth Kendall, 'Contemporary Jihadi Militancy in Yemen: How is the Threat Evolving?', *Middle East Institute*, Policy Paper 2018, no. 7, July 2018, pp. 1–10.

33. Gerald Feierstein, 'Is there a path out of the Yemen conflict? Why it matters', *Prism*, vol. 7 no. 1 (2017), pp. 16–31.

34. Dore Gold, 'Regional Challenges and Opportunities: The View from Saudi Arabia and Israel', *Council on Foreign Relations*, 4 June 2015, https://www.cfr.org/event/regional-challenges-and-opportunities-view-saudi-arabia-and-israel-0, last accessed 5 July 2019.

35. Shimnit Meir, 'Israel's ties with the Arab world are nothing to get excited over', *Yediot Aharanot*, 26 November 2018.

36. Amos Harel and Yarden Michaeli, 'Will Khashoggi's murder foil the Saudi–Israeli thaw?', *Ha'aretz*, 17 April 2019.

37. Noa Landau and Reuters, 'Netanyahu: Events at Istanbul consulate "horrendous", but Saudi stability must be maintained', *Ha'aretz*, 2 November 2018.

38. Chemi Shalev, 'Israel's Iron Dome defense of Saudi Arabia aims to avert collapse of Trump and Netanyahu's entire Middle East strategy', *Ha'aretz*, 22 November 2018.

39. 'US blocs UNSC statement on Israel's use of force on Land Day', *Al Jazeera English*, 1 April 2018, https://www.aljazeera.com/news/2018/04/blocks-unsc-statement-israel-force-land-day-180401054016894.html, last accessed 5 July 2019.

40. For a detailed (if colourful) account of the relationship

between Netanyahu, the Trump Administration and Crown Prince Mohammed bin Salman, see Adam Entous, 'Donald Trump's New World Order', *The New Yorker*, 18 June 2018, https://www.newyorker.com/magazine/2018/06/18/donald-trumps-new-world-order, last accessed 5 July 2019.

41. David D. Kirkpatrick, Ben Hubbard, Mark Landler and Mark Mazzetti, 'The Wooing of Jared Kushner: How the Saudis got a Friend in the White House', *The New York Times*, 8 December 2018.

42. Stig Stenslie, 'The End of Elite Unity and the Stability of Saudi Arabia', *The Washington Quarterly*, vol. 41 no. 4 (2018), pp. 68–73.

43. Amos Harel, 'Syria Pullout: Israel left with false Russian promises and a volatile US President', *Ha'aretz*, 23 December 2018.

44. Elie Podeh, 'Saudi Arabia and Israel: From Secret to Public Engagement, 1948–2018', *Middle East Journal*, vol. 72 no. 4 (2018), p. 585.

4. ARMS SALES AND THE NUCLEAR QUESTION

1. For two opposing views on the JCPOA itself, see Mark Fitzpatrick, 'Iran: A good deal', *Survival*, vol. 57 no. 5 (2015), pp. 47–52; Thomas C. Moore, 'Iran: Non-proliferation overshadowed', *Survival*, vol. 57 no. 5 (2015), pp. 53–8.

2. Julian Borger, Saeed Kamali Dehghan and Oliver Holmes, 'Iran deal: Trump breaks with European allies over "horrible, one-sided" nuclear agreement', *The Guardian*, 9 May 2018.

3. For the complete transcript of Netanyahu's speech to con-

gress, 3 March 2015, see https://www.washingtonpost.com/gdpr-consent/?destination=%2fnews%2fpost-polit ics%2fwp%2f2015%2f03%2f03%2ffull-text-netanyahus-address-to-congress%2f%3f&utm_term=.747a03727fc8, last accessed 5 July 2019.

4. See the comments of former director of Mossad, Efraim Halevy, during the course of a panel discussion with Crown Prince Turki al-Faisal. See 'Shared Security Challenges and Opportunities', Israel Policy Forum, New York, 23 October 2017, https://www.youtube.com/watch?v=RXM-atXc-QkA, last accessed 5 July 2019; Robin Wright, 'As Trump tries to kill the Iran deal, a former Israeli spy lobbies to save it', *The New Yorker*, 5 October 2017. Halevy has been particularly outspoken against successive Netanyahu governments and his approach to international diplomacy. See Dalie Karpel, 'A former spy chief is calling on Israelis to revolt', *Ha'aretz*, 1 October 2016.

5. Barak David, Amos Harel, Chaim Levinson and Amir Tabon, 'Netanyahu at odds with Israeli military and intelligence brass over whether to push Trump to scrap the Iran deal', *Ha'aretz*, 16 September 2017.

6. Yoav Zitun, 'Defense minister hints at cooperation with Gulf monarchies', *Yediot Aharanot*, 5 March 2016.

7. Ronen Bergman, 'Iran's great nuclear deception', *Yediot Aharanot*, 11 December 2018.

8. Yoel Guzansky and Azriel Bermant, 'The best of the worst: Why Iran's enemies support the nuclear deal', *Foreign Affairs*, 13 August 2015, https://www.foreignaffairs.com/articles/iran/2015–08–13/best-worst, last accessed 5 July 2019.

9. Mohammed Elmenshawy, 'The Arabs smitten by the Israeli

lobby', *Ahram Online*, 10 April 2014, http://english. ahram.org.eg/NewsContentP/4/98578/Opinion/The-Arabs-smitten-by-the-Israeli-lobby.aspx, last accessed 5 July 2019.

10. Israel Ziv, 'The real Iranian threat', *Yediot Aharanot*, 16 July 2015. See also the interview with Israeli Defence Minister Moshe Ya'alon in *Der Spiegel*; Ronen Bergman and Holger Stark,'We Can in No Way Tolerate an Iran with Nuclear Weapons', *Spiegel Online*, 8 July 2015, http://www.spiegel.de/international/world/israeli-defense-minister-moshe-yaalon-critizes-iran-deal-a-1047260-druck.html, last accessed 5 July 2019; Yaron Friedman, 'Yemen's Hezbollah: The Saudi–Israeli problem', *Yediot Aharanot*, 18 October 2016.

11. 'Netanyahu's Congress speech draws praise in Saudi Arabia, derision in the West', *Ha'aretz*, 4 March 2015.

12. For the most detailed account to date of Israel's preparations to attack Iran, see Daniel Sobelman, 'Restraining an ally: Israel, the United States and the Iran's nuclear programme 2011–12', *Texas National Security Review*, vol. 1 no. 4 (2018), pp. 11–38. See also Ehud Barak, *My Country: Fighting for Israel, Searching for Peace*, London: Macmillan, 2018, pp. 428–36. Barak was Defence Minister in Netanyahu's coalition government and a strong advocate of a preventive strike against Iran.

13. Sarah Yizraeli, 'Saudi-Israel Dialogue: What Lies Ahead?', *Strategic Assessment* (Institute for National Security Studies), vol. 10 no. 2 (2007), p. 69.

14. Anshel Pfeffer, 'Mossad Chief Reportedly Visited Saudi Arabia for Talks on Iran', *Ha'aretz*, 26 July 2010.

15. Many in the Israeli security establishment were opposed

to a strike on Iran without full co-ordination with the United States, and because some believed the nuclear agreement with Iran was actually in Israel's best interests. Author interview with Ambassador Efraim Halevy, Ramat Aviv, 1 August 2013. See also Clive Jones, 'Israel's Security Nexus as Strategic Restraint: The Case of Iran 2009–2013', *The Journal of Strategic Studies*, vol. 41 nos 1–2 (2018), pp. 160–80.

16. Gili Cohen, 'Gantz, Dempsey discuss security co-operation between Israel and Gulf monarchies', *Ha'aretz*, 31 March 2014.

17. Anshel Pfeffer, 'Mossad Chief Reportedly Visited Saudi Arabia for Talks on Iran', *Ha'aretz*, 26 July 2010.

18. Barak Ravid, 'Wikileaks blows cover off Israel's covert Gulf ties', *Ha'aretz*, 29 November 2010.

19. 'PM Netanyahu at the opening of the Knesset winter session', Israeli Ministry of Foreign Affairs, 27 October 2014, http://mfa.gov.il/MFA/PressRoom/2014/Pages/PM-Netanyahu's-remarks-at-the-opening-of-the-Knesset-winter-session-27-October-2014.aspx, last accessed 5 July 2019.

20. Matthew Kaminski, 'Prince Alwaleed bin Talal: An ally frets about American retreat', *The Wall Street Journal*, 22 November 2013.

21. 'Fars report: Saudi intelligence chief met with Israeli counterpart', *The Jerusalem Post*, 8 December 2013. Israel's former ambassador to Egypt, Zvi Mazel, also highlighted the growing intelligence ties between Israel and the Gulf monarchies that emerged over their shared concerns regarding Iran and, indeed, the Muslim Brotherhood. See Kristian Coates Ulrichsen, 'Israel and the Arab Gulf mon-

archies: Drivers and Directions of Change', *Centre for the Middle East/Rice University's Baker Institute for Public Policy* (September 2016), p. 7.

22. Pieter D. Wezeman *et al.*, 'Trends in International Arms Transfers, 2017', *Stockholm International Peace Research Institute Fact Sheet*, March 2018, p. 6.

23. See Yahel Arnon and Yoel Guzansky, 'A Conventional Arms Race', *INSS Insight* no. 1074, 11 July 2018. For a detailed overview of arms spending in the Gulf since 2011, see David B. Roberts, 'The Gulf Monarchies' Armed Forces at the Crossroads', *Études de L'Ifri focus stratégique* no. 80, 4 May 2018, https://www.ifri.org/en/publications/etudes-de-lifri/focus-strategique/gulf-monarchies-armed-forces-crossroads, last accessed 5 July 2019.

24. Yaakov Katz and Amir Bohbot, *The Weapon Wizards: How Israel became a High-Tech Military Superpower*, New York: St Martin's Press, 2017, p. 296.

25. Sharon Weinberger, 'China Has Already Won the Drone War', *Foreign Policy*, 10 May 2018.

26. 'Saudi Threatens Military Action if Qatar Deploys Anti-Aircraft Missiles: Report', *Reuters*, 2 June 2018.

27. Jeremy Binnie, 'Qatar Parades Chinese Ballistic Missiles', *HIS Janes Defense Weekly*, 20 December 2017.

28. Barbara Opall-Rome, 'Trump could let the UAE buy F-35 jets', *Defense News*, 4 November 4 2017; 'The Gulf's "little Sparta": The ambitious United Arab Emirates', *The Economist*, 6 April 2017.

29. Thomas Shanker, 'U.S. Arms Deal With Israel and 2 Arab Nations Is Near', *The New York Times*, 19 April 2013.

30. Barak David and Chaim Levinson, 'Arab states won't demand a vote on Israel's nuclear arms at IAEA conference in September', *Ha'aretz*, 18 August 2016.

31. Victor Kattan, 'Behind the extravagant hype of an Israeli–Saudi "courtship", Israel is setting the price for Riyadh to go nuclear', *Ha'aretz*, 14 February 2018; Zvi Bar'el, 'Iranian nuclear programme? Trump and Israel will soon have to worry about the Saudis too', *Ha'aretz*, 25 March 2018.

32. Yoel Guzansky, 'Nuclear Development in the Arabian Peninsula: The United Arab Emirates—A Harbinger of Things to Come?', *Tel Aviv Notes*, vol. 12 no. 8 (2018), pp. 1–3.

33. Carole Nakhle, 'Nuclear Energy's Future in the Middle East and North Africa', *Carnegie Middle East Center*, 28 January 2016, http://carnegie-mec.org/2016/01/28/nuclear-energy-s-future-in-middle-east-and-north-africa-pub-62562, last accessed 5 July 2019.

34. 'A Prince fails to charm', *The Economist*, 22 December 2018, pp. 81–2.

35. Nakhle, op. cit.

36. 'National poll shows strong support for UAE peaceful nuclear energy programme', *Emirates Nuclear Energy Corporation*, 20 June 2018, https://www.enec.gov.ae/news/latest-news/national-poll-shows-strong-support-for-uae-peaceful-nuclear-energy-program/, last accessed 5 July 2019.

37. The NWP is available at https://www.uae-embassy.org/sites/default/files/UAE_Policy_Peaceful_Nuclear_Energy_English.pdf, last accessed 5 July 2019.

38. Charles W. Dunne, 'The Middle East Nuclear Picture: Peaceful Programs or Not, Cause for Concern', Arab Center Washington DC, 2 February 2018, http://arab-centerdc.org/policy_analyses/the-middle-east-nuclear-

picture-peaceful-programs-or-not-cause-for-concern/, last accessed 5 July 2019.

39. Mari Luomi, 'The Economic and Prestige Aspects of Abu Dhabi's Nuclear Programme', in Mehran Kamrava (ed.), *The Nuclear Question in the Middle East*, London: Hurst, 2012, p. 127.

40. Ibid., pp. 135–6.

41. Scott Sagan, 'Why Do States Build Nuclear Weapons?: Three Models in Search of a Bomb', *International Security*, vol. 21 no. 3 (1996/97), pp. 73–6. On the breakdown of regional security, see Anoush Ehteshami, 'MENA De-Regionalisation: From Hegemonic Competition to Regional Fragmentation', unpublished paper, Durham University, 2017.

42. 'Growing popularity of nuclear power brings with it political controversy', *Gulf States News*, vol. 42 no. 1055, 8 March 2018, p. 10.

43. For a detailed analysis of the UAE's new-found assertiveness in foreign affairs, see Andrew England and Simeon Kerr, 'A display of power', *The Financial Times*, 25 October 2017; David Roberts, 'The Gulf Monarchies' Armed Forces at the Crossroads', *Études de L'Ifri focus stratégique* no. 80, 4 May 2018, https://www.ifri.org/en/publications/etudes-de-lifri/focus-strategique/gulf-monarchies-armed-forces-crossroads, last accessed 5 July 2019, pp. 23–8.

44. Quoted in Guzansky, op. cit., p. 2.

45. Luomi, op. cit., p. 156.

46. Shaul Shay, 'The Sunni Arab Countries going Nuclear', *IPS Publications*, Institute for Policy and Strategy/IDC Herzliya, February 2018, https://www.idc.ac.il/he/

research/ips/Documents/1/Nuclear-main.pdf, last accessed 4 July 2019.

47. 'King Abdullah City for Atomic and Renewable Energy, the Vision: Energy Sustainability for Future Generations', Government of Saudi Arabia, http://www.kacare.gov.sa/en/?page_id=84, last accessed 5 July 2019.

48. Glada Lahn and Paul Stevens, *Burning Oil to Keep Cool: The Hidden Energy Crisis in Saudi Arabia*, London: Chatham House/Royal Institute of International Affairs, 2011, pp. 1–33.

49. Quoted in Yoel Guzansky, 'Saudi Arabia: Walking the Nuclear Path', *Strategic Assessment*, vol. 21 no. 2 (2018), p. 76.

50. Nicholas L. Miller and Tristan A. Volpe, 'Geostrategic Nuclear Exports: The Competition for influence in Saudi Arabia', *Carnegie Endowment for International Peace*, 7 February 2018, http://carnegieendowment.org/2018/02/07/geostrategic-nuclear-exports-competition-for-influence-in-saudi-arabia-pub-75472, last accessed 5 July 2019.

51. 'Why Trump might bend nuclear security rules to help Saudi Arabia build reactors in the desert', *The Washington Post*, 19 February 2018.

52. Victor Gilinsky and Henry Sokolski, 'Don't give Saudi Arabia an easy path to Nukes', *Foreign Policy*, 1 March 2018, https://foreignpolicy.com/2018/03/01/dont-give-saudi-arabia-an-easy-path-to-nukes/, last accessed 5 July 2019.

53. Amir Tibon, '"Regional arms race": US congressmen want Trump to report on Saudi Arabia's nuclear ambitions', *Ha'aretz*, 3 October 2018.

54. Ed Crooks, 'US and Saudi Arabia move slowly towards nuclear deal', *The Financial Times*, 14 March 2019.
55. Bar'el, op. cit.
56. 'Israel Confident in U.S. Protections in any Saudi Nuclear Power Deal', *Ha'aretz*, 27 June 2018.
57. Victor Kattan, 'Behind the extravagant hype of an Israeli–Saudi "courtship", Israel is setting the price for Riyadh to go nuclear', *Ha'aretz*, 14 February 2018.
58. On the attack on the Iraqi nuclear reactor, see Amos Perlmutter, Michael I. Handel and Uri Bar-Joseph, *Two Minutes over Baghdad*, Abingdon: Frank Cass, 2003; Rafael Ofek, '"Operation Opera": Intelligence behind the Scenes', *IsraelDefense*, 4 September 2015, https://www.israeldefense.co.il/en/content/operation-opera-intelligence-behind-scenes, last accessed 5 July 2019. On the attack in Syria, see Amos Harel and Aluf Benn, 'No Longer a Secret: How Israel Destroyed Syria's Nuclear Reactor', *Ha'aretz*, 23 March 2018.

5. LIMITS OF COLLUSION: THE SYRIAN CIVIL WAR

1. Sources vary as to precise numbers and do not always include those killed in terrorist/militant attacks or in Israeli strikes. Even so, at the time of writing it is reckoned that around 91,000 Arabs and just under 25,000 Israelis have been killed in six main wars. Again, numbers for those killed in Syria vary but estimates lie between 369,000 and 560,000. Neither figure includes the wounded or the displaced. For figures on the Arab–Israeli conflict see https://www.jewishvirtuallibrary.org/total-casualties-arab-israeli-conflict, last accessed 5 July 2019; for figures on Syria, see Megan Specia, 'How Syria's death total is lost in the fog of war', *The New York Times*, 13 April 2018.

2. Matthew Rosenburg, 'In Reversal, Obama Says U.S. Soldiers Will Stay in Afghanistan to 2017', *The New York Times*, 16 October 2015.

3. 'PM Netanyahu at the WEF event hosted by Fareed Zakaria (CNN)', Davos, 21 January 2016, http://mfa. gov.il/MFA/PressRoom/2016/Pages/PM-Netanyahu-at-the-WEF-event-hosted-by-Fareed-Zakaria-21-Jan-2016.aspx, last accessed 5 July 2019.

4. Mohammed Elmenshawy, 'The Arabs smitten by the Israeli lobby', *Ahram Online*, 10 April 2014, http://english.ahram.org.eg/NewsContentP/4/98578/Opinion/The-Arabs-smitten-by-the-Israeli-lobby.aspx, last accessed 5 July 2019.

5. Oded Eran, 'Will changes in Riyadh lead to a new era in Israeli–Saudi Relations?', *Yediot Aharanot*, 10 November 2017.

6. Dan Williams, 'Israel says close to forging new ties across Arab world', *Reuters*, 14 April 2014, http://uk.reuters.com/article/uk-israel-arab-ties-idUKBREA3D0TT 20140414, last accessed 5 July 2019.

7. Ibid.

8. Ayelett Shani, 'Israel is shooting itself in the foot by declaring its ties to Saudi Arabia, expert warns', *Ha'aretz*, 30 November 2017; 'Steinetz reveals covert contacts with Saudi Arabia', *Yediot Aharanot*, 20 November 2017.

9. Helene Cooper, 'Converging Interests May Lead to Cooperation Between Israel and Gulf States', *The New York Times*, 31 March 2014.

10. 'A Selection of Military Operations by the Islamic State', *Dabiq* no. 12, al Hayat Media Center, 2015, http://www.clarionproject.org/docs/islamic-state-isis-isil-dabiq-magazine-issue-12-just-terror.pdf, last accessed 5 July 2019.

11. Daniel J. Roth, 'Hebrew speaking-ISIS jihadi threatens Israel, Jews worldwide in new video', *The Jerusalem Post*, 23 October 2015.

12. Jürgen Todenhöfer, 'Special Report: Behind enemy lines with ISIS: "We fear the IDF"'. 27 December 2015, http://www.jewishnews.co.uk/special%E2%80%88report-behind-enemy-lines-with-isis-we-fear-the-idf/, last accessed 4 July 2019.

13. Anshel Pfeffer, 'Amman warns: Jihadists hijacking Syria revolution, may target Israel, Jordan next', *Ha'aretz*, 20 December 2012.

14. Itamar Rabinovich, *Israel's View of the Syrian Crisis*, Analysis Paper 28, The Saban Center for Middle East Policy/Brookings Institution, 26 November 2012, https://www.brookings.edu/research/israels-view-of-the-syrian-crisis/, last accessed 5 July 2019, pp. 1–14.

15. Gili Cohen, 'IDF reinforces security along the border fence with Syria', *Ha'aretz*, 14 September 2012.

16. Jonathan Lis, 'IDF intelligence chief: Fall of Assad regime only a matter of time', *Ha'aretz*, 17 July 2012; Barak Ravid, 'Israel attacks target on Syria-Lebanon border, Western sources say', *Ha'aretz*, 30 January 2013; Lilach Shoval and Daniel Siryoti, 'IAF Chief: We are prepared to deal with Syrian chemical weapons', *Israel Hayom*, 20 December 2012.

17. Zvi Bar'el, 'In admitting Israeli attack, Hezbollah changed the rules', *Ha'aretz*, 27 February 2014. The IDF gave access to the BBC to highlight the type of medical support given by Israeli hospitals to wounded and traumatised Syrian refugees who were picked up by the Israeli troops along the border. See 'The Documentary: Inside

the Israeli Hospital', BBC World Service Radio, 29 May 2017, https://www.bbc.co.uk/programmes/p0531xq7, last accessed 5 July 2019.

18. Sheera Frankel and Hugh Tomlinson, 'Israeli tanks fire warning at Syria after 40 years of uneasy silence', *The Times*, 12 November 2012.

19. Amos Harel, 'Death of Iranian General brings Tehran back into the heart of Israel's conflict with the Hezbollah', *Ha'aretz*, 19 January 2015.

20. Alex Fishman, 'Killing three birds with one stone', *Yediot Aharanot*, 21 January 2015.

21. Zvi Bar'el, 'In admitting Israeli attack, Hezbollah changed the rules', *Ha'aretz*, 27 February 2014; 'Hezbollah threatens to attack Israel in response to Syrian border strike', *Ha'aretz*, 26 February 2014.

22. Muted but not entirely silent. Hezbollah is believed to have been behind the suicide bomb attack on a bus carrying Israel tourists in Burgas, Bulgaria, in 2012; it has launched its own UAV across Israel, and in 2012 the Israeli internal security service, Shin Bet, arrested fourteen Israeli Arabs who were later charged with smuggling explosive devices into Israel from Lebanon at the behest of Hezbollah. See Amos Harel, 'Why did Israel attack Syria now and why did the Syrians admit it?', *Ha'aretz*, 1 February 2013.

23. 'Israeli intelligence intercepted Syrian regime talk about the attack', *The Guardian*, 28 August 2013.

24. Michelle Nichols, 'Saudi rejects U.N. Security Council seat, opening way for Jordan', *Reuters*, 12 November 2013, http://www.reuters.com/article/us-un-saudi-jordan-idUSBRE9AB14720131112, last accessed 5 July 2019.

25. 'PM Netanyahu at the opening of the Knesset winter session', Israeli Ministry of Foreign Affairs, 27 October 2014, http://mfa.gov.il/MFA/PressRoom/2014/Pages/PM-Netanyahu's-remarks-at-the-opening-of-the-Knesset-winter-session-27-October-2014.aspx, last accessed 5 July 2019.

26. Liad Osmo, '"If Iran hits Tel Aviv, we'll hit Tehran" defense minister tells newspaper', *Yediot Aharanot*, 27 April 2018.

27. Alex Fishman, 'IDF Chief's Saudi Interview: A gesture from Riyadh', *Yediot Aharanot*, 19 November 2017; Jonathan Lis, 'When Jerusalem needs to talk to Riyadh: This Saudi newspaper is Israel's backchannel to the Arab world', *Ha'aretz*, 16 November 2017; Amos Harel, 'Israeli military chief gives unprecedented interview to Saudi media: 'Ready to share Intel on Iran'', *Ha'aretz*, 16 November 2017.

28. Daniel B. Shapiro, 'Is Saudi Arabia pushing Israel into war with Hezbollah and Iran?', *Ha'aretz*, 7 November 2017; author interview with Dan Shapiro, Tel Aviv, 22 March 2018.

29. Amos Harel, 'Saudi Arabia is opening a new front against Iran and wants Israel to do its dirty work', *Ha'aretz*, 9 November 2017.

30. On the deterrence relationship between Israel and Hezbollah, see Daniel Sobelman, 'Learning to Deter: Deterrence Failure and Success in the Israel-Hezbollah Conflict, 2006–16', *International Security*, vol. 41 no. 3 (2016/17), pp. 151–96.

31. See for example Sheera Frenkel and Martin Fletcher, 'Israeli airstrike destroys Syrian convoy "taking hi-tech weapons to Hezbollah"', *The Times*, 31 January 2013.

32. Amos Harel, 'The attack in Syria: Israel's policy of ambiguity is nearing an end', *Ha'aretz*, 27 April 2017; 'Israeli strikes inside Syria pick up tempo in proxy war', *Yediot Aharanot*, 27 April 2017.

33. 'Iran: Israelis and Saudis coordinating on certain issues in the region', *The Jerusalem Post*, 7 March 2017.

34. This allegedly includes Russian training of Hezbollah units in sophisticated missile systems, including the SA-22 surface-to-air missile and the Yakhont surface-to-sea missile that could hit Israeli gas rigs in the eastern Mediterranean. See Raphael D. Marcus, *Israel's Long War with Hezbollah*, Washington, D.C.: Georgetown University Press, 2018, pp. 269–70. On Russian–Israeli military co-ordination, see Zvi Bar'el, 'Israel's slow creep into the Syrian Civil War', *Ha'aretz*, 23 June 2017.

35. Amos Harel, 'Trump and Putin are the real targets of Israel's alleged strike in Syria', *Ha'aretz*, 7 September 2017.

36. Oliver Holmes, 'Israel retaliates after Iran "fire 20 rockets" at army in occupied Golan Heights', *The Guardian*, 10 May 2018.

37. 'Two IDF pilots hurt after F16 downed during retaliatory strike in Syria', *Yediot Aharanot*, 10 February 2018; Darya Korunskaya and Stephen Farrell, 'Putin sees chance circumstance behind downing of Russian plane off Syrian coast', *Reuters*, 18 September 2018, https://uk.reuters.com/article/uk-mideast-crisis-syria-russia/putin-sees-chance-circumstances-behind-downing-of-russian-plane-off-syrian-coast-idUKKCN1LY05J, last accessed 5 July 2019.

38. This was certainly the view of the former director of Mossad, Tamir Pardo. See Daniel Salami, 'Former Mossad

Chief doubts Russia could remove Iran from Syria', *Yediot Aharanot*, 14 August 2018; Amos Harel, 'With Russian presence in Syria, Israeli Air force has to be very precise', *Ha'aretz*, 21 September 2018.

39. Amos Yadlin, 'Assad must go', *Yediot Aharanot*, 18 May 2016.

40. Nir Boms and Karolina Zielińska, 'Israel and the Southen de-escalation zone: A closer look at the Israeli-Syrian border', *Tel Aviv Notes*, Moshe Dayan Center/Tel Aviv University, vol. 14 no. 12 (12 July 2018), p. 5.

41. For the most detailed account of Israel's aid to Syrian rebels, see Elizabeth Tsurkov, 'Inside Israel's Secret Program to back Syrian rebels', *Foreign Policy*, 6 September 2018; Daniel J. Levy, 'Israel just admitted arming anti-Assad Syrian rebels. Big mistake', *Ha'aretz*, 31 January 2019; Zvi Bar'el, 'Israel's slow creep in the Syrian civil war', *Ha'aretz*, 23 June 2017; Amos Harel, 'To push Iran back, Israel ramps up support for Syrian rebels, "arming 7 different groups"', *Ha'aretz*, 19 February 2018.

42. Noa Landau, 'Netanyahu, Putin to meet next week in Moscow', *Ha'aretz*, 3 July 2018.

43. 'Netanyahu tells Putin: Iranian missile factories in Lebanon are already in progress; we won't accept this threat', *Ha'aretz*, 29 January 2018.

44. Amos Yadlin, 'Israel's wars between wars', *Yediot Aharanot*, 7 September 2018; Yaniv Kubovich, 'Hezbollah built missile storehouses in the heart of Beirut's civilian population', *Ha'aretz*, 28 September 2018.

45. Amos Harel, '"Aerial and intelligence superiority": Army chief reveal's how Israel beat Iran's Solemeini in Syria', *Ha'aretz*, 13 January 2019.

46. Noa Landau, 'Russia-Israel deal clear: Iran away from border, Assad's rule accepted', *Ha'aretz*, 12 July 2018; Zvi Bar'el, 'Syria's Assad had become Israel's ally', *Ha'aretz*, 3 July 2018.

47. 'America and Syria: Disengagement', *The Economist*, 5 January 2019, p. 34.

48. Helene Cooper, 'Converging Interests May Lead to Cooperation Between Israel and Gulf Monarchies', *The New York Times*, 31 March 2014.

49. Yoel Guzansky, 'The Arab World and the Syrian Crisis', *INSS Insight*, vol. 461 no. 2 (2013), pp. 1–4.

50. Ibid., p. 2.

51. See Jacob Abadi, 'Saudi Arabia's rapprochement with Israel: The national security imperatives', *Middle Eastern Studies* (2019), p. 13.

CONCLUSION: REVEALED INTERESTS, HIDDEN PARTNERSHIPS

1. Herb Keinon, 'Ex-IDF deputy chief: Beware of Gulf monarchies; their values are different than ours', *The Jerusalem Post*, 11 December 2018.

2. 'Qatar: Governance, Security, and US Policy', *Congressional Research Service*, 11 April 2019, p. 7, https://fas.org/sgp/crs/mideast/R44533.pdf, last accessed 5 July 2019.

3. Efraim Halevy, email correspondence with Clive Jones, 7 May 2016.

4. See Ian Black, 'Just Below the Surface: Israel, the Arab Gulf States and the Limits of Cooperation', LSE Middle East Centre Report, March 2019, p. 37, http://eprints.lse.ac.uk/100313/, last accessed 5 July 2019.

5. Yair Ettinger, *Privatizing Religion: The Transformation of*

Israel's Religious-Zionist Community, Washington: D.C.: Brookings Center for Middle East Policy, March 2017, pp. 4–7, https://www.brookings.edu/research/privatizing-religion-the-transformation-of-israels-religious-zionist-community/, last accessed 5 July 2019.

6. On the ideo-theology of the settlers and religious nationalism, see Gadi Taub, *The Settlers*, Yale: Yale University Press, 2010; Idith Zertal and Akiva Eldar, *Lords of the Land: The War over Israel's Settlements in the Occupied Territories 1967–2007*, New York: Nation Books, 2007.

7. 'Saudi general tells Israeli TV of peace hopes', *The Times of Israel*, 5 June 2015.

8. The whole of the exchange can be viewed at 'Shared Security Challenges and Opportunities', Israel Policy Forum, New York, 23 October 2017, https://www.youtube.com/watch?v=RXM-atXcQkA, last accessed 5 July 2019.

9. Simon Henderson, 'Israel-GCC Ties Twenty-Five Years After the First Gulf War', *Policy Watch: Washington Institute for Near East Studies*, Fall 2015, http://www.washingtoninstitute.org/policy-analysis/view/israel-gcc-ties-twenty-five-years-after-the-first-gulf-war, last accessed 5 July 2019.

10. Michael Herzog, 'New IDF Strategy goes Public', *The Washington Institute for Near East Policy Policy Watch*, 28 August 2015, at http://www.washingtoninstitute.org/policy-analysis/view/new-idf-strategy-goes-public, last accessed 5 July 2019.

11. David Makovsky, 'The Silent Strike: How Israel bombed a nuclear installation and kept it secret', *The New Yorker*, 17 September 2012.

12. Paul Sonne, 'Can Saudi Arabia produce ballistic missiles? Satellite imagery raises suspicions', *The Washington Post*, 23 January 2019; AP, 'Saudi Arabia appears to be testing ballistic missiles program, satellite images show', *Ha'aretz*, 26 January 2019.

13. Zvi Bar'el, 'Does Iran really want to destroy Israel', *Ha'aretz*, 8 January 2019; Smadar Perry, 'Israel, Syria and the world through Iranian eyes', *Yediot Aharonot*, 1 February 2019.

14. Gawdat Bahgat, 'The Brewing War between Iran and Israel: Strategic Implications', *Middle East Policy*, vol. 25 no. 3 (2018), p. 75.

15. Author interview with Lieutenant-General Moshe Ya'alon (Res), Tel Aviv, 21 March 2018.

16. Amir Tibon, 'Two years in, Gulf monarchies disappointed in Trump on everything from Iran to peace', *Ha'aretz*, 25 January 2019.

17. Ibid.

18. Eric Posner, 'The case against human rights', *The Guardian*, 4 December 2014; Zachary Shapiro, 'Saudi Arabia is no ally of Israel', *Ha'aretz*, 2 April 2019.

19. 'Netanyahu: Countries flocking to forge ties with Israel', *The Times of Israel*, 7 March 2016. Israel did not just restrict its diplomatic endeavours to the Gulf Arab states. Under Netanyahu, it went all out to establish new ties and re-establish old ties across Africa. See Alhadji Bouba Nouhou, 'Israel tries to mend relations with Africa', *Le Monde Diplomatique* (English edition), December 2017, p. 7.

20. Raphael Ahren, 'PM: Renewal of Chad ties is proof of Israel's "rising standing" in the Muslim world', *The Times of Israel*, 20 January 2019.

21. 'A Conversation on Security and Peace in the Middle East: HRH Prince Turki al-Faisal, Saudi Arabia and Maj. Gen. (ret.) Yaakov Amidror, Israel', The Washington Institute for Near East Policy, 5 May 2016, https://www.washingtoninstitute.org/policy-analysis/view/a-conversation-on-security-and-peace-in-the-middle-east, last accessed 5 July 2019.

22. See David Remnick, 'Partners in Division', The New Yorker, 22 April 2019, pp. 13–14.

23. Amir Tabon, 'Saudi Arabia, UAE to attend Trump peace conference in Bahrain', Ha'aretz, 22 May 2019.

24. Yossi Beilin, 'US Bahrain conference premature', Al Monitor Online, 27 May 2019, https://www.al-monitor.com/pulse/originals/2019/05/israel-united-states-bahrain-palestinians-peace-process.html, last accessed 5 July 2019. See also Oliver Holmes, 'Political chaos in Israel disrupts Jared Kushner's peace plan', The Guardian, 30 May 2019.

25. Elior Levy and Itamar Eichner, 'Saudi calls on Israel to accept 2002 Arab peace initiative', Yediot Aharanot, 4 June 2016; Barak David, 'Saudi foreign minister rejects Netanyahu's demand to "update" Arab peace initiative', Ha'aretz, 3 June 2016.

26. 'Israeli official praises Saudi King for stance on Iran, economy', Yediot Aharanot, 16 June 2016.

BIBLIOGRAPHY

Primary Sources: Author Interviews

Ambassador Dan Shapiro, Tel Aviv, 22 March 2018.

Ambassador Efraim Halevy, Ramat Aviv, 1 August 2013.

Lieutenant-General (Res) Moshe Ya'alon, Tel Aviv, 21 March 2018.

Senior Omani Foreign Office Official, Muscat, 11 April 2011.

Online Resources

'Bahrain: Message to the Arab League', *WikiLeaks*, 16 March 2005, http://wikileaks.org/plusd/cables/05MANAMA397_a.html, last accessed 5 July 2019.

'Beirut Declaration on Saudi Peace Initiative-28-Mar-2002', Israeli Ministry of Foreign Affairs, 28 March 2002, http://www.mfa.gov.il/mfa/foreignpolicy/peace/guide/pages/beirut%20declaration%20on%20saudi%20peace%20initiative%20-%2028-.aspx, last accessed 5 July 2019.

'Doing business in Israel: Israel trade and export guide', UK Government Trade and Investment Report, 27 May 2015, https://www.gov.uk/government/publications/exporting-to-israel/exporting-to-israel, last accessed 5 July 2019.

FAQs, UAE Embassy in the Netherlands, 2015, http://www. uae-embassy.ae/Embassies/nl/faq's/5148, last accessed 24 February 2018.

'Israeli Delegation Discusses Cooperation with IRENA on Advancement of Renewable Energy', IRENA Press Office, 27 November 2015, https://www.irena.org/newsroom/ pressreleases/2015/Nov/Israeli-Delegation-Discusses-Cooperation-with-IRENA-on-Advancement-of-Renewable-Energy, last accessed 5 July 2019.

'King Abdullah City for Atomic and Renewable Energy, the Vision: Energy Sustainability for Future Generations', Government of Saudi Arabia, http://www.kacare.gov.sa/ en/?page_id=84, last accessed 5 July 2019.

'PM Netanyahu at the opening of the Knesset winter session', Israeli Ministry of Foreign Affairs, 27 October 2014, http://mfa.gov.il/MFA/PressRoom/2014/Pages/ PM-Netanyahu's-remarks-at-the-opening-of-the-Knesset-winter-session-27-October-2014.aspx, last accessed 5 July 2019.

'U/S Burns meeting at Israel's MFA on Lebanon, NATO, the Vatican, Moderate Arab States and India', 24 August 2007, http://wikileaks.org/plusd/cables/07TELAVIV2576_a. html, last accessed 5 July 2019.

Books

Alpher, Yossi, *Periphery: Israel's Search for Middle East Allies*, London: Rowman & Littlefield, 2015.

Barak, Ehud, *My Country: Fighting for Israel, Searching for Peace*, London: Macmillan, 2018.

Bergman, Ronen, *The Secret War with Iran: The 30-Year Covert Struggle for Control of a Rogue State*, Oxford: One World, 2008.

Blandford, Nicholas, *Killing Mr Lebanon: The Assassination of Rafik Hariri and its Impact on the Middle East*, London: I.B. Tauris, 2009.

Buzan, Barry, and Ole Wæver, *Regions and Powers: The Structure of International Security*, Cambridge: Cambridge University Press, 2003.

Chalcraft, John, *Popular Politics in the Making of the Modern Middle East*, Cambridge: Cambridge University Press, 2016.

Davidson, Christopher (ed.), *Power and Politics in the Persian Monarchies*, London: Hurst, 2011.

Eiran, Ehud, 'Israel's Response to the JCPOA', in Payam Mohseni (ed.), *Tipping the Balance? Implications of the Iran Nuclear Deal on Israeli Security*, Cambridge, MA: Harvard Kennedy School/Belfer Center for Science and International Affairs, 2015.

El Shazly, Saad, *The Arab Military Option*, San Francisco: American Mideast Research, 1986.

Guzansky, Yoel, *The Arab Gulf Monarchies and Reform in the Middle East*, Basingstoke: Palgrave-Macmillan, 2015.

Harel, Amos, and Avi Issacharoff, *34 Days: Israel, Hezbollah and the War in Lebanon*, Basingstoke: Palgrave-Macmillan, 2008.

Hill, Ginny, *Yemen Endures: Civil War, Saudi Adventurism and the Future of Arabia*, Hurst: London, 2017.

Holden, David, and Richard Johns, *The House of Saud: The Rise and Rule of the Most Powerful Dynasty in the Arab World*, New York: Holt, Rinehart, and Winston, 1981.

Inbar, Efraim (ed.), *Regional Security Regimes: Israel and Its Neighbors*, New York: SUNY Press, 1995.

Inbari, Motti, *Messianic Religious Zionism Confronts Israeli*

Territorial Compromises, Cambridge: Cambridge University Press, 2012.

Jervis, Robert, 'From Balance to Concert: A Study of the Concert of International Security Cooperation', in Kenneth Oye (ed.), *Cooperation under Anarchy*, Princeton, N.J.: Princeton University Press, 1985, pp. 58–79.

Jones, Clive, *Soviet Jewish Aliyah: Impact and Implications for Israel and the Middle East*, London: Frank Cass, 1996.

———, *Britain and the Yemen Civil War, 1962–1965*, Brighton: Sussex Academic Press, 2010.

———, and Tore. T Petersen (eds), *Israel's Clandestine Diplomacies*, London: Hurst, 2013.

Jones, Jeremy, and Nicholas Ridout, *Oman, Culture and Diplomacy*, Edinburgh: Edinburgh University Press, 2012.

Kahanov, Michael, *Saudi Arabia and the Conflict in Palestine*, Jerusalem: Carmel, 2012.

Kamrava, Mehran (ed), *The Nuclear Question in the Middle East*, London: Hurst, 2012.

Katz, Yaakov and Amir Bohbot, *The Weapon Wizards: How Israel became a High-Tech Military Superpower*, New York: St Martin's Press, 2017.

Kepel, Gilles, *The Prophet and the Pharaoh: Muslim Extremism in Egypt*, London: Al-Saqi Books, 1985.

Kinninmont, Jane, 'Bahrain', in Christopher Davidson (ed.), *Power and Politics in the Persian Monarchies*, London: Hurst, 2011.

Klieman, Aharon, 'The Israel-Jordan Tacit Security Regime', in Efraim Inbar (ed.), *Regional Security Regimes: Israel and its Neighbors*, New York: State University of New York Press, 1995.

Kostiner, Joseph, 'Coping with Regional Challenges: A case

study of Crown Prince Abdullah's Peace Initiative', in Paul Aarts and Gerd Nonneman (eds), *Saudi Arabia in the Balance*, London: Hurst, 2005.

———, *The Marginal Peace: The Attitudes of Persian Arabian Gulf Monarchies Towards Israel and the Peace Process*, Tel Aviv: Tel Aviv University Press, 2008.

———, 'The Roots of the Arab Peace Plan and its Reversals', in Ephraim Lavie (ed.), *Israel and the Arab Peace Initiative*, Tel Aviv: Tel Aviv University Press, 2010.

Krasner, Stephen, *International Regimes*, New York: Cornell University Press, 1983.

Lavie, Ephraim (ed), *Israel and the Arab Peace Initiative*, Tel Aviv: Tel Aviv University Press, 2010.

Lipson, Charles, 'Are Security Regimes Possible? Historical Cases and Modern Issues', in Efraim Inbar (ed.), *Regional Security Regimes: Israel and Its Neighbors*, New York: SUNY Press, 1995.

Luomi, Mari, 'The Economic and Prestige Aspects of Abu Dhabi's Nuclear Programme', in Mehran Kamrava (ed.), *The Nuclear Question in the Middle East*, London: Hurst, 2012.

Magen, Amichai (ed.), *The Crisis of Governance in the Middle East: Implications for Democracy, Development and Security*, Tel Aviv: IDC Herziliya/Konrad-Adenauer Stiftung, 2013.

Marcus, Raphael D., *Israel's Long War with Hezbollah*, Washington, D.C.: Georgetown University Press, 2018.

Michael, Kobi, and Yoel Guzansky, *The Arab World on the Road to State Failure*, Tel Aviv: Institute for National Security Studies, 2017.

Miller, Rory, *Desert Kingdoms to Global Powers: The Rise of the Arab Gulf*, London: Yale University Press, 2016.

Mohseni, Payam (ed.), *Tipping the Balance? Implications of the Iran Nuclear Deal on Israeli Security*, Cambridge, MA: Harvard Kennedy School/Belfer Center for Science and International Affairs, 2015.

Nevo, Joseph, *King Hussein and the Evolution of Jordan's Perception of a Political Settlement with Israel*, Brighton: Sussex Academic Press, 2006.

Oye, Kenneth (ed.), *Co-operation under Anarchy*, Princeton, N.J.: Princeton University Press, 1985.

Parsi, Trita, *Treacherous Alliance: The Secret Dealings of Iran, Israel, and the U.S.*, Yale: Yale University Press, 2007.

Perlmutter, Amos, Michael I. Handel and Uri Bar-Joseph, *Two Minutes over Baghdad*, Abingdon: Frank Cass, 2003.

Petersen, Tore T. *Anglo-American Policy toward the Persian Gulf, 1978–1985*, Brighton: Sussex Academic Press, 2015.

Podeh, Elie, *Chances for Peace: Missed Opportunities in the Arab–Israeli Conflict*, Austin TX: University of Texas Press, 2015.

Raviv, Dan, and Yossi Melman, *Spies Against Armageddon*, New York: Levant Books, 2012.

Safran, Nadav, *Saudi Arabia: The Ceaseless Quest for Security*, Cambridge, MA: The Belknap Press of Harvard University Press, 1985.

Sayigh, Yezid, *Armed Struggle and the Search for State: The Palestinian National Movement, 1949–1993*, Oxford: Oxford University Press, 1999.

Taub, Gadi, *The Settlers*, Yale: Yale University Press, 2010.

Tripp, Charles, *The Power and the People: Paths of Resistance in the Middle East*, Cambridge: Cambridge University Press, 2013.

Zertal, Idith, and Akiva Eldar, *Lords of the Land: The War over Israel's Settlements in the Occupied Territories 1967–2007*, New York: Nation Books, 2007.

Journal Articles

Abadi, Jacob, 'Saudi Arabia's rapprochement with Israel: The national security imperatives', *Middle Eastern Studies*, vol. 55 no. 3 (2019).

Adamsky, Dmitry, 'The Israeli Odyssey toward its National Cyber Security Strategy', *The Washington Quarterly*, vol. 40 no. 2 (2017).

Ahram, Ariel I., and Ellen Lust, 'The Decline and Fall of the Arab State', *Survival*, vol. 58 no. 2 (2016).

al-Saud, Naef Bin Ahmed, 'The Evolution of Saudi Security and Enforcement on Communication', *Joint Force Quarterly*, vol. 65, 2nd Quarter (2012).

Bahgat, Gawdat, 'The Brewing War between Iran and Israel: Strategic Implications', *Middle East Policy*, vol. 25 no. 3 (2018).

Bianco, Cinzia, and Gareth Stansfield, 'The Intra-GCC Crises: Mapping GCC fragmentation after 2011', *International Affairs*, vol. 94 no. 3 (2018).

Cooper, Andrew F., and Bessma Momani, 'Qatar and Expanded Contours of Small State Diplomacy, The International Spectator', *Italian Journal of International Affairs*, vol. 46 no. 3 (2011).

Ehteshami, Anoush, 'Saudi Arabia as a Resurgent Regional Power', *The International Spectator: Italian Journal of International Affairs*, vol. 53 no. 5 (2018).

Fitzpatrick, Mark, 'Iran: A good deal', *Survival*, vol. 57 no. 5 (2015).

Gal, Yitzhak, 'Israeli Trade with Middle East Markets in

2011', *Middle East Economy, Moshe Dayan Center for Middle East and African Studies*, vol. 22 no. 1 (2012).

Gross Stein, Janice, 'Detection and Defection: Security Regimes and the Management of International Conflict', *International Journal*, vol. 40 no. 4 (1985).

Guzansky, Yoel, 'Defence Cooperation in the Arabian Gulf: The Peninsula Shield Force put to the Test', *Middle Eastern Studies*, vol. 50 no. 4 (2014).

———, and Clive Jones, 'Israel's Relations with the Gulf Monarchies: Towards the Emergence of a Tacit Security Regime?', *Contemporary Security Policy* vol. 38 no. 3 (2017).

———, 'Nuclear Development in the Arabian Peninsula: The United Arab Emirates—A Harbinger of Things to Come?', *Tel Aviv Notes*, vol. 12 no. 8 (2018).

Inbar, Efraim, and Shmuel Sandler, 'The changing Israeli strategic equation: Toward a Security Regime', *Review of International Studies*, vol. 21 no. 1 (1995).

Jones, Clive, and Beverley Milton-Edwards, 'Missing the "devils" we knew? Israel and Political Islam amid the Arab Awakening', *International Affairs*, vol. 89 no. 2 (2013), pp. 399–415.

———, 'Israel's Security Nexus as Strategic Restraint: The Case of Iran 2009–2013', *The Journal of Strategic Studies*, vol. 41 nos 1–2 (2018).

Khatib, Lina, 'Qatar's foreign policy: The limits of pragmatism', *International Affairs*, vol. 89 no. 2 (2013).

Kramer, Martin, 'Israel and the Post-American Middle East', *Foreign Affairs*, vol. 95 no. 4 (2016).

Moore, Thomas C., 'Iran: Non-proliferation overshadowed', *Survival*, vol. 57 no. 5 (2015).

Orkaby, Asher, 'The 1964 Israeli airlift to Yemen and the expansion of weapons diplomacy', *Diplomacy and Statecraft*, vol. 26 no. 4 (2016).

Perry, Glenn E., 'Israeli involvement in Inter-Arab Politics', *International Journal of Islamic and Arab Studies*, vol. 1 no. 1 (1984).

Podeh, Elie., 'Israel and the Arab Peace Initiative 2002–2014: A Plausible Missed Opportunity', *Middle East Journal*, vol. 68 no. 4 (2014).

———, 'Saudi Arabia and Israel: From Secret to Public Engagement 1948-2018', *Middle East Journal*, vol. 72 no. 4 (2018).

Rabi, Uzi, 'Oman and the Arab–Israeli conflict: The reflection of a pragmatic foreign policy', *Israel Affairs*, vol. 11 no. 3 (2005).

———, 'Qatar's relations with Israel: Challenging Arab and Gulf norms', *Middle East Journal*, vol. 63 no. 3 (2009).

Roberts, David B., 'Understanding Qatar's Foreign Policy Objectives', *Mediterranean Politics*, vol. 17 no. 2 (2012).

Rosman-Stollman, Elisheva, 'Balancing Acts: The Gulf States and Israel', *Middle Eastern Studies*, vol. 40 no. 4 (2004).

Sagan, Scott, 'Why Do States Build Nuclear Weapons?: Three Models in Search of a Bomb', *International Security*, vol. 21 no. 3 (1996/97).

Stenslie, Stig, 'The End of Elite Unity and the Stability of Saudi Arabia', *The Washington Quarterly*, vol. 41 no. 4 (2018).

Valbjørn, Morten, and André Bank, 'The New Arab Cold War: Rediscovering the Arab dimension of Middle East regional politics', *Review of International Studies*, vol. 38 no. 1 (2012).

Yizraeli, Sarah, 'Saudi-Israel Dialogue: What Lies Ahead?', *Strategic Assessment* (Institute for National Security Studies), vol. 10 no. 2 (2007).

Research Papers and Policy Reports

'A Conversation on Security and Peace in the Middle East: HRH Prince Turki al-Faisal, Saudi Arabia and Maj.-Gen (ret.) Yaakov Amidror, Israel', *The Washington Institute for Near East Policy*, 5 May 2016 at https://www.washington-institute.org/policy-analysis/view/a-conversation-on-security-and-peace-in-the-middle-east, last accessed 5 July 2019.

'Assessing Israel's Trade with its Arab Neighbours', Report for the Tony Blair Institute for Global Change, 14 August 2018, http://institute.global/insight/middle-east/assessing-israels-trade-its-arab-neighbours, last accessed 5 July 2019.

Beilin, Yossi, 'US Bahrain conference premature', *Al Monitor Online*, 27 May 2019, https://www.al-monitor.com/pulse/originals/2019/05/israel-united-states-bahrain-palestinians-peace-process.html, last accessed 5 July 2019.

Black, Ian, 'Just Below the Surface: Israel, the Arab Gulf States and the Limits of Cooperation', LSE Middle East Centre Report, March 2019, pp. 1–37, http://eprints.lse.ac.uk/100313/, last accessed 5 July 2019.

Boms, Nirand Karolina Zielińska, 'Israel and the Southen de-escalation zone: A closer look at the Israeli-Syrian border', *Tel Aviv Notes*, Moshe Dayan Center/Tel Aviv University, vol. 14 no. 12, 12 July 2018.

Burson-Martseller, Asda'a, 'Inside the hearts and minds of Arab youth', Arab Youth Survey, 13 April 2016, https://

www.arabyouthsurvey.com/pdf/whitepaper/en/2016-AYS-White-Paper.pdf, last accessed 5 July 2019.

Cordesman, Anthony H., 'The War in Yemen: Hard Choices in a Hard War', Center for Strategic and International Studies Report, 9 May 2017, pp. 1–7, https://www.csis.org/analysis/war-yemen-hard-choices-hard-war, last accessed 5 July 2019.

Craig, Alan, and Clive Jones, *Discovery of Israel's Gas Fields and their Geopolitical Implications—The Emirates Occasional Papers No. 81*, Abu Dhabi: ECSSR, 2013.

Dunne, Charles W., 'The Middle East Nuclear Picture: Peaceful Programs or Not, Cause for Concern', Arab Center, Washington, D.C., 2 February 2018, http://arab-centerdc.org/policy_analyses/the-middle-east-nuclear-picture-peaceful-programs-or-not-cause-for-concern/, last accessed 5 July 2019.

Ettinger, Yair, *Privatizing Religion: The Transformation of Israel's Religious-Zionist Community*, Washington, D.C.: Brookings Center for Middle East Policy, March 2017, pp. 4–7, https://www.brookings.edu/research/privatizing-religion-the-transformation-of-israels-religious-zionist-community/, last accessed 5 July 2019.

Gilinsky, Victor, and Henry Sokolski, 'Don't give Saudi Arabia an easy path to Nukes', *Foreign Policy*, 1 March 2018, https://foreignpolicy.com/2018/03/01/dont-give-saudi-arabia-an-easy-path-to-nukes/, last accessed 5 July 2019.

'Growing popularity of nuclear power brings with it political controversy', *Gulf States News*, vol. 42 no. 1055, 8 March 2018.

Gold, Dore, 'Regional Challenges and Opportunities: The

View from Saudi Arabia and Israel', *Council on Foreign Relations*, 4 June 2015, https://www.cfr.org/event/regional-challenges-and-opportunities-view-saudi-arabia-and-israel-0, last accessed 5 July 2019.

Guzansky, Yoel, 'The Arab World and the Syrian Crisis', *INSS Insight*, vol. 461 no. 2 (2013).

———, and Azriel Bermant, 'The best of the worst: Why Iran's enemies support the nuclear deal', *Foreign Affairs*, 13 August 2015, https://www.foreignaffairs.com/articles/iran/2015–08–13/best-worst, last accessed 5 July 2019.

———, 'The Islamic State vs the Saudi State', in Yoram Schweitzer and Omer Eliav (eds), *The Islamic State: How Viable Is It?*, Tel Aviv: INSS, 2016, pp. 173–9.

———, and Erez Striem, 'Saudi Arabia: A Build-up of Internal and External Challenges', *INSS Insight*, no. 768, November 2015, https://www.inss.org.il/publication/saudi-arabia-a-buildup-of-internal-and-external-challenges/, last accessed 5 July 2019.

———, and Kobi Michael, 'Israel's Qatari Dilemma', *INSS Insight*, no. 1034 14 March 2018, http://www.inss.org.il/publication/israels-qatari-dilemma/?offset=13&posts=114&subject=263, last accessed 5 July 2019.

Hassan, Hassan, 'Qatar won the Saudi Blockade', *Foreign Policy*, 4 June 2018, https://foreignpolicy.com/2018/06/04/qatar-won-the-saudi-blockade/, last accessed 5 July 2019.

Henderson, Simon, 'Israel-GCC Ties Twenty-Five Years After the First Gulf War', *Policy Watch: Washington Institute for Near East Studies*, Fall 2015, http://www.washingtoninstitute.org/policy-analysis/view/israel-gcc-ties-twenty-five-years-after-the-first-gulf-war, last accessed 5 July 2019.

———, 'Israel's Gulf Breakthrough', *The Washington Institute Policy Brief*, 30 November 2015, http://www.washington-institute.org/policy-analysis/view/israels-gulf-break-through, last accessed 5 July 2019.

Herzog, Michael, 'New IDF Strategy goes Public', *The Washington Institute for Near East Policy Policy Watch*, 28 August 2015, at http://www.washingtoninstitute.org/policy-analysis/view/new-idf-strategy-goes-public, last accessed 5 July 2019.

Kaye, Dalia Dassa, Alireza Nader and Parisa Roshan, *Israel and Iran: A Dangerous Rivalry*, Santa Monica: RAND/National Defense Research Institute, 2011, https://www.rand.org/pubs/monographs/MG1143.html, last accessed 5 July 2019.

Kendall, Elizabeth, 'Contemporary Jihadi Militancy in Yemen: How is the Threat Evolving?', *Middle East Institute*, Policy Paper 2018, no. 7, July 2018, pp. 1–10.

Lahn, Glada, and Paul Stevens, *Burning Oil to Keep Cool: The Hidden Energy Crisis in Saudi Arabia*, London: Chatham House/Royal Institute of International Affairs, 2011.

Miller, Nicholas L., and Tristan A. Volpe, 'Geostrategic Nuclear Exports: The Competition for Influence in Saudi Arabia', *Carnegie Endowment for International Peace*, 7 February 2018, http://carnegieendowment.org/2018/02/07/geostrategic-nuclear-exports-competition-for-influence-in-saudi-arabia-pub-75472, last accessed 5 July 2019.

Nakhle, Carole, 'Nuclear Energy's Future in the Middle East and North Africa', *Carnegie Middle East Center*, 28 January 2016, http://carnegie-mec.org/2016/01/28/nuclear-energy-s-future-in-middle-east-and-north-africa-pub-62562, last accessed 5 July 2019.

Neubauer, Sigurd, 'Qatar's Changing Foreign Policy', *Sada Analysis: Carnegie Endowment for International Peace*, 8 April 2014, https://carnegieendowment.org/sada/55278, last accessed 5 July 2019.

———, 'Oman: The Gulf's Go-between', *The Arab Gulf Institute in Washington*, Issue Paper no. 1, 5 February 2016, http://www.agsiw.org/oman-the-gulfs-go-between/, last accessed 5 July 2019.

Podeh, Elie, 'From Fahd to 'Abdallah: The Origins of the Saudi Peace Initiatives and their Impact on the Arab System and Israel', Harry S. Truman Research Institute for the Advancement of Peace, Gitelson Peace Publications, Hebrew University of Jerusalem, July 2003.

Pollock, David, 'New Poll Shows Majority of Saudis, Kuwaitis, Emiratis Reject ISIS, Back Two-State Solution with Israel', 23 October 2014, http://www.washingtoninstitute.org/policy-analysis/view/new-poll-shows-majority-of-saudis-kuwaitis-emiratis-reject-isis-back-two-st, last accessed 5 July 2019.

Rabinovich, Itamar, *Israel's View of the Syrian Crisis*, Analysis Paper 28, The Saban Center for Middle East Policy/Brookings Institution, 26 November 2012, pp. 1–12, https://www.brookings.edu/research/israels-view-of-the-syrian-crisis/, last accessed 5 July 2019.

———, and Itai Brun, 'Israel and the Arab Turmoil', The Hoover Institution, Stanford University, 10 October 2017, https://www.hoover.org/research/israel-and-arab-turmoil-0, last accessed 5 July 2019.

Redman, Nicholas, 'Oman: Small State, Big Voice', 30 October 2018, https://www.iiss.org/blogs/analysis/2018/10/oman-alawi-speech, last accessed 5 July 2019.

Roberts, David, 'Qatar and the Muslim Brotherhood: Pragmatism or Preference?', *Middle East Policy Council*, vol. 21 no. 3, Fall 2017, https://www.mepc.org/qatar-and-muslim-brotherhood-pragmatism-or-preference, last accessed 5 July 2019.

―――, 'The Gulf Monarchies' Armed Forces at the Crossroads', *Études de L'Ifri focus stratégique* no. 80 4 May 2018, https://www.ifri.org/en/publications/etudes-de-lifri/focus-strategique/gulf-monarchies-armed-forces-crossroads, last accessed 5 July 2019.

Salisbury, Peter, *Yemen: National Chaos, Local Order*, London: Royal Institute for International Affairs, 2017, pp. 9–23, https://www.chathamhouse.org/publication/yemen-national-chaos-local-order, last accessed 5 July 2019.

Shay, Shaul, 'The Sunni Arab Countries going Nuclear', *IPS Publications*, Institute for Policy and Strategy/IDC Herzliya, February 2018, https://www.idc.ac.il/he/research/ips/Documents/1/Nuclear-main.pdf, last accessed 5 July 2019.

Teitelbaum, Joshua, *The Arab Peace Initiative: A Primer and Future Prospects*, Jerusalem: Jerusalem Centre for Public Affairs, 2009, http://www.jcpa.org/text/Arab-Peace-Initiative.pdf, last accessed 5 July 2019.

Ulrichsen, Kristian Coates, 'Israel and the Arab Gulf Monarchies: Drivers and Directions of Change', *Center for the Middle East/Rice University's Baker Institute for Public Policy*, September 2016.

Wasser, Becca, 'Israel and the Gulf States', IISS Voices, *International Institute for Strategic Studies*, 22 August 2013.

Wezeman, Pieter D., et al., 'Trends in International Arms

Transfers, 2017', *Stockholm International Peace Research Institute Fact Sheet*, March 2018.

Zetelny, Itay, 'The Israeli Hi-Tech Industry', EY Report, Tel Aviv, January 2014, https://ec.europa.eu/assets/jrc/events/20140120-tto-circle/jrc-20140120-tto-circle-zetelny.pdf, last accessed 5 July 2019.

Unpublished Paper

Ehteshami, Anoush, 'MENA De-Regionalisation: From Hegemonic Competition to Regional Fragmentation', unpublished paper, Durham University, 2017.

Online News Sources

Allilou, Aziz, 'Saudi Arabia's Al-Waleed Bin Talal to Pay Official Visit to Israel', 5 July 2015, http://www.moroccoworldnews.com/2015/07/162534/saudi-arabias-al-waleed-bin-talal-to-pay-official-visit-to-israel/, last accessed 4 July 2019.

'A Selection of Military Operations by the Islamic State', *Dabiq* no. 12, al-Hayat Media Center, 2015, http://www.clarionproject.org/docs/islamic-state-isis-isil-dabiq-magazine-issue-12-just-terror.pdf, last accessed 5 July 2019.

Bergman, Ronen, and Holger Stark, 'We Can in No Way Tolerate an Iran with Nuclear Weapons', *Spiegel Online*, 8 July 2015, http://www.spiegel.de/international/world/israeli-defense-minister-moshe-yaalon-critizes-iran-deal-a-1047260-druck.html, last accessed 4 July 2019.

Donaghy, Rori, 'Falcon Eye: The Israeli-installed mass civil surveillance system of Abu Dhabi', *Middle East Eye*, 28 February 2015, http://www.middleeasteye.net/news/uae-israel-surveillance-2104952769, last accessed 5 July 2019.

Dunne, Charles W., 'The Middle East Nuclear Picture: Peaceful Programs or Not, Cause for Concern', Arab Center, Washington, D.C., 2 February 2018, http://arab-centerdc.org/policy_analyses/the-middle-east-nuclear-picture-peaceful-programs-or-not-cause-for-concern/, last accessed 5 July 2019.

Eldar, Akiva, 'Why cancelled Arab League summit should worry Israelis', 3 March 2016, http://www.al-monitor.com/pulse/originals/2016/03/marrakesh-arab-league-summit-arab-peace-initiative-netanyahu.html#ixzz450ob1eUv, last accessed 5 July 2019.

Elmenshawy, Mohammed, 'The Arabs smitten by the Israeli lobby', *Ahram Online*, 10 April 2014, http://english.ahram.org.eg/NewsContentP/4/98578/Opinion/The-Arabs-smitten-by-the-Israeli-lobby.aspx, last accessed 5 July 2019.

'Emirates "has security links with Israel"', *UPI*, 27 January 2012, http://www.upi.com/Business_News/Security-Industry/2012/01/27/Emirates-has-security-links-with-Israel/73471327687767/, last accessed 5 July 2019.

Entous, Adam, 'Donald Trump's New World Order', *The New Yorker*, 18 June 2018, https://www.newyorker.com/magazine/2018/06/18/donald-trumps-new-world-order, last accessed 5 July 2019.

'Exclusive: Israel hosted UAE military delegation to review F-35s, sources say', *i24News*, 4 July 2018, https://i24news.tv/en/news/israel/178686–180704-sources-tell-i24news—israel-hosted-uae-military-delegation-to-review-f-35s, last accessed 5 July 2019.

Ferziger, Jonathan, and Peter Waldman, 'How do Israel's Tech Firms Do Business in Saudi Arabia? Very Quietly',

Bloomberg News Online, 2 February 2017, https://www.bloomberg.com/news/features/2017–02–02/how-do-israel-s-tech-firms-do-business-in-saudi-arabia-very-quietly, last accessed 5 July 2019.

Goldberg, Jeffrey, 'Saudi Crown Prince: Iran's Supreme Leader "Makes Hitler Look Good"', *The Atlantic*, 2 April 2018, https://www.theatlantic.com/international/archive/2018/04/mohammed-bin-salman-iran-israel/557036/, last accessed 5 July 2019.

'Israeli culture minister visits Abu Dhabi's Sheikh Zayed mosque', *The National* (UAE), 29 October 2018, https://www.thenational.ae/uae/government/israeli-cultural-minister-visits-abu-dhabi-s-sheikh-zayed-grand-mosque-1.785540, last accessed 5 July 2019.

Israel Ministry of Foreign Affairs, 'Address by FM Livni to the 8th Doha Forum on Democracy, Development and Free Trade', 14 April 2008, https://mfa.gov.il/MFA/PressRoom/2008/Pages/Address%20by%20FM%20Livni%20to%20the%20Doha%20Conference%2014-Apr-2008.aspx, last accessed 5 July 2019.

'Israel to sever ties with Qatar', *Agence France Presse*, 26 August 2011, http://www.dailystar.com.lb//News/Middle-East/2011/Aug-26/147209-israel-to-sever-ties-with-qatar.ashx, last accessed 5 July 2019.

'Kerry calls new Arab League peace stance "big step forward"' *Reuters*, 30 April 2013, http://www.reuters.com/article/us-palestinians-israel-usa-idUSBRE93T16Z20130430, last accessed 5 July 2019.

Korunskaya, Darya, and Stephen Farrell, 'Putin sees chance circumstance behind downing of Russian plane off Syrian coast', *Reuters*, 18 September 2018, https://uk.reuters.

com/article/uk-mideast-crisis-syria-russia/putin-sees-chance-circumstances-behind-downing-of-russian-plane-off-syrian-coast-idUKKCN1LY05J, last accessed 5 July 2019.

'Kuwaiti Writer to Muslims: Stop Cursing Jews and Christians in The Friday Sermons', *MEMRI*, 5 April 2016, https://www.memri.org/reports/kuwaiti-writer-muslims-stop-cursing-jews-and-christians-friday-sermons, last accessed 5 July 2019.

Makovsky, David, 'The Silent Strike: How Israel bombed a nuclear installation and kept it secret', *The New Yorker*, 10 September 2012, https://www.newyorker.com/magazine/2012/09/17/the-silent-strike, last accessed 5 July 2019.

Melhem, Ahmad, 'Why is the Palestinian Authority angry over Iran's offer of aid?', *Al-Monitor*, 9 March 2016, http://www.al-monitor.com/pulse/originals/2016/03/iran-aid-palestinian-victims-intifada-anger-pa.html, last accessed 5 July 2019.

Moore, Jack, 'Iran ceases financial aid to Hamas in Gaza official claims', *Newsweek Magazine*, 28 July 2015, http://europe.newsweek.com/iran-ceases-financial-aid-hamas-gaza-official-claims-330889, last accessed 5 July 2019.

'Morocco "cancels" Arab League summit: Useless and hypocritical', *The New Arab*, 20 February 2016, https://www.alaraby.co.uk/english/news/2016/2/20/morocco-cancels-arab-league-summit-useless-and-hypocritical, last accessed 5 July 2019.

'National poll shows strong support for UAE peaceful nuclear energy programme', *Emirates Nuclear Energy Corporation*', 20 June 2018, https://www.enec.gov.ae/

news/latest-news/national-poll-shows-strong-support-for-uae-peaceful-nuclear-energy-program/, last accessed 5 July 2019.

Netanyahu, Binyamin, 'PM Netanyahu at the WEF event hosted by Fareed Zakaria (CNN)', 21 January 2016, http://mfa.gov.il/MFA/PressRoom/2016/Pages/PM-Netanyahu-at-the-WEF-event-hosted-by-Fareed-Zakaria-21-Jan-2016.aspx, last accessed 5 July 2019.

———, 'Innovation Nation: The World in 2018', *The Economist*, December 2017, www.theworldin.com/article/14441/edition2018innovation-nation, last accessed 5 July 2019.

Netanyahu's speech to Congress, 3 March 2015, https://www.washingtonpost.com/gdpr-consent/?destination=%2fnews%2fpost-politics%2fwp%2f2015%2f03%2f03%2ffull-text-netanyahus-address-to-congress%2f%3f&utm_term=.747a03727fc8, last accessed 5 July 2019.

Nichols, Michelle, 'Saudi rejects U.N. Security Council seat, opening way for Jordan', *Reuters*, 12 November 2013, http://www.reuters.com/article/us-un-saudi-jordan-idUSBRE9AB14720131112, last accessed 5 July 2019.

Ofek, Rafael, '"Operation Opera": Intelligence behind the Scenes', *Israel Defense*, 4 September 2015, https://www.israeldefense.co.il/en/content/operation-opera-intelligence-behind-scenes, last accessed 5 July 2019.

Opall-Rome, Barbara, and Awad Mustafa, 'Israel's Angst over Qatar Sale could End Boeing's F-15 Line', *Defense News*, 28 February 2016, http://www.defensenews.com/story/defense/air-space/air-force/2016/02/28/israels-angst-over-qatar-sale-could-end-boeings-f-15-line/80895346/, last accessed 5 July 2019.

Podosky, Philip, 'Official to i24NEWS: "Bahrain will be first Gulf state to form ties with Israel"', *i24 News*, 20 June 2018, https://www.i24news.tv/en/news/israel/diplomacy-defense/177564–180620-bahrain-doesn-t-view-israel-as-enemy-will-be-first-gulf-state-to-establish-ties, last accessed 5 July 2019.

Shezaf, Haga, and Rori Donaghy, 'Israel eyes improved ties with Gulf monarchies after "foothold" gained in the UAE', *Middle East Eye*, 18 January 2016, http://www.middleeasteye.net/news/israel-eyes-improved-gulf-states-relationship-ties-flourish-uae-895004700, last accessed 5 July 2019.

Todenhöfer, Jürgen, 'Special Report: Behind enemy lines with ISIS: "We fear the IDF"', 27 December 2015, http://www.jewishnews.co.uk/special%E2%80%88report-behind-enemy-lines-with-isis-we-fear-the-idf/, last accessed 5 July 2019.

'UAE and Israel are like 'brothers' says senior general', *Middle East Monitor*, 17 November 2017, https://www.middleeastmonitor.com/20171117-uae-and-israel-are-like-brothers-says-senior-general/, last accessed 5 July 2019.

'UAE buying arms from Israel', *Middle East Monitor*, 5 February 2018, https://www.middleeastmonitor.com/20180205-uae-buying-arms-from-israel/, last accessed 5 July 2019.

'UAE offered to fund Israel's Gaza offensive', Doha Desk, *The Peninsula Qatar*, http://thepeninsulaqatar.com/news/qatar/292061/uae-offered-to-fund-israel-s-gaza-offensive, last accessed 24 February 2016.

'US blocs UNSC statement on Israel's use of force on Land Day', *Al Jazeera English*, 1 April 2018, https://www.aljazeera.com/news/2018/04/blocks-unsc-statement-israel-force-land-day-180401054016894.html, last accessed 5 July 2019.

Williams, Dan, 'Israel says close to forging new ties across Arab world', *Reuters*, 14 April 2014, http://uk.reuters.com/article/uk-israel-arab-ties-idUKBREA3D0TT20140414, last accessed 5 July 2019.

Yanover, Yori, 'Israelis risk flying through enemy countries to save buck', *The Jewish Press*, 1 March 2012, http://www.jewishpress.com/news/breaking-news/to-save-a-buck-israelis-risk-flying-through-enemy-countries/2012/03/01/, last accessed 5 July 2019.

Younes, Ali, 'Israel to open office for renewable energy in Abu Dhabi', *Al Jazeera English*, 27 November 2015, http://www.aljazeera.com/news/2015/11/israel-open-office-renewable-energy-abu-dhabi-151127184424647.html, last accessed 5 July 2019.

Online Broadcast Events

'A Conversation on Security and Peace in the Middle East: HRH Prince Turki al-Faisal, Saudi Arabia and Maj.-Gen (ret.) Yaakov Amidror, Israel', The Washington Institute for Near East Policy, 5 May 2016, https://www.washington-institute.org/policy-analysis/view/a-conversation-on-security-and-peace-in-the-middle-east, last accessed 5 July 2019.

'Israel and the Middle East: Seeking Common Ground: A Conversation with HRH Prince Turki bin Faisail Al Saud and General Amos Yadlin', The German Marshall Fund of the United States, Brussels, 26 May 2014, https://www.youtube.com/watch?v=TOHmgzbh7XA, last accessed 5 July 2019.

'Shared Security Challenges and Opportunities', Israel Policy Forum, New York, 23 October 2017, https://www.youtube.com/watch?v=RXM-atXcQkA, last accessed 5 July 2019.

'The Documentary: Inside the Israeli Hospital', BBC World Service Radio, 29 May 2017, https://www.bbc.co.uk/programmes/p0531xq7, last accessed 5 July 2019.

Newspapers

France:

Le Monde Diplomatique

Israel:

Ha'aretz
Israel Hayom
The Israel Times
The Jerusalem Post
Yediot Aharonot

United Kingdom:

The Daily Telegraph
Financial Times
The Guardian
The Times

United States of America:

The New York Times
The Wall Street Journal
The Washington Post

BIBLIOGRAPHY

Periodicals

Der Spiegel
The Atlantic
The Economist
The New Yorker

INDEX

Note: Page numbers followed by "*n*" refer to notes.